Eyewitness Accounts of the American Revolution

Travels in North-America

Marquis de Chastellux

The New York Times & Arno Press

Reprinted from a copy in the library of the
General Society of Mechanics and Tradesmen
of the City of New York

*

*

Library of Congress Catalog Card No. 67-29046

*

Manufactured in the U.S.A.

TRAVELS
IN
NORTH-AMERICA,

IN THE YEARS 1780, 1781, AND 1782.

BY THE

MARQUIS DE CHASTELLUX,

ONE OF THE FORTY MEMBERS OF THE FRENCH ACADEMY, AND MAJOR-GENERAL IN THE FRENCH ARMY, SERVING UNDER THE COUNT DE ROCHAMBEAU.

TRANSLATED FROM THE FRENCH
BY AN ENGLISH GENTLEMAN,
WHO RESIDED IN AMERICA AT THAT PERIOD.

WITH NOTES BY THE TRANSLATOR.

SECOND EDITION.

Πολλων δ' ανθρωπων ιδεν αϛεα και νοον εγνω. Odyſſey, B. I.
Multorumque hominum vidit urbes, & mores cognovit.

VOLUME II.

LONDON:
PRINTED FOR G. G. J. AND J. ROBINSON,
PATER-NOSTER-ROW.
M DCC LXXXVII.

CONTENTS

TO THE

SECOND VOLUME.

Description

Defcription

Road

The

TRA-

TRAVELS

IN

NORTH-AMERICA.

Journal of a Journey in Upper-Virginia, in the Apalachian Mountains, and to the Natural Bridge.

FROM the moment the French troops were eſtabliſhed in the quarters they occupied in Virginia, I formed the project of travelling into the upper parts of that province, where I was aſſured that I ſhould find objects worthy of exciting the curioſity of a ſtranger; and faithful to the principles, which from my youth I had lain down, never to neglect ſeeing every country in my

 power,

power, I burned with impatience to ſet out. The ſeaſon however was unfavourable, and rendered travelling difficult and laborious; beſides, Experience taught me that travelling in winter never offered the greateſt ſatisfaction we can enjoy; that of ſeeing Nature, ſuch as ſhe ought to be, and of forming a juſt idea of the general face of a country; for it is eaſier for the imagination to deprive a landſcape of the charms of ſpring, than to cloath with them, the hideous ſkeleton of winter; as it is eaſier to imagine what a beauty at eighteen may be at eighty, than to conceive what eighty was at eighteen.—Monſieur de Rochambleau being abſent likewiſe during the month of February, and Monſieur le Chevalier de la Luzerne having choſen the month of March to pay us a viſit, politeneſs and my duty obliged me to wait till April, before I could begin my travels.—On the 8th of that month I ſet out with Mr. Lynch, then my Aide de Camp and Adjutant, now General; Mr. *Frank Dillon*, my ſecond Aide de Camp* and Mr.

* Monſieur le Baron de Monteſquieu went to Europe after the ſiege of York, and did not return until the month of September following.

Mr. le Chevalier d'Oyrè of the engineers: ſix ſervants and a led horſe compoſed our train: ſo that our little caravan conſiſted of four maſters, ſix ſervants, and eleven horſes. I regulated my journey by the ſpring, and gave it time ſufficient to precede us. For though in the 37th degree of latitude, one might expect to find it in the month of April, I ſaw no trace of it in the wood through which we paſſed; the verdure being hardly diſcoverable on the thorns, the ſun notwithſtanding was very ardent, and I regretted to find ſummer in the heavens, whilſt the earth afforded not the ſmalleſt appearance of the ſpring. The eighteen miles through which we paſſed, before we baited our horſes at *Bird*'s tavern, were ſufficiently known to me, for it was the ſame road I travelled laſt ſummer in coming from Williamſburgh. The remaining ſixteen, which compleated our days work, and brought us to *New-Kent-Court Houſe*, offered nothing curious; all I learnt by a converſation with Mr. Bird was, that he had been pillaged by the Engliſh when they paſſed his houſe in their march to *Weſtover*, in purſuit of Monſieur de la

 Fayette,

Fayette, and in returning to Williamſburgh, after endeavouring in vain to come up with him. It was comparatively nothing to ſee their fruits, fowls and cattle carried away by the light troops which formed the van-guard, * the army collected what the van-guard

* It is with great reluctance that truth compels me to confirm the horrid depredations committed by the Engliſh army in their progreſs through many parts of America. Much has been ſaid on this ſubject, both in and out of parliament, but I am ſorry to ſay, that future hiſtorians of this unhappy war, will find the fact too well eſtabliſhed to refuſe a deciſive verdict. Happy if *the reſult* may tend henceforth to alleviate the miſeries of mankind, and mitigate the horrors of a civil conteſt. The wife of an Engliſhman, one of the principal merchants of Philadelphia, having retired with her family to the neighbourhood of Mountholſy in the Jerſeys, aſſured me, that ſhe found the country in general well-affected to the Engliſh, until the arrival of their army, whoſe indiſcriminate and wanton enormities ſoon alienated their moſt zealous friends, for even the officers were contaminated with the inſatiable ſpirit of revenge and plunder. Amongſt various anecdotes, ſhe related to me the circumſtance of the cruel treatment of a lady of her acquaintance, who was devoted to the Britiſh intereſt, and gave up her houſe with exultation to ſome officers of *Clinton*'s army in

guard had left, even the officers ſeized the rum and all kinds of proviſions, without paying a farthing for them; this hurricane which deſtroyed every thing in its paſſage, was followed by a ſcourge yet more terrible, a numerous rabble, under the title of *Refugees* and *Loyaliſts*, followed the army, not to aſſiſt in the field, but to partake of the

their retreat from Philadelphia. But not only was her zeal repaid with inſult and her own houſe plundered; ſhe had the mortification to ſee it made the receptacle of the pillage of her poorer neighbours. Obſerving ſome of the officers make frequent excurſions, and return, followed by ſoldiers, laden with various articles, ſhe had at length the curioſity to paſs into the garden, and looking through the window, ſaw four of them, and *the Chaplain*, emptying a ſack containing ſtockings, ſhirts, ſhifts, counterpanes, ſheets, ſpoons, and women's trinkets. The booty was regularly ſhared, and the diſtribution of theſe unhallowed ſpoils, to her utter aſtoniſhment and horror, was no other than the miniſter of virtue and religion. The detail of this war is a hiſtory of ſuch iniquity: was it poſſible therefore to expect a more favourable termination of it, either on the principle of a Divine Providence, or of human conduct?

TRANSLATOR.

plunder *. The furniture and cloaths of the inhabitants were in general the ſole booty

* The Loyaliſts, no doubt, no more merit indiſcriminate cenſure than any other body of men; the Tranſlator, who thinks he underſtands the true principles of liberty, for which he has ever been a zealous and unſhaken advocate, admits however, and admires the virtue, honour, and ſteadfaſt attachment of many illuſtrious individuals to a cauſe, directly deſtructive of his own wiſhes; but with every fair allowance for the violence inſeparable from civil conteſts, he cannot help bearing his teſtimony to the wanton outrages committed by an unprincipled banditti who attached themſelves to the royal cauſe, and branded it with ruin and diſgrace. The root of this evil originated in the *Board of Loyaliſts* eſtabliſhed by Lord George Germain at the inſtigation of ſkulking Refugees, who flying themſelves, from the ſcene of danger, took up their reſidence in London, and were in the inceſſant purſuit of perſonal and intereſted vengeance. He does not aſſert that their councils loſt America, but it is now paſt doubt, that they formed a ſtrong ſecondary cauſe of precipitating that event, and of embittering the ſeparation. General Clinton, the whole army at New-York, can witneſs the inſolence and indirect menaces of this incorporated rabble of marauders, in the affair of *Captain Huddy*, and the ſubſequent claim of the Congreſs. Had the war continued, this *imperium in imperio* muſt have been attended with the moſt fatal conſequences; this illiberal narrow mind-

booty left to ſatisfy their avidity; after they had emptied the houſes, they ſtript the proprietors; and Mr. Bird, repeated with indignation, that they had taken from him by force, the very boots from off his legs. In my way hither I had the ſatisfaction however of recalling to mind the firſt puniſhment inflicted on theſe robbers. Six miles from Williamſburgh I paſſed near a place where two croſs roads interſecting each other, leave an open ſpace; one leading to Williamſburgh, the other to *James-town*. On the 25th of June, Monſieur de la Fayette here ordered the vanguard to attack that of Lord Cornwallis; *Sincoe*, who commanded it, was left behind to collect the cattle, whilſt Lord Cornwallis was encamping at Williamſburgh, where he arrived the preceding evening. Monſieur de la Fayette's cavalry with ſome infantry mounted behind them, arrived ſoon

ed ſet of men, became the ſpies and cenſors of Britiſh policy, and Britiſh conduct, and the commander in Chief himſelf, was ſtruck with horror at their unenlightened, blood-thirſty tribunal.

TRANSLATOR.

enough to force *Sincoe* to an engagement, and was ſoon after joined by the reſt of the American light infantry. *Sincoe* fought with diſadvantage, till Lord Cornwallis marching to his aſſiſtance, the Americans retired, after having killed or wounded near 150 men, with the loſs only of ſeven or eight. Colonel *Butler*, an American officer, who commanded a battalion of light infantry, and Colonel *Galvan** a French officer, who commanded another, diſtinguiſhed themſelves very much on this occaſion. The recollection of this event, the preſage of that ſucceſs which crowned our campaign, employed my thoughts ſo much the more agreeably the whole evening, as we had taken up our lodgings in a good inn, where we were ſerved with an excellent ſupper, compoſed chiefly of ſturgeon, and I had two kinds of fiſh, at leaſt as good in Virginia as in Europe, but which make their appearance only in the ſpring.

The next morning I had an enjoyment of another kind. I roſe with the ſun, and whilſt

* The ſame who afterwards ſhot himſelf at Philadelphia. See notes to 1ſt vol. TRANSLATOR.

whilſt breakfaſt was preparing, took a walk round the houſe; the birds were heard on every ſide, but my attention was chiefly attracted by a very agreeable ſong, which appeared to proceed from a neighbouring tree. I approached ſoftly, and perceived it to be a mocking bird, ſaluting the riſing ſun. At firſt I was afraid of frightening it, but my preſence on the contrary gave it pleaſure; for apparently delighted at having an auditor, it ſung better than before, and its emulation ſeemed to increaſe, when it perceived a couple of dogs, which followed me, draw near to the tree on which it was perched. It kept hopping inceſſantly from branch to branch, ſtill continuing its ſong, for this extraordinary bird is not leſs remarkable for its agility, than its charming notes; it keeps perpetually riſing and ſinking, ſo as to appear not leſs the favourite of Terpſichore, than Polihymnia. This bird cannot certainly be reproached with fatiguing its auditors, for nothing can be more varied than its ſong, of which it is impoſſible to give an imitation, or even to furniſh any adequate idea. As it had every

every reaſon to be contented with my attention, it concealed from me no one of its talents; and one would have thought, that after having delighted me with a concert, it was deſirous of entertaining me with a comedy. It began to counterfeit different birds; thoſe which it imitated the moſt naturally, at leaſt to a ſtranger, were the jay, the raven, the cardinal, and the lapwing *. It appeared deſirous of retaining me near it, for after having liſtened, for a quarter of an hour, on my return to the houſe, it followed me, flying from tree to tree, always ſinging, ſometimes its natural ſong, at others, thoſe which it had learned in Virginia, and in its travels; for this bird is one of thoſe which change climate, altho' it ſometimes appears here during the winter. As the next day's journey was to be longer than that of the preceding one, we left *New-Kent-Court-Houſe* before eight o'clock, and

* Or rather the painted plover, which is the lapwing of America. It differs from ours, by its plumage, mixt with grey, white and yellow gilt; it differs alſo a little in its ſong, but it has the ſhape and manners, and is abſolutely the ſame ſpecies.

and rode twenty miles to *Newcaſtle*, where I reſolved to give our horſes two hours repoſe; the road was not ſo level as that we had travelled the day before, and was rendered more agreeable by being diverſified with ſome little hillocks. From the top of them you had a view to the diſtance of ſome miles, and at times one might perceive *Pamunkey* River, which runs at the bottom of a deep valley, covered with wood. As you approach Newcaſtle, the country becomes more gay. This little capital of a ſmall diſtrict, contains twenty-five or thirty houſes, ſome of which are pretty enough. When our horſes were repoſed, and the heat already troubleſome in the middle of the day, was a little abated, we continued our journey, that we might arrive, before dark, at *Hanover-Court-Houſe*, from which we were yet ſixteen miles. The country through which we paſſed is one of the fineſt of lower Virginia. There are many well cultivated eſtates, and handſome houſes, amongſt others, one belonging to Mr. *Jones*, ſituated near the road, two miles from Newcaſtle, of a very elegant appearance, which, we were informed, was furniſhed with infinite

finite taſte, and what is ſtill more uncommon in America, that it was embelliſhed with a garden, laid out in the Engliſh ſtyle *. It is even pretended, that this kind of park, through which the river flows, yields not in beauty to thoſe, the model of which the French have received from England, and are now imitating with ſuch ſucceſs †.

The

* The Author has ſince ſeen this garden, which anſwers the deſcription given, and is really very elegant.

† The gardens I have hitherto ſeen in France profeſſedly laid out on the Engliſh model, are with great deference to the Author, but very *unſucceſsful imitations* of the Engliſh ſtyle; thoſe of the Comte de Artois at *Bagatelle*, and of the Duke of Orleans at *Mouſſeaux* near Paris, are indeed no imperfect imitations of *Mr. Sterling*'s in the comedy of the Clandeſtine Marriage, of the Spaniard's at Hampſtead, of Bagnigge-wells, or a Common Council-man's retreat upon the Wandſworth road. They preſent a fantaſtic, and crouded groupe of Chineſe pagodas, gothic ruins, immoveable windmills, molehill-mounts, thirty graſs patches, dry bridges, pigmy ſerpentines, cockleſhell caſcades, and ſtagnant duck-pools. The gardens of the Thuilleries and Marly,

Three miles from Hanover, there are two roads, that which we were to follow winds a little towards the north, and approaches the Pamunkey. We arrived before sunset and alighted at a tolerable handsome inn; a very large saloon and a covered portico, are destined to receive the company who assemble every three months at the *Court-house*, either on private or public affairs. This asylum is the more necessary, as there are no other houses in the neighbourhood. Travellers make use of these establishments, which are indispensable in a country so thinly inhabited, that the houses are often at a distance of two or three miles from each other. Care is generally taken to place the Court-house in the center of the county. As there are a great many counties in Virginia, they are seldom more than six or seven leagues diameter; thus every man can return home after he has finished his affairs.

The

with all their undisguised, artificial labours, are at least noble, magnificent, and useful; their terraces are grand, and their lofty *Berceaus* beautiful, and well adapted to the climate.

TRANSLATOR.

The county of Hanover, as well as that of New Kent, had ſtill reaſon to remember the paſſage of the Engliſh. Mr. *Tilghman*, our landlord, though he lamented his misfortune in having lodged and boarded Lord Cornwallis and his retinue, without his Lordſhip's having made him the leaſt recompenſe, could not yet help laughing at the fright which the unexpected arrival of Tarleton ſpread amongſt a conſiderable number of gentlemen, who had come to hear the news, and were aſſembled in the Court-houſe. A negro on horſeback came full gallop, to let them know that Tarleton was not above three miles off. The reſolution of retreating was ſoon taken, but the alarm was ſo ſudden, and the confuſion ſo great, that every one mounted the firſt horſe he could find, ſo that few of thoſe curious gentlemen returned upon their own horſes. The Engliſh, who came from Weſtover, had paſſed the *Chilkahominy* at *Button's-bridge*, and directed their march towards the *South Anna*, which Mr. de la Fayette had put between them and himſelf.

Mr.

Mr. Tilghman having had time to renew his provisions since the retreat of Lord Cornwallis, we supped very well, and had the company of Mr. *Lee*, brother to Colonel *Henry Lee* *; who long commanded a legion, and often distinguished himself, particularly in Carolina †. We set

* Colonel Harry Lee is a smart, active young man, first cousin to Mr. Arthur Lee, and Mr. William Lee, late Alderman of London. He rendered very essential services to his country, particularly in the southern war. His corps was mounted on remarkably fine, high-priced horses, mostly half-blood English stallions, and officered principally by his own family and relations. Had the war continued, there is every reason to believe that the American cavalry would have taken some consistence, and have become very formidable in the field; Mr. Tarleton received many severe checks in his exploits from the corps under Colonel Washington, and that of Colonel Harry Lee. Towards the close of the war, he had to encounter an enemy very different from flying militia, and scattered bodies of broken, half-disciplined infantry, of whom slaughter *may* be service, but conquest no honour. TRANSLATOR.

† Lord Cornwallis was unquestionably the English General whose courage, talents and activity, occasioned the greatest loss to the Americans; it is not astonishing therefore he should not have inspired them with sentiments similar to those of his own

ſet out at nine the next morning, after having breakfaſted much better than our horſes, which had nothing but oats, the country being ſo deſtitute of forage, that it was not poſſible to find a truſs of hay, or a few leaves of Indian corn, though we had ſought for it for two miles round. Three miles and a half from Hanover we croſſed the South Anna on a wooden bridge. I obſerved

troops, whoſe attachment, and admiration of his character, were unbounded. Yet they never accuſed him of rapine, nor even of intereſted views; and the complaints of Mr. Tilghman only prove the ſad conſequences of a war, in the courſe of which the Engliſh ſuffered more from want, in the midſt of their ſucceſs, than in their diſaſters; the former carrying them far from the fleet, and the latter obliging them to approach it. But the moſt painful of theſe conſequences was the neceſſity which compelled a man of my Lord Cornwallis's birth and character, to conduct, rather than command, a numerous band of traitors and robbers, which Engliſh policy decorated with the name of *Loyaliſts*. This rabble preceded the troops in plunder, taking ſpecial care never to follow them in danger. The progreſs was marked by fire, devaſtation, and outrages of every kind; they ravaged ſome part of America 'tis true, but ruined England, by inſpiring her enemies with an irreconcileable hatred.

obſerved that the river was deeply embanked, and from the nature of the ſoil concluded it was the ſame during a great part of its courſe: it appears to me therefore that would have been a good defence, if Monſieur de la Fayette, who paſſed it higher up, had arrived in time to deſtroy the bridge. On the left ſide of the river the ground riſes, and you mount a pretty high hill, the country is barren, and we travelled almoſt always in the woods, till one o'clock, when we arrived at *Offly*, and alighted at General *Nelſon*'s, formerly Governor of Virginia. I had got acquainted with him during the expedition to York, at which critical moment he was Governor, and conducted himſelf with the courage of a brave ſoldier, and the zeal of a good citizen. At the time when the Engliſh armies were carrying deſolation into the heart of his country, and our troops arrived unexpectedly to ſuccour and revenge it, he was compelled to exert every means, and to call forth every poſſible reſource, to aſſiſt Monſieur de la Fayette to make ſome reſiſtance; and furniſh General Waſhington with horſes, car-

 riages,

riages, and provisions: but I am sorry to add, what will do but little honour to Virginia, that the only recompence of his labours was the hatred of a great part of his fellow citizens. At the first assembly of the province, held after the campaign, he experienced from them neither the satisfaction he had a right to expect, at being freed from servitude, nor that emulation which is the general consequence of success; but instead of these sentiments, so natural in such circumstances, a general discontent arising from the necessity under which he had often laboured, of pressing their horses, carriages and forage. Those laws and customs which would have ceased to exist by the conquest of the province, were put in force against its defender, and General Nelson, worn out at length by the fatigues of the campaign, but still more by the ingratitude of his fellow citizens, resigned the place of Governor, which he had held for six months, but not without enjoying the satisfaction of justifying his conduct, and of seeing his countrymen pardon the momentary injuries he had done their laws, by endeavouring

deavouring to ſave the ſtate. If to the character I have juſt given of General Nelſon, I ſhould add, that he is a good and gallant man, in every poſſible ſituation of life, and has ever behaved with the utmoſt politeneſs to the French, you will be ſurpriſed that I ſhould go to viſit him in his abſence, like *Mathwin* in the comedy of *Roſe and Colas*; for though I knew he was not at home, as I had met him near Williamſburgh, where he was detained by public buſineſs, the viſit I intended to pay him formed a part of my journey I undertook—beſides that I was deſirous of ſeeing his family, particularly his younger brother, Mr. William Nelſon, with whom I was intimately connected at Williamſburgh, where he paſſed the greateſt part of the winter. *Offly* is far from correſponding with the riches of General Nelſon, or with his high conſideration in Virginia; it is but a moderate plantation, where he has contented himſelf with erecting ſuch buildings as are neceſſary for the improvement of his lands, and for the habitation of his *overſeers*; his general reſidence is at *York*, but that he was obliged to abandon: and Offly being beyond the South Anna, and ſituated far back in the country, he thought that this lonely houſe would be at leaſt a ſafe retreat for his family; it was not ſecure however from the viſits of Lord Cornwallis, who, in his peregrinations thro' Virginia, advanced even ſo far, though without doing much miſchief. In the abſence of the General, his mother and wife received us with all the politeneſs, eaſe, and cordiality natural to his family. But as in America the ladies are never thought ſufficient to do the honors of the houſe, five or ſix Nelſons were aſſembled to receive us; amongſt others, the *Secretary* Nelſon, uncle to the General, with his two ſons, and two of the General's brothers. Theſe young men were all married, and ſeveral of them were accompanied by their wives and children, all called Nelſon, and diſtinguiſhed only by their chriſtian names *, ſo that during the two days which I paſſed in this truly patriarchal houſe, it was

* The French in general aſſume the ſurname, by which they chuſe to be diſtinguiſhed in the world, ſo that the name which, with us, is a real bond

was impoſſible for me to find out their degrees of relationſhip. When I ſay that we paſſed two days in this houſe, it may be underſtood in the moſt literal ſenſe, for the weather was ſo bad, there was no poſſibility of ſtirring out. The houſe being neither convenient nor ſpacious, company aſſembled either in the parlour or ſaloon, eſpecially the men, from the hour of breakfaſt, to that of bed-time, but the converſation was always agreeable and well ſupported. If you were deſirous of diverſifying the ſcene, there were ſome good French and Engliſh authors at hand. An excellent breakfaſt at nine in the morning, a ſumptuous dinner at two o'clock, tea and punch in the afternoon, and an elegant little ſupper, divided the day moſt happily, for thoſe whoſe ſtomachs were never unprepared. It is worth obſerving, that on this occaſion, where fifteen or twenty people, (four of whom were ſtrangers to the family

of affection, is ſoon loſt with them. I was long acquainted with four brothers in France, without knowing they were related to each other.

TRANSLATOR.

or country) were aſſembled together, and by bad weather forced to ſtay within doors, not a ſyllable was mentioned about play. How many parties of *trictrac*, *whiſt*, and *lotto* would with us have been the conſequence of ſuch obſtinate bad weather? Perhaps too, ſome more rational amuſements might have varied the ſcene agreeably; but in America, muſic, drawing, public reading, and the work of the ladies, are reſources as yet unknown, though it is to be hoped they will not long neglect to cultivate them; for nothing but ſtudy was wanting to a young Miſs Tolliver who ſung ſome airs, the words of which were Engliſh, and the muſic Italian. Her charming voice, and the artleſs ſimplicity of her ſinging, were a ſubſtitute for taſte, if not taſte itſelf; that natural taſte, always ſure, when confined within juſt limits, and when timid in its weakneſs, it has not been altered, or ſpoiled by falſe precepts and bad examples.

Miſs Tolliver had attended her ſiſter, Mrs. William Nelſon, to Offly, who had juſt miſcarried, and kept her bed. She was brought up in the middle of the woods by

her

her father, a great fox-hunter, consequently could have learned to sing from the birds only, in the neighbourhood, when the howling of the dogs permitted her to hear them. She is an agreeable figure, as well as Mrs. Nelson her sister, tho' less pretty than a third daughter, who remained with her father. These young ladies came often to Williamsburgh to attend the balls, where they appeared as well dressed as the ladies of the town, and always remarkable for their decency of behaviour. The young military gentlemen, on the other hand, had conceived a great affection for Mr. Tolliver their father, and took the trouble sometimes to ride over to breakfast and talk with him of the chace. The young ladies, who appeared from time to time, never interrupted the conversation. These pretty nymphs more timid and wild than those of Diana, though they did not conduct the chace, inspired the taste for it into the youth: they knew however how to defend themselves from fox-hunters, without destroying, by their arrows, those who had the presumption to look at them.

After this little digreſſion, which requires ſome indulgence, I ſhould be at a loſs for a tranſition to an old magiſtrate, whoſe white locks, noble figure, and ſtature, which was above the common ſize, commanded reſpect and veneration. *Secretary Nelſon*, to whom this character belongs, owes this title to the place he occupied under the Engliſh Government. In Virginia the Secretary, whoſe office it was to preſerve the regiſters of all public acts, was, by his place, a member of the council, of which the Governor was the chief. Mr. Nelſon, who held this office for thirty years, ſaw the morning of that bright day which began to ſhine upon his country; he ſaw too the ſtorms ariſe which threatened its deſtruction, though he neither endeavoured to collect, or to foment them.

Too far advanced in age to deſire a revolution, too prudent to check this great event, if neceſſary, and too faithful to his countrymen to ſeparate his intereſt from theirs, he choſe the criſis of this alteration, to retire from public affairs. Thus did he opportunely quit the theatre, when new pieces

pieces demanded fresh actors, and took his seat among the spectators, content to offer up his wishes for the success of the Drama, and to applaud those who acted well their part. But in the last campaign, chance produced him on the scene, and made him unfortunately famous. He lived at *York*, where he had built a very handsome house, from which neither European taste nor luxury was excluded; a chimney-piece and some bass reliefs of very fine marble, exquisitely sculptured, were particularly admired, when fate conducted Lord Cornwallis to this town to be disarmed, as well as his till then victorious troops. Secretary Nelson did not think it necessary to fly from the English, to whom his conduct could not have made him disagreeable, nor have furnished any just motive of suspicion. He was well received by the General, who established his head-quarters in his house, which was built on an eminence, near the most important fortifications, and in the most agreeable situation of the town. It was the first object which struck the sight as you approached the town, but inſtead of travellers, it ſoon drew the attention of our bombardiers and cannoniers, and was almoſt entirely deſtroyed. Mr. Nelſon lived in it at the time our batteries tried their firſt ſhot, and killed one of his negroes at a little diſtance from him; ſo that Lord Cornwallis was ſoon obliged to ſeek another aſylum. But what aſylum could be found for an old man, deprived of the uſe of his legs by the gout? But, above all, what aſylum could defend him againſt the cruel anguiſh a father muſt feel at being beſieged by his own children; for he had two in the American army. So that every ſhot, whether fired from the town, or from the trenches, might prove equally fatal to him; I was witneſs to the cruel anxiety of one of theſe young men, when after the flag was ſent to demand his father, he kept his eyes fixed upon the gate of the town, by which it was to come out, and ſeemed to expect his own ſentence in the anſwer. Lord Cornwallis had too much humanity to refuſe a requeſt ſo juſt, nor can I recollect, without emotion, the moment in which

I ſaw

I ſaw this old gentleman alight at General Waſhington's. He was ſeated, the fit of the gout not having yet left him; and whilſt we ſtood around him, he related to us, with a ſerene countenance, what had been the effect of our batteries, and how much his houſe had ſuffered from the firſt ſhot.

The tranquillity which has ſucceeded theſe unhappy times, by giving him leiſure to reflect upon his loſſes, has not embittered the recollection; he lives happily in one of his plantations, where, in leſs than ſix hours, he can aſſemble thirty of his children, grand children, nephews, nieces, &c. amounting in all to ſeventy, the whole inhabiting Virginia. The rapid increaſe of his own family juſtifies what he told me of the population in general, of which, from the offices he has held all his life, he muſt have it in his power to form a very accurate judgment. In 1742 the people *ſubject to pay taxes* in the State of Virginia, that is to ſay, the white males above ſixteen, and the male and female blacks of the ſame age, amounted only to the number of 63,000; by by his account they now exceed 160,000 *.

After paſſing two days very agreeably with this intereſting family, we left them the 12th at ten in the morning, accompanied by the Secretary, and five or ſix other Nelſons, who conducted us to *Little River Bridge*, a ſmall creek on the road about five miles from Offly. There we ſeparated, and having rode about eleven miles further through woods, and over a barren country, we arrived at one o'clock at *Willis*'s inn or ordinary; for the inns which in the other provinces of America are known by the name of taverns, or public-houſes, are in Virginia called *ordinaries*. This conſiſted of a little houſe placed in a ſolitary ſituation in the middle of the woods, notwithſtanding which we there found a great deal of company. As ſoon as I alighted, I enquired what might be the reaſon of this numerous aſſembly, and was informed it was a *cock-match*. This diverſion is much in faſhion

* This calculation is much below that given by other writers, and I have reaſon to believe that it is conſiderably below the mark. TRANSLATOR.

faſhion in Virginia, where the Engliſh cuſtoms are more prevalent than in the reſt of America. When the principal promoters of this diverſion, propoſe to watch their champions, they take great care to announce it to the public; and although there are neither poſts, nor regular conveyances, this important news ſpreads with ſuch facility, that the planters for thirty or forty miles round, attend, ſome with cocks, but all with money for betting, which is ſometimes very conſiderable. They are obliged to bring their own proviſions, as ſo many people with good appetites could not poſſibly be ſupplied with them at the inn. As for lodgings, one large room for the whole company, with a blanket for each individual, is ſufficient for ſuch hearty countrymen, who are not more delicate about the conveniencies of life, than the choice of their amuſements.

Whilſt our horſes were feeding, we had an opportunity of ſeeing a battle. The preparation took up a great deal of time; they arm their cocks with long ſteel ſpurs, very ſharp, and cut off a part of their feathers,

thers, as if they meant to deprive them of their armour. The ſtakes were very conſiderable; the money of the parties was depoſited in the hands of one of the principal perſons, and I felt a ſecret pleaſure in obſerving that it was chiefly French *. I know

* The prodigious quantity of French money brought into America by their fleets and armies, and the loans made to Congreſs, together with the vaſt return of dollars from the Havannah, and the Spaniſh, Portugueze and Engliſh gold which found its way into the country from the Britiſh lines, rendered ſpecie very plentiful towards the concluſion of the war; and the arrival of the army of the Comte de Rochambeau was particularly opportune, as it happened at the very diſtreſſing criſis of the death of the paper currency. The French money alone in circulation in the United States, in the year 1782, was eſtimated after very accurate calculations, at thirty-five millions of livres, or near a million and a half ſterling. Although it is impoſſible to aſcertain with any degree of preciſion the quantity of Britiſh money circulating in the revolted part of the continent, under the forms of Spaniſh, Portugal, and Engliſh coin, yet ſome general idea may be entertained that the quantity was very conſiderable, from the following extract from the *ſeventh report of the commiſſioners of public accounts*: "We obtained by requiſition from the office of the Paymaſter General "of the forces, an account of the money iſſued to

know not which is the most astonishing, the insipidity of such diversion, or the stupid

" Messrs. Hartley and Drummond, pursuant to his " Majesty's warrants, for the *extraordinary* services " of his Majesty's forces serving in North America " *from the* 1st of January 1776, to *the 31st of De-* " *cember* 1781. This sum amounts to 10,083,863l. " 2s. 6d. — There are two ways by which this " money goes from these remitters into the hands " of their agents : the one is by bills drawn by them " on the remitters, which bills they receive the va- " lue for in America, and the remitters discharge " when presented to them in London; the other is " by sending out *actual cash*, whenever it becomes " necessary to support the exchange, by increasing " the quantity of current cash in the hands of the " agents."—Now the votes of Parliament will shew the reader, the vast sums *annually* granted to Messrs. Hartley and Drummond, for the specific purpose of purchasing Spanish and Portugal gold alone, to supply " this quantity of current cash," besides the vast exportation of English guineas: nor is it to be doubted, that a great proportion of this supply found its way into the heart of the United States, in return for provisions, in payment of their captive armies, &c. &c. The British navy too is not included in this estimate. Great sums 'tis true, returned to Britain directly or indirectly for goods, &c. but much specie remained incontestably in the country. With respect to the Spanish dollars from the Havannah and the West Indies, no just calculation can

pid intereſt with which it animates the parties. This paſſion appears almoſt innate amongſt the Engliſh, for the Virginians are yet Engliſh in many reſpects. Whilſt the intereſted parties animated the cocks to battle, a child of fifteen, who was near me, kept leaping for joy, and crying, Oh! it is a *charming diverſion*.

We had yet ſeven or eight and twenty miles to ride, to the only inn where it was poſſible to ſtop, before we reached Mr. Jefferſon's; for Mr. de Rochambeau, who had travelled the ſame road but two months before, cautioned me againſt ſleeping at *Louiſa Court-houſe*, as the worſt lodging he had found in all America. This public-houſe is ſixteen miles from Willis's ordinary. As he had given me a very forcible deſcription not only of the houſe, but of

be formed, but the amount muſt have been very conſiderable, as they appeared to me to circulate in the proportion of at leaſt *three* or *four* to *one* of all the other coined ſpecie.—When the Tranſlator added this note, he had not ſeen *Lord Sheffield*'s obſervations on the ſubject. In theſe however, he thinks his lordſhip diſcovers *deep prejudices*, mixed with much excellent reaſoning and a great deal of truth.

TRANSLATOR.

of the landlord, I had a curiosity to judge of it by my own experience. Under the pretence of enquiring for the road, therefore, I went in, and observed, that there was no other lodging for travellers than the apartment of the landlord. This man, called *Johnson*, is become so monstrously fat, that he cannot move out of his arm-chair. He is a good-humoured fellow, whose manners are not very rigid, who loves good cheer, and all sorts of pleasure, insomuch that at the age of fifty he has so augmented his bulk, and diminished his fortune, that by two opposite principles he is near seeing the termination of both; but all this does not in the least affect his gaiety. I found him contented in his arm-chair, which serves him for a bed; for it would be difficult for him to lie down, and impossible to rise. A stool supported his enormous legs, in which were large fissures on each side, a prelude to what must soon happen to his belly. A large ham and a bowl of grog served him for company, like a man resolved to die surrounded by his friends. He called to my

 mind,

mind, in ſhort, the country ſpoken of by Rabelais, where the men order their bellies to be hooped to prolong their lives, and eſpecially the Abbé, who having exhauſted every poſſible reſource, reſolved to finiſh his days by a great feaſt, and invited all the neighbourhood to his *burſting*.

The night was already cloſed in, when we arrived at the houſe of Colonel *Boſwell*, a tall, ſtout Scotſman, about ſixty years of age, and who had been about forty years ſettled in America, where, under the Engliſh government, he was a Colonel of militia. Although he kept a kind of tavern, he appeared but little prepared to receive ſtrangers. It was already late indeed, beſides that this road, which leads only to the mountains, is little frequented. He was quietly ſeated near the fire, by the ſide of his wife, as old, and almoſt as tall as himſelf, whom he diſtinguiſhed by the epithet of, "honey," which in French correſponds with *mon petit cœur*. Theſe honeſt people received us cheerfully, and ſoon called up their ſervants, who were already gone to bed. Whilſt they were preparing

ſupper,

ſupper, we often heard them call *Roſe, Roſe,* which at length brought to view the moſt hideous negreſs I ever beheld. Our ſupper was rather ſcanty, but our breakfaſt the next morning better; we had ham, butter, freſh eggs, and coffee by way of drink: for the whiſkey or corn-ſpirits we had in the evening, mixt with water, was very bad; beſides that we were perfectly reconciled to the American cuſtom of drinking coffee with meat, vegetables, or other food.

We ſet out the next morning at eight o'clock, having learned nothing in this houſe worthy of remark, except that notwithſtanding the hale and robuſt appearance of Mr. and Mrs. Boſwell, not one of fourteen of their children had attained the age of ten years. We were now approaching a chain of mountains of conſiderable height, called the *South-weſt mountains,* becauſe they are the firſt you meet in travelling weſtward, before you arrive at the chain known in France by the name of the *Apalachians,* and in Virginia by that of the Blue Ridge, North Ridge, and Allegany mountains. As the country was much covered with woods, we had a view of them but very ſeldom; and travelled a long time without ſeeing any habitation, at times greatly perplexed to chooſe among the different roads, which croſſed each other*. At laſt we overtook a traveller who preceded us, and ſerved not only as a guide, but by his company helped to abridge our journey. He was an Iriſhman †, who though but lately arrived

* The difficulty of finding the road in many parts of America is not to be conceived, except by thoſe ſtrangers who have travelled in that country. The roads, which are not through the woods, not being kept in repair, as ſoon as one is in bad order, another is made in the ſame manner, that is, merely by felling the trees; and the whole interior parts are ſo covered, that without a compaſs it is impoſſible to have the leaſt idea of the courſe you are ſteering. The diſtances too are ſo uncertain, as in every country where they are not meaſured, that no two accounts reſemble each other. In the back parts of Penſylvania, Maryland, and Virginia, I have frequently travelled thirty miles for ten, though frequently ſet right by paſſengers and negroes; but the great communications between the large towns, through all the well-inhabited parts of the continent, are as practicable and eaſy as in Europe. TRANSLATOR.

† An Iriſhman, the inſtant he ſets foot on American ground, becomes, *ipſo facto*, an American; this

ed in America, had made ſeveral campaigns, and received a conſiderable wound

was uniformly the caſe during the whole of the late war. Whilſt Engliſhmen and Scotſmen were regarded with jealouſy and diſtruſt, even with the beſt recommendation, of zeal and attachment to their cauſe, a native of Ireland ſtood in need of no other certificate than his dialect; his ſincerity was never called in queſtion, he was ſuppoſed to have a ſympathy of ſuffering, and every voice decided as it were intuitively, in his favour. Indeed their conduct in the late revolution amply juſtified this favourable opinion; for whilſt the Iriſh emigrant was fighting the battles of America by ſea and land, the Iriſh merchants, particularly at Charles-Town, Baltimore and Philadelphia, laboured with indefatigable zeal, and at all hazards, to promote the ſpirit of enterprize, to increaſe the wealth, and maintain the credit of the country; their purſes were always open, and their perſons devoted to the common cauſe. On more than one imminent occaſion, Congreſs owed their exiſtence, and America poſſibly her preſervation, to the fidelity and firmneſs of the Iriſh. I had the honour of dining with the Iriſh Society, compoſed of the ſteadieſt whigs upon the continent, at the city tavern in Philadelphia, on St. Patrick's day; the members wear a medallion ſuſpended by a riband, with a very ſignificant device, which has eſcaped my memory, but was ſo applicable to the American revolution, that until I was aſſured that it

in his thigh by a musquet ball; which, though it could never be extracted, had not in the least affected either his health or gaiety. He related his military exploits, and we enquired immediately about the country which he then inhabited. He acquainted us that he was settled in North Carolina, upwards of eighty miles from *Catawbaw*, and were then 300 from the sea. These new establishments are so much the more interesting, as by their distance from all commerce, agriculture is their sole resource; I mean that patriarchal agriculture, which consists in producing only what is sufficient for their own consumption, without the hope of either sale or barter. These Colonies therefore must necessarily

subsisted prior to that event, and had a reference only to the oppression of Ireland by her powerful sister, I concluded it to be a temporary illusion. General Washington, Mr. Dickinson, and other leading characters, are adopted members of this Society, having been initiated by the ceremony of an exterior application of a whole bottle of claret poured upon the head, and a generous libation to liberty and good living, of as many as the votary could carry off.

TRANSLATOR.

ceſſarily be rendered equal to all their wants. It is eaſy to conceive that there is ſoon no deficiency of food, but it is alſo neceſſary, that their flocks and their fields ſhould furniſh them with clothing; they muſt manufacture their own wool, and flax, into clothes and linen, they muſt prepare the hides to make ſhoes of them, &c. &c *. as to drink, they are obliged to content themſelves with milk and water, until their apple-trees are large enough to bear fruit, or until they have been able to procure themſelves ſtills, to diſtil their grain.—In theſe troubleſome times we ſhould ſcarcely imagine in Europe, that nails are the articles the moſt wanted in theſe new colonies: for the axe and the ſaw can ſupply every other want. They contrive however to erect huts, and conſtruct roofs without nails, but the work is by this means rendered much more tedious, and in ſuch circum-

* It is a natural ſuppoſition that workmen of all ſorts (at leaſt the moſt neceſſary) ſhould form a part of every new colony, and follow their particular trade as the moſt beneficial employment.

TRANSLATOR.

ſtances every body knows the value of time and labour. It was a natural queſtion to aſk ſuch a cultivator what could bring him four hundred miles from home, and we learned from him that he carried on the trade of horſe-ſelling, the only commerce of which his country was ſuſceptible *, and by which people in the moſt eaſy circumſtances endeavoured to augment their fortunes. In fact, theſe animals multiply very faſt in a country where there is abundant paſture; and as they are conducted without any expence, by grazing on the road, they become the moſt commodious article of exportation, for a country ſo far from any road or commerce. The converſation continued and brought us inſenſibly to the foot of the mountains. On the ſummit of one of them we diſcovered the houſe of Mr. Jefferſon, which ſtands pre-eminent in

* Conſiderable quantities of peltry are likewiſe brought from the back parts of North Carolina; and I have met with ſtrings of horſes laden with that article paſſing through Virginia to Philadelphia from the diſtance of ſix hundred miles.

TRANSLATOR.

in theſe retirements; it was himſelf who built it and preferred this ſituation; for although he poſſeſſed conſiderable property in the neighbourhood, there was nothing to prevent him from fixing his reſidence whereever he thought proper. But it was a debt Nature owed to a philoſopher and a man of taſte, that in his own poſſeſſions he ſhould find a ſpot, where he might beſt ſtudy and enjoy her. He calls his houſe *Monticello*, (in Italian, *Little Mountain*) a very modeſt title, for it is ſituated upon a very lofty one, but which announces the owner's attachment to the language of Italy; and above all to the fine arts, of which that country was the cradle, and is ſtill the aſylum. As I had no farther occaſion for a guide, I ſeparated from the Iriſhman; and after aſcending by a tolerably commodious road, for more than half an hour, we arrived at *Monticello*. This houſe, of which Mr. Jefferſon was the architect, and often one of the workmen, is rather elegant, and in the Italian taſte, though not without fault; it conſiſts of one large ſquare pavilion, the entrance of which is by two por-

ticoes

ticoes ornamented with pillars. The ground floor confifts chiefly of a very large lofty faloon, which is to be decorated entirely in the antique ftyle: above it is a library of the fame form, two fmall wings, with only a ground floor, and attic ftory, are joined to this pavilion, and communicate with the kitchen, offices, &c. which will form a kind of bafement ftory over which runs a terrace. My object in this fhort defcription is only to fhew the difference between this, and the other houfes of the country; for we may fafely aver, that Mr. Jefferfon is the firft American who has confulted the fine arts to know how he fhould fhelter himfelf from the weather. But it is on himfelf alone I ought to beftow my time. Let me defcribe to you a man, not yet forty, tall, and with a mild and pleafing countenance, but whofe mind and underftanding are ample fubftitutes for every exterior grace. An American, who without ever having quitted his own country, is at once a mufician, fkilled in drawing; a geometrician, an aftronomer, a natural philofopher, legiflator, and ftatefman. A fenator

tor of America, who ſat for two years in that famous Congreſs which brought about the revolution; and which is never mentioned without reſpect, though unhappily not without *regret*: a governor of Virginia, who filled this difficult ſtation during the invaſions of *Arnold*, of *Philips*, and of *Cornwallis*; a philoſopher, in voluntary retirement, from the world, and public buſineſs, becauſe he loves the world, inaſmuch only as he can flatter himſelf with being uſeful to mankind; and the minds of his countrymen are not yet in a condition either to bear the light, or to ſuffer contradiction. A mild and amiable wife, charming children, of whoſe education he himſelf takes charge, a houſe to embelliſh, great proviſions to improve, and the arts and ſciences to cultivate; theſe are what remain to Mr. Jefferſon, after having played a principal character on the theatre of the new world, and which he preferred to the honourable commiſſion of Miniſter Plenipotentiary in Europe*. The viſit which I made him was

* Mr. Jefferſon having ſince had the misfortune to loſe his wife, has at laſt yielded to the intreaties of

was not unexpected, for he had long ſince invited me to come and paſs a few days with him, in the center of the mountains; notwithſtanding which I found his firſt appearance ſerious, nay even cold; but before I had been two hours with him we were as intimate as if we had paſſed our whole lives together; walking, books, but above all, a converſation always varied and intereſting, always ſupported by that ſweet ſatisfaction experienced by two perſons, who in communicating their ſentiments and opinions, are invariably in uniſon, and who underſtand each other at the firſt hint, made four days paſs away like ſo many minutes.

This

his country, and accepted the place of Miniſter Plenipotentiary at the court of France, and is now at Paris. It is neceſſary to obſerve that Mr. Jefferſon, who juſtly ſtands in the higheſt ſituation in America, was one of the five Miniſters Plenipotentiary for concluding a peace in Europe, named by Congreſs full two years before it took place; Meſſrs. Franklin, Adams, Laurens, and Jay were the other four.

TRANSLATOR.

This conformity of ſentiments and opinions on which I inſiſt, becauſe it conſtitutes my own eulogium, (and ſelf-love muſt ſomewhere ſhew itſelf) this conformity, I ſay, was ſo perfect, that not only our taſte was ſimilar, but our predilections alſo, thoſe partialities which cold methodical minds ridicule as enthuſiaſtic, whilſt ſenſible and animated ones cheriſh and adopt the glorious appellation. I recollect with pleaſure that as we were converſing one evening over a bowl of punch, after Mrs. Jefferſon had retired, our converſation turned on the poems of *Oſſian*. It was a ſpark of electricity which paſſed rapidly from one to the other; we recollected the paſſages in thoſe ſublime poems, which particularly ſtruck us, and entertained my fellow travellers, who fortunately knew Engliſh well, and were qualified to judge of their merit, though they had never read the poems. In our enthuſiaſm the book was ſent for, and placed near the bowl, where, by their mutual aid, the night far advanced imper-

imperceptibly upon us. Sometimes natural philoſophy, at others politicks or the arts were the topicks of our converſation, for no object had eſcaped Mr. Jefferſon; and it ſeemed as if from his youth he had placed his mind, as he has done his houſe, on an elevated ſituation, from which he might contemplate the univerſe.

The only ſtranger who viſited us during our ſtay at Monticello, was Colonel *Armand*, whom I have mentioned in my firſt Journal; he had been in France the preceding year with Colonel *Laurens*, but returned ſoon enough to be preſent at the ſiege of York, where he marched as a volunteer at the attack of the redoubts. His object in going to France, was to purchaſe clothing and accoutrements compleat for a regiment he had already commanded, but which had been ſo roughly handled in the campaigns to the ſouthward, that it was neceſſary to form it anew: he made the advance of the neceſſaries to Congreſs, who engaged to provide men and horſes. *Charlotteville*, a riſing little town ſituated in a valley two leagues from Monticello, being the quarter aſſigned

aſſigned for aſſembling this legion, Colonel Armand invited me to dine with him the next day, where Mr. Jefferſon and I went, and found the legion under arms. It is to be compoſed of 200 horſe and 150 foot. The horſe was almoſt compleat and very well mounted; the infantry was ſtill feeble, but the whole were well clothed, well armed, and made a very good appearance. We dined with Colonel Armand, all the officers of his regiment, and a *wolf* he amuſes himſelf in bringing up, which is now ten months old, and is as familiar, mild, and gay as a young dog; he never quits his maſter, and has conſtantly the privilege of ſharing his bed. It is to be wiſhed that he may always anſwer ſo good an education, and not reſume his natural character as he advances to maturity. He is not quite of the ſame kind with ours, his ſkin is almoſt black, and very gloſſy; he has nothing fierce about the head, ſo that were it not for his upright ears, and pendent tail, one might readily take him for a dog. Perhaps he owes the ſingular advantage of not exhaling a bad ſmell, to the care which is

taken

taken of his toilet; for I remarked that the dogs were not in the leaſt afraid of him, and that when they croſſed his trace, they paid no attention to it. But it appears improbable, that all the neatneſs in the world can deceive the inſtinct of thoſe animals, which have ſuch a dread of wolves, that they have been obſerved, in the King's garden at Paris, to raiſe their coats and howl at the ſmell only of two mongrels, engendered by a dog and a ſhe-wolf. I am inclined therefore to believe, that this peculiarity belongs to the ſpecies of black wolf, for they have our ſpecies alſo in America; and in Europe we may poſſibly have the black kind, for ſo it may be conjectured at leaſt from the old proverb: "He is as much afraid of me as of a *grey* wolf," which implies that there are alſo black ones.

Since I am on the ſubject of animals, I ſhall mention here ſome obſervations which Mr. Jefferſon enabled me to make upon the wild beaſts which are common in this country. I have been a long time in doubt whether to call them roebucks, ſtags, or deer, for in Canada they are known by the

the firſt name, in the eaſtern provinces by the ſecond, and in the ſouthern by the third. Beſides, in America, their nomenclatures are ſo inaccurate, and their obſervations ſo ſlight, that no information can be acquired by examining the people of the country. Mr. Jefferſon amuſed himſelf by raiſing a ſcore of theſe animals in his park; they are become very familiar, which happens to all the animals of America; for they are in general much eaſier to tame than thoſe of Europe. He amuſes himſelf by feeding them with Indian corn, of which they are very fond, and which they eat out of his hand. I followed him one evening into a deep valley, where they are accuſtomed to aſſemble towards the cloſe of the day, and ſaw them walk, run, and bound: but the more I examined their paces, the leſs I was inclined to annex them to any particular ſpecies in Europe; they are abſolutely of the ſame colour as the roebuck, and never change even when they are tamed, which often happens to deer. Their horns, which are never more than a foot and a half long, and have more than four branches on each ſide, are more open and broader than thoſe of the roebuck; they take an oblique direction in front; their tails are from eight to ten inches long, and when they leap they carry them almoſt vertical like the deer; reſembling thoſe animals not only in their proportions, but in the form of their heads, which are longer and leſs frizzled than thoſe of the roebuck. They differ alſo from that ſpecies, as they are never found in pairs. From my own obſervations, in ſhort, and from all I have been able to collect on the ſubject, I am convinced that this kind is peculiar to America, and that it may be conſidered ſomething between the deer and roebuck*. Mr. Jefferſon being no ſportſman, and not having croſſed the ſeas, could have no decided opinion on this part of natural hiſtory; but he has not neglected the other branches. I ſaw with pleaſure that he had applied himſelf particularly to meteorological obſervation,

* I have been lately aſſured, that when theſe animals grow old, their horns are as large as thoſe of the ſtag, but their fleſh has certainly the ſame taſte with that of the deer in England.

ſervation, which, in fact, of all the branches of philoſophy, is the moſt proper for the Americans to cultivate, from the extent of their country, and the variety of their ſituations, which give them in this point a great advantage over us, who in other reſpects have ſo many over them. Mr. Jefferſon has made, with Mr. *Maddiſon*, a well informed profeſſor of mathematics, ſome correſpondent obſervations on the reigning winds at *Williamſburgh*, and Monticello; and although theſe two places are at the diſtance only of fifty leagues, and not ſeparated by any chain of mountains, the difference of their reſults was, that for 127 obſervations on the N. E. wind at Williamſburgh, there were only 32 at Monticello, where the N. W. wind in general ſupplies the place of the N. E. This latter appears to be a ſea-wind, eaſily counteracted by the ſlighteſt obſtacle, inſomuch that twenty years ſince it was ſcarcely ever felt beyond *Weſt-point*; that is to ſay beyond the conflux of the *Pawmunkey* and the *Matapony*, which unite and form York river, near

 thirty-

thirty-five miles from its mouth.* Since the progreſs of population and agriculture has conſiderably cleared the woods, it penetrates ſo far as Richmond, which is thirty miles further. It may hence be obſerved, firſt, that the winds vary infinitely in their obliquity, and in the height of their region.

* The rapid changes of the temperature of the air in America, and particularly to the ſouthward, are apt to deſtroy the beſt European conſtitutions. In the middle of the hotteſt day in July and Auguſt, when the heat was ſo intolerable as almoſt to prevent reſpiration, I have frequently known the wind ſhift ſuddenly round to the N. W. attended with a blaſt, ſo cold and humid, as to make it immediately neceſſary to ſhut all the doors and windows, and light large fires. It is impoſſible to conceive any thing more trying for the human body, relaxed and open at every pore, from a continuance of burning heat, than this raw, piercing wind, which blows over ſuch immenſe boundleſs tracts of lakes and foreſts; but the melioration of the climate, even from the partial, and comparatively inconſiderable deſtruction of the woods in many parts of the continent, is ſo rapid, as to be ſtrikingly perceptible even in the courſe of a very few years; and its ſalubrity in proportion to the progreſs of theſe improvements, will probably approach much nearer to thoſe of Europe under the ſame latitudes. TRANSLATOR.

region. Secondly, that nothing is more essential than the manner in which we proceed in the clearing of a country, for the salubrity of the air, nay even the order of the seasons, may depend on the access which we allow the winds, and the direction we may give them. It is a generally received opinion at Rome, that the air is less healthy since the felling of a large forest situated between that city and Ostia, which defended it from the winds known in Italy by the names of the *Scirocco* and the *Libico*. It is believed in Spain also, that the excessive droughts, of which the Castilians complain more and more, are occasioned by the cutting down of the woods, which used to attract and break the clouds in their passage. There is yet a very important consideration upon which I thought it my duty to fix the attention of the learned in this country, whatever diffidence I may have of my own knowledge in philosophy, as well as on every other subject. The greatest part of Virginia is very low and flat, and so divided by creeks and great rivers, that it appears absolutely redeemed from the ſea, and an entire new creation; it is conſequently very ſwampy, and can be dried only by the cutting down a great quantity of wood; but as on the other hand it can never be ſo drained as not ſtill to abound with mephitical exhalations; and of whatever nature theſe exhalations may be, whether partaking of fixed or inflammable air, it is certain that vegetation abſorbs them equally, and that trees are the moſt proper to accompliſh this object *. It appears equally dangerous either to cut down or to preſerve a great quantity of wood; ſo that the beſt manner of proceeding to clear the country, would be to diſperſe the ſettlements as much as poſſible, and to leave ſome groves of trees ſtanding between them. In this manner the ground inhabited would be always healthy; and as there yet remain conſiderable marſhes which they cannot drain, there is no riſk of admitting the winds too eaſily, as they would ſerve to carry off the exhalations.

But

* This diſcovery the world owes to Doctor Franklin.

But I perceive my journal is ſomething like the converſation I had with Mr. Jefferſon; I paſs from one object to another, and forget myſelf as I write, as it happened not unfrequently in his ſociety. I muſt now quit the Friend of Nature, but not Nature herſelf, who expects me in all her ſplendour at the end of my journey; I mean the famous *Bridge* of *Rocks*, which unites two mountains, the moſt curious object I ever yet beheld, as its conſtruction is the moſt difficult of ſolution. Mr. Jefferſon would moſt willingly have conducted me thither, although this wonder is upwards of eighty miles from him, and he had often ſeen it; but his wife being expected every moment to lie in, and himſelf as good a huſband, as he is an excellent philoſopher and a virtuous citizen, he only acted as my guide for about ſixteen miles, to the paſſage of the little river *Mechum*, where we parted, and I preſume, to flatter myſelf, with mutual regret.

We walked our horſes ſeventeen miles further in the defiles of the weſtern mountains, before we could find a place to bait them; at laſt we ſtopped at a little lonely houſe, a Mr. *Mac Donnel's*, an Iriſhman, where we found eggs, bacon, chickens, and whiſkey, on which we made an excellent repaſt. He was an honeſt, obliging man; and his wife, who had a very agreeable and mild countenance, had nothing ruſtic either in her converſation or her manner. For in the center of the woods, and wholly occupied in ruſtic buſineſs, a Virginian never reſembles an European peaſant: he is always a freeman, participates in the government, and has the command of a few negroes. So that uniting in himſelf the two diſtinct qualities of citizen and maſter, he perfectly reſembles the bulk of individuals who formed what were called *the people* in the ancient republics; a people very different from that of our days, though they are very improperly confounded, in the frivolous declamations of our half philoſophers, who, in comparing ancient with modern times, have invariably miſtaken the word *people*, for mankind in general; and believing themſelves its defenders, have beſtowed their praiſes on the oppreſſors of humanity.

How

How many ideas have we ſtill to rectify? How many words, the ſenſe of which is yet vague and indeterminate? The dignity of man has been urged a hundred times, and the expreſſion is univerſally adopted. Yet after all, the dignity of man is relative; if taken in an individual ſenſe, it is in proportion to the inferior claſſes; the plebeian conſtitutes the dignity of the noble, the ſlave that of the plebeian, and the negro that of his white maſter. If taken in a general acceptation, it may inſpire man with ſentiments of tyranny and cruelty, in his relative ſituation with reſpect to other animals; deſtroying thus the general beneficence, by counteracting the orders and the views of Nature. What then is the principle on which Reaſon, eſcaped from ſophiſts and rhetoricians, may at laſt rely? The equality of rights; the general intereſt which actuates all; private intereſt, connected with the general good; the order of society; as neceſſary as the ſymmetry of a bee-hive; &c. if all this does not furniſh matter for eloquence, we muſt conſole ourſelves, and prefer genuine morality to that which is fallacious.

fallacious *. We had reason to be contented with that of Mr. Mac Donnel; he presented us with the best he had, did not make us pay too dear, and gave us every instruction necessary to continue our journey; but not being able to set out until half past four o'clock, and having twelve miles to go before we passed the *Blue Bridges*, we were happy in meeting on the road with an honest traveller, who served us for a guide, and with whom we entered into conversation. He was an inhabitant of the county of *Augusta*, who had served in Carolina

* The *Marquis de Chastellux* has distinguished himself very honourably in the literary world by several productions, but particularly by his treatise *De la Felicité Publique*, wherein he breathes the generous, enlightened language of philanthropy and freedom. He was chosen a member of the French academy at a very early age, by dint of his own merit, and not by a court mandate, or intrigue; and was, *if I mistake not*, when very young, in correspondence with, and a favourite of, the illustrious Pope *Ganganelli*. He has lately translated into French, Colonel Humphreys's poem, *The Campaign*, mentioned in the notes to the first volume of this work.

TRANSLATOR.

lina as a common *rifleman**, notwithſtanding which, he was well mounted, and appeared much at his eaſe. In America the militia is compoſed of all the inhabitants without diſtinction, and the officers are elected

* The riflemen are a Virginian militia, compoſed of the inhabitants of the mountains, who are all expert hunters, and make uſe of rifle guns. Towards the end of the war little uſe was made of them, as it was found that the difficulty of loading their pieces more than equalled the advantages derived from their exactneſs. The Americans had great numbers of riflemen in ſmall detachments on the flanks of General Burgoyne's army, many of whom took poſt on high trees *in the rear of their own line*, and there was ſeldom a minute's interval of ſmoke without officers being taken off by ſingle ſhot. Captain Green of the 31ſt regiment, Aide de Campe to General Philips, was ſhot through the arm by one of thoſe markſmen as he was delivering a meſſage to General Burgoyne. After the convention, the commanding officer of the riflemen informed General Burgoyne that the ſhot was meant for him; and as Captain Green was ſeen to fall from his horſe, it was for ſome hours believed in the American army that General Burgoyne was killed. His eſcape was owing to the Captain's having laced furniture to his ſaddle, which made him to be miſtaken for the General. General Burgoyne ſays, in his Narrative, that not an Indian could be brought within the ſound of a rifle ſhot.

TRANSLATOR.

elected by them without respect either to service or experience. Our fellow-traveller had been at the battle of *Cowpens*, where General *Morgan*, with 800 militia, entirely defeated the famous *Tarleton*, at the head of his legion, a regiment of regular troops, and of different pickets drawn from the army, forming near 1200 men, of whom upwards of 800 were killed or made prisoners *. This event, the most extraordinary

* *Lord Cornwallis*, in his answer to *Sir Henry Clinton*'s Narrative, published in 1783, gives the following state of his army before the defeat of Tarleton, and subsequent to that event, from which we may authenticate the loss of men, and deduce the importance of Morgan's victory to America.

January 15th, 1781, the rank and file of his Lordship's army was,

Guards, - - -	690
7th regiment, - -	167
16th, three companies, -	41
23d regiment, - -	286
33d regiment, - -	328
71st, 1st battalion, -	249
71st, 2d battalion, -	237
71st, light company, -	69
German regiment of Bose, -	347
Yagers, - - -	103
Carried over	2517

nary of the whole war, had always excited my curioſity. The modeſty and ſimplicity with

Brought over	2517
Tarleton's legion,	451
N. Carolina volunteers,	256
Total before the battle,	3224

February 1ſt, 1781, after the defeat of Tarleton,

Guards,	690
7th regiment,	——
16th,	——
23d,	279
33d,	334
71ſt, 1ſt battalion,	——
71ſt, 2d ditto,	234
71ſt, light company,	——
German regiment of Boſe,	345
Yagers	97
Tarleton's legion	174
N. Carolina volunteers,	287
Total after the defeat of Tarleton,	2440

Total loſs with the detachment of artillery 800 out of 1050 men, the real number of Tarleton's force.

The names of the regiments that have no numbers annexed to them in the laſt column; are thoſe which were totally deſtroyed, that is, killed, wounded, or taken, in the battle of Cowpens, on the 17th of January, between Morgan and Tarleton. Lord Cornwallis

with which General Morgan gave the account of it, have been generally admired. But one circumſtance in this relation had always aſtoniſhed me. Morgan drew up his troops in order of battle, in an open wood, and divided his riflemen upon the two wings, ſo as to form, with the line, a kind of *tenaille*, which collected the whole fire, both directly and obliquely, on the center of the Engliſh. But after the firſt diſcharge, he made ſo dangerous a movement, that had he commanded the beſt diſciplined troops in the world, I ſhould be at

in his Gazette account, immediately after the affair, ſtated the loſs only at 400, but the truth at length appears, when the purpoſes of miſrepreſentation are at an end, and the detail becomes neceſſary to the General's own honour.

Lord Cornwallis, in his account of Tarleton's defeat, mentions a very honourable circumſtance for the corps of artillery, but which was by no means unexamined by this brave body of men, in ſeveral actions in America: he ſays, "In juſtice to the detachment of royal artillery, I muſt here obſerve, that no terrors could induce them to abandon their guns, and they were *all* either killed or wounded in defence of them."

TRANSLATOR.

at a loſs to account for it. He ordered the whole line to wheel to the right, and after retreating thirty or forty paces, made them halt, face about, and recommence the fire. I begged this witneſs, whoſe depoſition could not be ſuſpected, to relate what he had ſeen, and I found his account perfectly conformable to Morgan's own relation. But as he could aſſign no reaſon for this retrograde motion, I enquired if the ground behind the firſt poſition was not more elevated and advantageous, but he aſſured me it was abſolutely the ſame; ſo that if it was this action which tempted the Engliſh (whoſe attack is not hot, but conſiſts in general of a briſk fire, rather than in cloſing with the enemy) to break their line, and advance inconſiderately into a kind of focus of ſhot poured from the center and the wings, it depended on General Morgan alone to have claimed the merit, and to have boaſted of one of the boldeſt ſtratagems ever employed in the art of war. This is a merit however he never claimed, and the relation of this rifleman leaves no doubt with me, that the General, dreading

the

the ſuperiority of the Engliſh, had at firſt deſigned to give up gradually the field of battle, and retreat to covered ground, more advantageous for inferior forces; but finding himſelf cloſely preſſed, he had no other reſource but to riſk every thing and give battle on the ſpot. Whatever was the motive of this ſingular manœuvre, the reſult of it was the defeat of Tarleton, whoſe troops gave way on all ſides, without a poſſibility of rallying them. Fatigued by a very long march, they were ſoon overtaken by the American militia, who, aſſiſted by ſixty horſe under Colonel Waſhington, made upwards of 500 priſoners, and took two pair of colours and two pieces of cannon.

It is natural to enquire how Tarleton's cavalry were employed during the engagement, and after the defeat; whilſt the infantry were engaged, they endeavoured to turn the flanks of General Morgan's army, but were kept in awe by ſome riflemen, and by the American horſe detached by Colonel Waſhington, to ſupport them, in two little ſquadrons. After the battle, they fled

fled full gallop, without ever thinking of the infantry, or taking the leaſt precaution to cover their retreat. As to the Engliſh General, God knows what became of him. And this is that Tarleton who with Cornwallis was to finiſh the conqueſt of America; who with Cornwallis had received the thanks of the Houſe of Commons, and whom all England admired as the hero of the army and the honour of the nation *.

In reflecting on the fate of war, let us recollect, that two months after this victory

* Colonel Tarleton has given ſo many proofs not only of courage but of great bravery and firmneſs, that every ſoldier ought to approve the eulogiums beſtowed upon his valour. It were to be wiſhed that he had always made good uſe of thoſe qualities, and that he had ſhewn himſelf as humane and ſenſible, as brave and determined. The deſign of theſe reflections is to ſhow, how much the Engliſh, in this war, have been obliged to ſwell their ſucceſſes, and diminiſh their defeats. The more rare they became, the more they were diſpóſed to ſolemnize the former. Howe and Burgoyne were diſgraced for not conquering America, whilſt others have obtained promotion for gaining ſome trifling advantages.

gained by the militia * over 1200 veteran troops, General Greene, after having aſſembled near 5000 men, half militia, half continentals, made choice of an excellent poſition, and employed all the reſources of military art, was beaten by 1800 men, abandoned by his militia †, and forced to limit

* Earl Cornwallis in his letter in the London Gazette of March 31ſt, 1781, ſays that Morgan had with him, " By the beſt accounts he could get, about 500 men, Continental and Virginia ſtate troops, 103 cavalry under Colonel Waſhington, and 6 or 700 militia; but that body is ſo fluctuating, that it is impoſſible to aſcertain its number *within ſome hundreds*, for three days following." This account ſeems to have been intended to qualify the defeat of Tarleton, who was a great favourite; but the fact is nearly as the Marquis de Chaſtellux ſtates it, for Morgan had very few continentals with him, and his whole body did not exceed 800 men.

† The *returns* of Lord Cornwallis's army taken a fortnight before the battle were, } 2213

The returns ſeventeen days after it, - 1723

His loſs conſequently may be ſtated at about the difference, - - } 490

Several attempts have been likewiſe made to prove that General Greene had with him at Guildford an army of 9 or 10,000 men, but Lord Cornwallis himſelf, in his letter to Lord Rawdon, dated Camp at

limit all his glory to the making the Engliſh pay dear for the field of battle, which

F 2 the

Guildford, March 17, 1781, and publiſhed in the *London Gazette* of May 10, 1781, expreſsly ſays, "General Greene having been *very conſiderably* reinforced from Virginia by *eight months men and militia*, and having collected *all the militia of this province*, advanced with an army of *about* 5 or 6000 men, and 4 ſix-pounders, to this place." From this *unexpected* account we may collect pretty clearly the indifferent compoſition of General Greene's force, and muſt render juſtice to the fairneſs of the French General's detail which calls them 5000 men, *half* militia, *half* continentals; and ſtates the conquering army *only* at 1800 men. The Tranſlator hopes the reader will not find theſe compariſons ſuperfluous, as ſuch ſcrutinies tend to elucidate the intereſting events of an ever memorable revolution, and to enlighten hiſtory. General Gates ſhewed me, at his houſe in Virginia, a letter from General Greene, wherein he took occaſion in the moſt liberal manner to reconcile him to the unfortunate affair of *Camden*, by a detail of the bad conduct of *the ſame militia*, at the battle of *Guildford*, the *Eutaws*, &c. He touched upon the matter with a delicacy and condour which did equal honour to his ſenſibility and judgment. Such a tribute of juſtice from the officer who had ſuperſeded him in his command, could not but be highly grateful to General Gates, poſſeſſing, as he does, in the moſt emi-

the reſt of his troops defended foot by foot, and yielded with reluctance *. Our conversation

nent degree, the warlike virtues, a pure diſintereſted attachment to the cauſe of freedom, and all the generous ſuſceptibility of an amiable private gentleman. Whilſt under a cloud himſelf, I heard him with admiration uniformly expatiate with all the diſtreſſed warmth of public virtue on the ſucceſſes of other Generals, and inſtead of jealous repining and diſguſt, pay his tribute of applauſe to the merits even of thoſe he could not love, and prognoſticate, with confidence, the final ſucceſs of America. It was with real joy therefore, that I ſaw his honour vindicated by the deliberate voice of Congreſs, himſelf reſtored to his former rank, and that harmony which never ſhould have been diſturbed, renewed between this true patriot and General Waſhington, under whom I left him ſecond in command at the camp at Verplanks on the North River in October, 1782. TRANSLATOR.

* Since the Journal was written, the author has had an opportunity of ſeeing General Morgan; he is a man about fifty, tall, and of a very martial appearance. The ſervices he rendered the ſtate during the war, were very numerous, and his promotion rapid. It is pretended that he was formerly *a carter*; and from the ſame unacquaintance with the cuſtoms and language of the country, another General is ſaid to have been *a farmer*, becauſe he employed himſelf in cultivation, and a third to have been *a*

'verſation on war and battles brought us to the foot of the *gap*, or, as it is called, the

butcher, becauſe he dealt in cattle. General Morgan was formerly engaged in waggons, undertook the tranſport of goods ſent by land, and often put himſelf at the head of theſe little convoys. The Marquis de Ch——, the firſt time he had an opportunity of ſeeing him, commanded the French troops in the abſence of the Comte de Rochambeau at Philadelphia, during the march from Williamſburgh to Baltimore. The Marquis de Ch—— was then at Colcheſter, with the firſt diviſion of the troops, after paſſing in boats the river which runs near the town. The carriages and artillery had taken another road, to gain an indifferent ford. General Morgan met them when they were engaged in a very narrow paſſage, and finding the carters did not underſtand their buſineſs, he ſtopped, and ſhewed them how they ought to drive. Having put every thing in order, he alighted at the Marquis's, and dined with him. The ſimplicity of his deportment, and the nobleneſs of his behaviour, recalled to mind the ancient Gallic and German chiefs, who, when in peace with the Romans, came to viſit and offer them aſſiſtance. He expreſſed a great attachment to the French nation, admired our troops, and never ceaſed looking at them; often repeating, that the greateſt pleaſure of his life would be, to ſerve in numerous and brilliant armies. It will eaſily be conjectured that his hoſt aſked him many queſtions,

neck of *Rock-Fiſh*, which, in an extent of more than fifty miles, is the only paſſage

particularly reſpecting the affair of Cowpens. His anſwer confirmed what the rifleman had ſaid; he owned alſo very candidly that the retrograde movement he had made, was not permeditated. His troops were intimidated, when the Engliſh, with more confidence than order, advanced to the attack: obſerving them keep their ranks, he ſuffered them to retreat a hundred paces, and then commanded them to halt and face the enemy, as if the retrograde movement had been really preconcerted *. Though this account, which is more recent and ſurer than in the text, might render thoſe reflections uſeleſs, it was thought proper to preſerve them, becauſe on one hand they are not unintereſting to the ſoldier, and on the other, they may teach philoſophers and critics to ſuſpect thoſe who have written hiſtory; above all, thoſe who, like Titus Livius, Dionyſius of Halicarnaſſus, and all the copious and elegant hiſtorians, delight in multiplying and varying the deſcriptions of battles; or, what is yet more reprehenſible, who like Frontin, Pollien, and other

* General Morgan by thus dexterouſly availing himſelf of the circumſtances of his very critical poſition, has perhaps more real merit, than if he had really preconceived the manœuvre which has given him ſo much fame; a manœuvre, from which, unleſs juſtified by a neceſſity ſuch as his, he had no right to expect ſucceſs, in the face of a *ſkilful* enemy; but Tarleton never was a *commander*. TRANSLATOR.

ſage to croſs the Blue Ridges, at leaſt in a carriage. We aſcended very commodiouſly, for about two miles, and on arriving at the top of the mountain, were ſurpriſed to find a little cottage lately built and inhabited by white people. I enquired of my fellow traveller what could engage them to ſettle in ſo barren and deſert a place; he told me they were poor people, who expected to get ſome aſſiſtance from paſſengers.

I expected this anſwer, and was ſorry to find in a new country, where the earth wants inhabitants, and agriculture, hands, white people under the neceſſity of begging. I ſtopped a moment to view the wild but unintereſting proſpect of the weſtern mountains, from the ſummit of the Blue Ridges. But as the ſun was near ſetting, I haſtened to reach the only inn where

other compilers, borrow from hiſtorians the events and ſtratagems of war, which they endeavour to collect.

General Morgan has not ſerved ſince the affair of Cowpens; he lives in the county of Fairfax and on the eſtate which he had either purchaſed or increaſed, waiting till opportunity ſhall preſent him with ſome command.

lodgings could be had, on the other side of the mountains. Notwithstanding which, I stopped once more, nor had I any reason to regret it. My servant always followed me with a fowling-piece, and as it frequently happened that I was obliged to alight to fire at a partridge, or some other game, our conversation did not prevent me from being always upon the watch. I perceived a large bird which crossed the road, and by the instinct of a sportsman, I concluded it to be what the inhabitants of the mountains called a *pheasant*, but which resembles much more a *woodhen*. To alight, call my dog, and take my gun, was the work of a moment; as I was preparing to follow the *woodhen* among the bushes, one of my servants pointed out to me two others, perched upon a tree behind him, and which looked at me with great tranquillity. I fired at the one nearest to me, nor did it require much address to kill it. Except that it was perhaps a little bigger, it resembled the one I had seen at Newport, where the Americans carry them sometimes to market, in winter, when they descend from

from the mountains, and are more eaſily killed. This one, before, it was plucked, was of the ſize of a capon; its plumage on the back and wings reſembled that of a hen pheaſant, and, on the belly and thighs, the large winter thruſh. It was booted like the rough-footed pigeon, to its feet, and the plumage of its head formed a kind of aigrette: take it altogether, it is a beautiful bird, and good eating; but when ſtript of its feathers, it was not larger than the red-footed partridge, or bartavelle. After ordering the woodhen I had killed, for ſupper, I tried to find the firſt I had ſeen run into the underwood. I raiſed it once, and although I ran immediately, and had an excellent dog, it was impoſſible to find it; theſe birds running very faſt, like the pheaſant and the rail. The mode which the inhabitants of the mountains make uſe of to kill them, is to walk in the woods at ſun-riſing and ſun-ſetting, to attend to the noiſe they make in beating their ſides with their wings, which may be heard above a mile; they then approach ſoftly, and uſually find them ſitting upon the trunk of ſome

old

old tree. It was perhaps lucky that my ſhooting did not continue with more ſucceſs; for it was almoſt night when we arrived at the ford of *South River*, and the waters, conſiderably augmented by the late rains, were very high. I was proud of fording the famous *Potowmack*, which had taken me an hour in a boat, at the *ferry* of *Alexandria* *.

South

* In travelling from Frederick-Town to Leeſburgh, in a ſingle-horſe chaiſe for one perſon, called in America *a ſulky*, the ſhafts of my carriage broke about a mile from the Potowmack, on the Maryland ſide, and I was reduced to the neceſſity, having no ſervant, of leaving it with all my papers, money, fire-arms, &c. and of mounting my horſe in ſearch of aſſiſtance. Night was coming on in a moſt difficult country, to which I was an utter ſtranger, and not even a negro-hut was to be met with. In theſe circumſtances I approached the Potowmack, on the other ſide of which I diſcovered a ſmoke in the woods, which gave me hopes of its proceeding from a houſe, but the river was near a mile broad, and my horſe barely fourteen hands high. Whilſt I was thus ſtanding in ſuſpence, two travellers arrive on horſeback and puſh into the river, a little higher up. I flew to follow them, but ſcarcely had they advanced one hundred yards before they returned, declaring it not fordable, and,

South river in fact is only a branch of the Potowmack, the ſource of which is in the

to add to my diſtreſs, they aſſured me that I was at a great diſtance from any houſe on that ſide, but, on the other, I ſhould find an ordinary kept by a Scotſman. They excuſed themſelves from aſſiſting me on the plea of urgent buſineſs, and left me with the conſoling aſſurance that the river might poſſibly be fordable, though they who were inhabitants of the country, did not chuſe to venture it. Perceiving the bottom of a good gravel, and free from rocks, I attempted the paſſage as ſoon as they left me, and in about twenty dangerous and irkſome minutes reached the other ſide, where I obtained the cheerful aid of two native negroes at the Scotſman's hut, for it was no better, and recroſſing the river, went in ſearch of my broken carriage, which we found in ſecurity. It was ten o'clock before I paſſed the river a third time, always up to my waiſt, and reached my quarters for the night, where at leaſt I met with as hoſpitable a reception as the houſe afforded; but the conſequence of this adventure, wherein I was ſucceſſively wet and dry three times, in the hot month of July, was a fever and ague, which tormented me for five months. At Alexandria, about fifty miles lower down, the Potowmack rolls its majeſtic ſtream with ſublimity and grandeur, ſixty gun ſhips may lie before the town, which ſtands upon its lofty banks, commanding, to a great extent,

the moutains, and like all other rivers is humble in its riſe; but it may be looked upon as the proudeſt of its branches, as at the diſtance of thirty leagues, it is above a mile broad, and reſembles more an arm of the ſea, than a river. Two hundred paces from the ford, but more than forty miles from the place from which I ſet out, I found the inn which Mr. Jefferſon had deſcribed to me; it was one of the worſt in all America. Mrs. Teaze, the miſtreſs of the houſe, was ſome time ſince left a widow; ſhe appears alſo to be in fact the widow of her furniture, for ſurely never was houſe ſo badly furniſhed. A ſolitary tin veſſel was the only bowl for the family, the ſervants and ourſelves; I dare not ſay for what other uſe it was propoſed to us on our going to bed *. As we were four maſters, without

the flatter ſhore of Maryland. This town, which ſtands above 200 miles from the ſea, is rapidly on the increaſe, and from the laviſh prodigality of Nature, cannot fail of becoming one of the firſt cities in the new world. TRANSLATOR.

* The Marquis's diſtreſs on this occaſion, reminds me naturally of a ſimilar, but ſtill worſe ſituation, in

without reckoning the rifleman, who had followed, and whom I had engaged to ſupper, the hoſteſs and the family were obliged to reſign to us their beds. But at the moment we were inclined to make uſe of them, a tall young man entering the chamber, where we were aſſembled, opened a cloſet, and took out of it a little bottle. I enquired what it was; it is, ſaid he, ſomething which the Doctor in the neighbourhood has ordered me to take every day. And for what complaint, ſaid I? Oh! not much, he replied, only a *little itch*. I own his

which I found myſelf on my return from America towards the end of the war, with four officers of the army of the Comte de Rochambeau. Our captain being obliged ſuddenly to take advantage of one of thoſe violent north weſters which blow in December, to get clear of the coaſt, beſet with New-York Privateers, forgot all his crockery ware, ſo that in default of plates, mugs, &c. we were obliged, during a winter's voyage of ſeven weeks, to apply two tin jugs we had purchaſed to drink our cyder, to every uſe; and, in ſpite of my repreſentations, even to ſome purpoſes I am unwilling to repeat; for in bad weather, theſe excellent *land-officers* would not be prevailed upon to look on deck.

TRANSLATOR.

his confeſſion was inguenuous, but I was by no means ſorry that I had ſheets in my portmanteau. It may eaſily be imagined we were not tempted to breakfaſt in this houſe. We ſet out therefore very early on the 18th, in hopes (as we had been told) that we ſhould find a better inn, at the diſtance of ten miles, but thoſe hopes were vain. Mr. *Smith*, a poor planter, to whom we were recommended, had neither forage for our horſes, nor any thing for ourſelves. He only aſſured us, that eight miles further we ſhould find a mill, the proprietor of which kept a public-houſe, and we found accordingly the mill and the miller. He was a young man, twenty-two years of age, whoſe charming face, fine teeth, red lips, and roſy cheeks, recalled to mind the pleaſing portrait which Marmontel gives of *Lubin*. His walk and carriage did not however correſpond with the freſhneſs of his looks, for he appeared ſluggiſh and inactive. I enquired the reaſon, and he told me he had been in a languiſhing ſtate ever ſince the battle of *Guildford*, in which he had received fifteen or ſixteen wounds with a hanger.

He

He had not, like the Romans, a crown to atteſt his valour; nor, like the French, either penſion or certificate of honour; inſtead of them, he had a piece of his ſkull, which his wife brought to ſhew me. I certainly little thought of finding, amidſt the ſolitudes of America, ſuch lamentable traces of European ſteel; but I was the moſt touched to learn, that it was after he had received his firſt wound, and was made priſoner, that he had been thus cruelly treated. This unhappy young man acquainted me, that overcome with wounds, and wallowing in his blood, he yet retained his preſence of mind, and imagining his cruel enemies would not leave exiſting a ſingle witneſs or victim of their barbarity, there remained no other way of ſaving his life, than by appearing as if he had loſt it.

The all-ſeeing eye of Divine Juſtice alone can diſcover and make known the authors of ſuch a crime; but, if diſcovered—Oh! for the voice of a Stentor and the trumpet of Fame, to devote the vile perpetrators to preſent and future horror! And to announce to all ſovereigns, generals and chiefs, that the

enormities

enormities which they tolerate, or leave unpuniſhed, will accumulate upon their heads, and, at ſome future time, render them the execration of a poſterity ſtill more ſenſible, and more enlightened than we yet are!

Even if Mr. *Steel*, our landlord, had been more active, and his wife, who was young and handſome, more induſtrious, they could not have ſupplied the total want in which they then were, of bread, and of every thing to drink; the bread was juſt kneaded, but not yet put into the oven; and as for liquors, the houſe made uſe of none; the ſame ſtream which turned the mill, was the only cellar of the young couple, ſo that we might apply to Mrs. Steel thoſe verſes of *Guarini*,

Quel fonte on d'ella beve
Quel ſolo aneo la bagna, e la conſiglia.

But theſe paſtoral manners are but ill ſuited to travellers. A few cakes, however, baked upon the cinders, excellent butter, good milk, and above all, the intereſt with which Mr. Steel inſpired us, made us paſs agreeably the time which was neceſſary to put our horſes in a condition to perform a long

long and difficult day's journey. About five o'clock in the evening, after we had travelled thirty-eight miles, we found ſome houſes, where we learned that we were yet ſix miles from *Praxton's Tavern*, where we intended to ſleep; that we had two fords to paſs, the laſt of which was impracticable on account of the late rains; but that we ſhould not be ſtopped, as we ſhould find a canoe to take us acroſs, and our horſes would ſwim behind. The night, and a black ſtorm which was brewing, made us haſten our ſteps. Notwithſtanding which, we were obliged to mount and deſcend a very high mountain; ſcarcely was there remaining the leaſt twilight when we arrived at the ſecond river, which is as large as James's, but near its ſource, and at a place where it deſcends from the mountains under the name of the *Fluvanna*. The difficulty was to paſs ten men and as many horſes with the help of a ſingle canoe, ſuch as is made uſe of by the ſavages, which at moſt could contain only four or five perſons and a ſingle negro, armed with a paddle inſtead of an oar. We put into the canoe

 our

our ſaddles and baggage, and made ſeveral trips, at each of which two horſes were ſwam acroſs, held by the bridle. It was night, and very dark before this buſineſs was finiſhed. But after we had, not without great trouble, reſaddled and reloaded our horſes, the difficulty was to reach the inn, which was half a mile from the place where we landed; for the river flows between two precipices, and as the canoe could not land us at the ford, nor conſequently at the road, we were obliged to climb up the mountain, by a path but little uſed, and very difficult even by daylight; nor ſhould we ever have found our way, had I not engaged the waterman to conduct us. We clambered up as well as we could, every one leading his horſe through the trees and branches, which we could not perceive, from the obſcurity of the night, until they ſtruck us on the face. At laſt we arrived at Praxton's tavern; but it was ten o'clock, and the houſe already ſhut up, or more properly the houſes, for there are two. I approached the firſt that offered, and knocked at the door, which they opened,

opened, and we ſaw five or ſix little negroes lying upon a mat before a large fire. We then went to the other, and there found five or ſix white children lying in the ſame manner; two or three grown-up negroes preſided over each of theſe little troops*. They told us that Mr. Praxton, his wife, and all his family, were invited to a wedding, but not far off, and that they would go and fetch them. As for us, we were invited to ſupper by a very voracious appetite, after a long journey and a great deal of fatigue, and were very differently ſituated from the new married couple and their

 company,

* It was a ſingular ſight for an European to behold the ſituation of the negroes in the ſouthern provinces during the war, when clothing was extremely ſcarce. I have frequently ſeen in Virginia, on viſits to gentlemen's houſes, young negroes and negroeſſes running about or baſking in the court-yard naked as they came into the world, with well characterized marks of perfect puberty; and young negroes from ſixteen to twenty years old, with not an article of clothing, but a looſe ſhirt, deſcending half way down their thighs, waiting at table where were ladies, without any apparent embarraſſment on one ſide, or the ſlighteſt attempt at concealment on the other.

TRANSLATOR.

company, and had no ſmall apprehenſions of ſeeing our hoſt and hoſteſs return compleatly drunk. But in this we were deceived; they arrived perfectly ſober, were polite and deſirous to pleaſe, and a little after midnight we had an excellent ſupper. Though the apartments and beds were not exactly what we wiſhed, they were better than at Mrs. *Teaze*'s, and we had no right to complain. Beſides, we enjoyed the ſatisfaction of having accompliſhed the object of our journey; for the *Natural Bridge* was not above eight miles off, and we had obtained every information neceſſary to find the road. The next morning our breakfaſt was ready betimes, and ſerved by the daughters of Captain Praxton; they had not appeared to advantage the preceding evening; notwithſtanding which, ſo far as the obſcurity of the room we ſupped in, our appetites, and the immenſe caps in which they were muffled up for the marriage, had permitted us to judge of them, we thought them tolerably handſome; but when we ſaw them by day-light, with their hair only turned up, without any other

other head-drefs, after the repofe of the night, their fole ornament, and for every grace, their natural fimplicity, we were confirmed in the opinion we had already formed, that the people of the mountains are, in general, handfomer and healthier than thofe on the fea-coaft *. There was in the houfe a young man alfo, tolerably well dreffed, and of an agreeable countenance, whom I concluded to be an intended match for one of our young hofteffes. But I foon difcovered that he was come for matches of another kind. In fact, one of my fellow-travellers inviting me to go and fee a very fine horfe, which ftood alone in a little ftable, I was informed it was a ftallion, which this young man had brought upwards of eighty miles, to difpofe of his favours to the mares

* The South Carolina gentlemen with whom I was acquainted, affured me, that the inhabitants of the back parts of that State, which is one of the moft unhealthy on the continent, are a vigorous and beautiful race of people, and poffefs all that hale ruddinefs which characterizes the natives of northern climates. TRANSLATOR.

of the country *. His price was twenty ſhillings Virginia currency †, or eighteen livres of our money, (about ſifteen ſhillings ſterling) for each viſit, or double if the connection was of longer duration, which is much leſs than is paid in the other parts of Virginia. Theſe details, which may

* Great attention is paid to the breed of blood-horſes to the ſouthward, and particularly in Virginia, and many ſecond-rate race horſes are annually ſent from England to ſerve as ſtallions. There were two or three in the ſtables of one *Bates* near Philadelphia, which I had ſeen win plates in England. This Bates is a native of Morpeth in Northumberland, and went to America before the war to diſplay feats of horſemanſhip; but he had the good fortune to marry a widow poſſeſſed of five hundred pounds a year, and is now maſter of a moſt beautiful villa on the banks of the Delaware, four or five miles from Philadelphia, ſtill following however the occupation of breeding and ſelling horſes, and keeping ſtallions, for there are no reſources for idleneſs in that country. TRANSLATOR.

† The difference of currency is one of the moſt puzzling and diſagreeable circumſtances for a ſtranger in America, the value of *the pound* varying in every State; an inconvenience which exiſted under the Britiſh government, and I am afraid, is ſtill likely to ſubſiſt. TRANSLATOR.

may appear trifling, will however ſerve to make the reader acquainted with a country, the inhabitants of which, diſperſed in the woods, are ſeparated only for the purpoſes of domeſtic comfort, which renders them independent of each other, but who readily communicate for the general intereſt, or their mutual wants. But I am too near the Natural Bridge to ſtop at other objects. We ſet out at nine o'clock in the morning, and to ſay the truth, rather heedleſsly; for in theſe mountains, where there are either too many or too few roads, people always think they have given ſufficient directions to travellers, who ſeldom fail to go aſtray. This is the common fault of thoſe who inſtruct others in what they themſelves are well acquainted with, nor are the roads to ſcience exempt from this inconvenience. After riding about two miles however, we luckily met a man who had juſt got his horſe ſhod, at a neighbouring forge, and was returning home, followed by two or three couple of hounds *. We ſoon entered in-

* Stopping one day at a ſmith's ſhop near *Wincheſter*, in the interior of Virginia, I found one of the work-

to converſation with him, and what ſeldom happens in America, he was curious to know who I was, and whither I was going*. My quality of a General Officer in the

men to be a Scotch Highlander in his Galic dreſs, and ſoon ſaw ſeveral more returning from harveſt; theſe men had been ſoldiers, and were then priſoners, but they were all peaceable, induſtrious labourers, and I could not find that any of them thought of returning to the barren hills of Caledonia. General Gates had ſeveral of them in his employ, and they were diſperſed over the whole country, where they appeared compleatly naturalized and happy. I afterwards ſaw many of them working at mills, and as quarry-men, on the picturesque banks of that ſublime river the Suſquehannah, a circumſtance which tranſported my imagination to the well-known borders of the Tay, and of Loch Lomond. TRANSLATOR.

* I am apt to think that the experience of every perſon who has viſited North-America, as well as my own country, will riſe in judgment againſt this obſervation of the Author; for my part, were I ſearching for a general characteriſtic of that part of the Continent, I ſhould not ſcruple to diſtinguiſh it, κατ' ἐξοχὴν, by the name of *the country of the curious*. Wherever you bend your courſe, to whomſoever you addreſs yourſelf, you are indiſpenſibly ſubject to a good humoured, inoffenſive, but *mighty* troubleſome inquiſition. Do you enquire your road? you are anſwered by a queſtion, " I ſuppoſe you

the French ſervice, and the deſire I expreſſed of ſeeing the wonders of his country, inſpiring

come from the Eaſtward, don't you?" Oppreſſed with fatigue, hunger, and thirſt, and drenched perhaps with rain, you anſwer ſhortly in the affirmative, and repeat your enquiry.—"Methinks you are in a mighty haſte—What news is there to the Eaſtward?" The only ſatisfaction you can obtain till you have opened your real, or pretended budget of news, and gratified the demander's curioſity. At an inn, the ſcrutiny is more minute; your name, quality, the place of your departure, and object of your journey, muſt all be declared to the good family in ſome way or other, (for their credulity is equal to their curioſity) before you can ſit down in comfort to the neceſſary refreſhment. This curious ſpirit is intolerable in the Eaſtern States; and I have heard Dr. Franklin, who is himſelf a Boſtonian, frequently relate with great pleaſantry, that in travelling when he was young, the firſt ſtep he took for his tranquillity, and to obtain immediate attention at the inns, was to anticipate enquiry, by ſaying, "My name is Benja-"min Franklin, I was born at Boſton, am a printer "by profeſſion, am travelling to Philadelphia, ſhall "return at ſuch a time, and have no news—Now "what can you give me for dinner?" The only cauſe which can be aſſigned for the Author's error in this reſpect, is the ſtate in which he travelled, his being a foreigner, and the facility of obtaining information from the perſons of his retinue.

TRANSLATOR

inſpiring him with a kind of affection for me, he offered to be our conductor, leading us ſometimes through little paths, at others through woods, but continually climbing or deſcending mountains; ſo that without a guide, nothing ſhort of witchcraft could have enabled us to find the road. Having thus travelled for two hours, we at laſt deſcended a ſteep declivity, and then mounted another; during which time he endeavoured to render the converſation more intereſting. At laſt, puſhing his horſe on briſkly, and ſtopping ſuddenly, he ſaid to me, " You deſire to ſee the *Natural Bridge*, don't you Sir? You are now upon it, alight and go twenty ſteps either to the right or left, and you will ſee this prodigy." I had perceived that there was on each ſide a conſiderable deep hollow, but the trees had prevented me from forming any judgment, or paying much attention to it.—Approaching the precipice, I ſaw at firſt two great maſſes or chains of rocks, which formed the bottom of a ravin, or rather of an immenſe abyſs; but placing myſelf, not without precaution, upon the brink of the

precipice,

precipice, I ſaw that theſe two buttreſſes were joined under my feet, forming a vault, of which I could yet form no idea but of its height. After enjoying this magnificent but tremendous ſpectacle, which many perſons could not bear to look at, I went to the weſtern ſide, the aſpect of which was not leſs impoſing, but more pictureſque. This *Thebais*, theſe ancient pines, theſe enormous maſſes of rocks, ſo much the more aſtoniſhing as they appear to poſſeſs a wild ſymmetry, and rudely to concur, as it were, in forming a certain deſign; all this apparatus of rude and ſhapeleſs Nature, which Art attempts in vain, attacks at once the ſenſes and the thoughts, and excites a gloomy and melancholy admiration. But it is at the foot of theſe rocks, on the edge of a little ſtream which flows under this immenſe arch, that we muſt judge of its aſtoniſhing ſtructure; there we diſcover its immenſe ſpurs, its backbendings, and thoſe profiles which architecture might have given it. The arch is not compleat, the eaſtern part of it not being ſo large as the weſtern, becauſe the mountain

mountain is more elevated on this than on the opposite side. It is very extraordinary that at the bottom of the stream there appear no considerable ruins, no trace of any violent laceration, which could have destroyed the kernel of the rock, and have left the upper part alone subsisting; for that is the only hypothesis that can account for such a prodigy. We can have no possible recourse either to a volcano or a deluge, no trace of a sudden conflagration, or of a slow and tedious undermining by the water.

The rock is of the calcareous kind, and its different strata are horizontal; a circumstance which excludes even the idea of an earthquake, or subterraneous cavern. It is not, in short, for a small number of travellers to give a decided opinion for the public on this phænomenon of Nature. It belongs to the learned of both worlds to judge of it, and they will now be enabled to attempt the discussion. The necessary steps are taken to render it as public as its singularity deserves; an officer of the engineers, the Baron de Turpin, an excellent mathematician and an accurate draughtsman,

man, is gone to take the principal aſpects and dimenſions. His labours will ſupply the deficiency of my deſcription *. Though unacquainted with the powers of Nature, we may at leaſt have ſome idea of our own. I ſhall therefore leave to more able hands the care of finiſhing this picture, of which I have given only an imperfect ſketch, and continue the relation of our journey, which, though the principal object be already accompliſhed, is not near being terminated, for the *Natural Bridge* is more than 250 miles from Williamſburgh.

Whilſt I was examining on all ſides, and endeavouring to take ſome drawings, my fellow-travellers had learned from our conductor that he kept a public-houſe, about ſeven or eight miles from the place where we were, and not more than two from the road which muſt be taken next day to leave the mountains. Mr. *Griſby*, (the name of our guide) had expreſſed his wiſhes to receive us, aſſuring us we ſhould be as well as at the tavern recommended by Mr.

* See at the end of this Journal the deſcription and the plans.

Mr. Praxton; but had this been otherwise, we had too many obligations to Mr. Grisby not to give him the preference. We renewed our journey therefore, under his guidance, through the woods, which were very lofty; strong robust oaks, and immense pines, sufficient for all the fleets of Europe, here grow old, and perish on their native soil; from which they have never yet been drawn even by the hand of industry *. One is surprized to find every where in these immense forests, the traces of conflagrations. These accidents are sometimes occasioned by the imprudence of travellers, who light a fire when they go to sleep and neglect

* The quality of the American oak is found by repeated experience to be by no means equal to, or so durable as that of Britain. A general survey of the American woods was taken by order of the government of England, previous to the war, and the different qualities ascertained by the surveyors, who, on their general report, gave the preference to the southern oak on the Apalachians, and in the interior of Georgia and Florida; but in the English yards, even the Dantzick plank, which grows in Silesia, and that of Stettin, is still preferred to the American. TRANSLATOR.

neglect afterwards to extinguiſh it. Little attention is paid them when the woods alone are the victims ; but as there are always ſome cultivated parts, the fire often reaches the fences, by which the fields are ſurrounded, and ſometimes the houſes themſelves, which is inevitable ruin to the cultivators.

I recollect that during my ſtay at Monticello, from which one may diſcover an extent of thirty or forty leagues of wood, I ſaw ſeveral conflagrations three or four leagues diſtant from each other, which continued burning until a heavy rain fell luckily and extinguiſhed them †. We arrived at

† Conflagrations which take their riſe in this manner, ſometimes ſpread to a prodigious extent in America, in the moraſſes, as well as in the woods ; in travelling from Eaſton on the Delaware over the *Muſconetgung* mountains in the Upper Jerſey, in 1782, I ſaw immenſe tracts of country lying in aſhes from one of theſe accidental fires ; and, during the ſame ſummer, Philadelphia was ſometimes covered with ſmoke, from a vaſt moraſs which had taken fire in the Jerſeys, and kept burning to a great depth from the ſurface, and for an extent of many miles around, for ſeveral months ; the progreſs of which

at Mr. Grifby's a little before five o'clock, having met with nothing on the road but a wild turkey, which rofe fo far off, that it was impoffible to find it again. The houfe was not large, but neat and commodious; we found it already taken up by other travellers, to whom we affuredly owed every token of refpect, if pre-eminence betwixt travellers were to be meafured by the length of their refpective journies.

The other guefts were a healthy good humoured young man of eight and twenty, who fet out from Philadelphia with a pretty wife of twenty, and a little child in her arms, to fettle 500 miles beyond the mountains, in a country lately inhabited, bordering on the *Ohio*, called the country of *Kentucket*. His whole retinue was a horfe, which carried his wife and child. We were aftonifhed at the eafy manner with which he proceeded on his expedition, and took the liberty of mentioning our furprize to him. He told us

could not be ftopped by the large trenches dug by the labour of the whole country, nor until it was extinguifhed by the autumnal rains.

TRANSLATOR.

as that the purchaſe of good land in Penſylvania was very-extravagant, that proviſions were too dear, and the inhabitants too numerous, in conſequence of which he thought it more beneficial to purchaſe for about fifty guineas the grant of a thouſand acres of land in *Kentucket*. This territory had been formerly given to a Colonel of militia, until the King of England thought proper to order the diſtribution of thoſe immenſe countries; part of which was ſold, and the other reſerved to recompenſe the American troops who had ſerved in Canada *

* The Author means the ſoldiers who ſerved in Canada againſt the French in the war before the laſt. *Kentucket* is at preſent peopled by above fifty thouſand ſettlers, and is on the point of being admitted into the union, as an independent ſtate. Kentucket is a ſettlement on the creek, or rather river of that name, which falls into the Ohio, and is 627¾ miles diſtant from Fort Pitt; but is extending in every direction over a tract of the fineſt and moſt fertile country in the world: and as it is from the interior ſettlements of this vaſt country, that America will derive her future greatneſs, and eſtabliſh new empires to rival, and perhaps outdo the antient world, I hope I ſhall be pardoned for

But, ſaid I, where are the cattle? The implements of huſbandry with which you
muſt

tranſcribing the following ſhort but intereſting account of the banks of the Ohio from Captain *Hutchins*'s Topographical Deſcription of that country, accompanying his Maps—“ The lands upon the *Ohio*,
“ and its branches, are differently timbered according
“ to their quality and ſituation. The high and
“ dry lands are covered with *red*, *white*, and *black*
“ oak, *hickery*, *walnut*, *red* and *white mulberry*, and
“ *aſh* trees, grape vines, &c. The low and mea-
“ dow lands are filled with *ſycamore*, *poplar*, *red* and
“ *white mulberry*, *cherry*, *beech*, *elm*, *aſpen*, *maple*, or
“ *ſugar* trees, *grape vines*, &c. And below, or ſouth-
“ wardly of the *Rapids*, are ſeveral large *cedar* and
“ *cypreſs ſwamps*, where the cedar and cypreſs-trees
“ grow to a remarkable ſize, and where alſo is great
“ abundance of canes, ſuch as grow in South Carolina.
“ There is a great variety of game, viz. buffaloes, bear,
“ deer, &c. as well as *ducks*, *geeſe*, *ſwans*, *turkies*, *phea-*
“ *ſants*, *partridges*, &c. which abound in every part of
“ this country. The *Ohio*, and the rivers emptying
“ into it, afford green, and other *turtle*, and fiſh of
“ various ſorts; particularly *carp*, *ſturgeon*, *perch*
“ and *catfiſh*; the two latter of an uncommon ſize;
“ viz. perch from eight to twelve pounds weight, and
“ *catfiſh* from fifty to one hundred pounds weight.
“ The country on both ſides of the Ohio, extending
“ ſouth-eaſterly and ſouth-weſterly from *Fort Pitt*
“ to the *Miſſiſippi*, and watered by the Ohio river
“ and its branches, contains at leaſt A MILLION OF

muſt begin to clear the land you have purchaſed?—In the country itſelf, replied he.

" SQUARE MILES ; and it may with truth be affirm-
" ed, that no part of the globe is bleſſed with a
" more healthful air or climate; watered with more
" navigable rivers, and branches communicating
" with the *Atlantic* ocean, by the rivers *Potowmack*,
" *James*, *Rapahannock*, *Miſſiſippi*, and *St. Lawrence*;
" or capable of producing, with leſs labour and ex-
" pence, *wheat*, *Indian corn*, *buck wheat*, *rye*, *oats*,
" *barley*, *flax*, *hemp*, *tobacco*, *rice*, *ſilk*, *pot-aſh*, &c.
" than the country under conſideration; and it
" may be added, that no ſoil can yield larger
" crops of *red* and *white clover*, and other uſeful
" graſs, than this does."——Colonel GORDON, in his *Journal*, gives the following deſcription of this ſoil and climate: " The country on the *Ohio*, &c.
" is every where pleaſant, with large level ſpots of
" rich land, remarkably healthy. One general re-
" mark of this nature may ſerve for the whole
" tract comprehended between the weſtern ſkirts
" of the Allegheney mountains, beginning at *Fort*
" *Ligonier*, thence bearing ſouth-weſterly to the
" diſtance of 500 miles oppoſite to the Ohio falls,
" then croſſing them northerly to the heads of the
" rivers that empty themſelves into the *Ohio*;
" thence eaſt along the ridge that ſeparates the lakes
" and *Ohio*'s ſtreams to *French Creek*, which is op-
" ſite to the abovementioned *Fort Ligonier* nor-
" therly. This country may, from a proper know-

I carry nothing with me, but I have money in my pocket, and ſhall want for nothing.

I began

" ledge, be affirmed to be the moſt healthy, the " moſt pleaſant, the moſt commodious, and moſt " fertile ſpot of earth *known to European people*."[a] To which may be added the following extract of a letter addreſſed to the Earl of Hillſborough, in the year 1772, then Secretary of State for the North American department.

" No part of North America will require leſs en- " couragement for the production of *naval ſtores*, " and *raw materials* for manfactures in Europe, " and for ſupplying the Weſt India iſlands with " *lumber*, *proviſions*, *&c.* than the country of the Ohio, " and for the following reaſons: Firſt, the lands " are excellent, the climate temperate, the native " grapes, *ſilk-worms* and *mulberry-trees* abound every " where; *hemp*, *hops*, and *rye* grow ſpontaneouſly in " the vallies and low-lands; *lead* and *iron* ore, " *coal* alſo, are plenty in the hills; ſalt and freſh " ſprings are innumerable; and no ſoil is bet- " ter adapted to the culture of tobacco, flax and " *cotton* than that of the Ohio. Secondly, the " country is well watered by ſeveral *navigable rivers* " communicating with each other; by which, and " a ſhort land carriage, the produce of the lands of " the Ohio can *even now* (in the year 1772) be ſent " cheaper to the ſea-port town of *Alexandria*, on " the Potowmack in Virginia, than any kind of mer- " chandize is ſent from *Northampton* to London.

I began to reliſh the reſolution of this young man, who was active, vigorous, and free

“ Thirdly, the Ohio is, at *all ſeaſons* of the year, na-
“ vigable with large boats like the *weſt country*
“ *barges*, rowed only by four or five men; and
“ from the month of February to April, large ſhips
“ may be built on the Ohio, and ſent to *ſea* laden
“ with hemp, iron, flax, ſilk, rice, tobacco, cotton,
“ pot-aſhes, &c. Fourthly, corn, beef, ſhip-plank,
“ and other uſeful articles can be ſent *down the*
“ *ſtream* of *Ohio* to Weſt Florida, and from thence
“ to the Weſt-Indies, much *cheaper*, and in better
“ order than from *New-York* or Philadelphia.
“ Fifthly, hemp, tobacco, iron, and ſuch bulky ar-
“ ticles may alſo be ſent *down* the Ohio to the ſea,
“ at leaſt 50 per cent. *cheaper* than theſe articles
“ were ever carried by a land carriage of only ſixty
“ miles in Penſylvania, where waggonage is cheaper
“ than in any other part of North America. Sixthly,
“ the expence of tranſporting *European manufac-*
“ *tures from the ſea to the Ohio*, will not be ſo much
“ as is now paid, and muſt ever be paid, to a
“ great part of the counties of *Penſylvania*, *Virgi-*
“ *nia*, and *Maryland*, as there is ſcarce a place be-
“ tween *Fort Pitt* and the *Rapids*, a diſtance of 705
“ computed miles, where good roads may not be
“ made, on the banks, which are *not liable to crumble*
“ *away*, and horſes employed in drawing up large
“ barges, as is done on the margin of the *Thames*
“ in *England*, and the *Seine* in *France*, againſt a

from care; but the pretty woman, twenty years of age only, I doubted not but ſhe was in

" ſtream remarkably gentle, except in high freſhes. " Whenever the *farmers* or merchants of *Ohio* " ſhall properly underſtand the buſineſs of tranſpor- " tation, they will build ſchooners, ſloops, &c. on " the *Ohio*, ſuitable for the *Weſt-India* or *European* " markets; or by having black walnut, cherry-tree, " oak, &c. properly ſawed for foreign markets, and " formed into *rafts*, as is now practiſed by the ſet- " tlers near the upper parts of the Delaware river, " and thereon ſtow their hemp, tobacco, &c. and " proceed with them to *New Orleans*. It may not " be amiſs perhaps to obſerve, that large quanti- " ties of flour are made in the diſtant (*weſtern*) " counties of Penſylvania, and ſent by an expen- " ſive land carriage to the city of Philadelphia, and " from thence ſhipped to South Carolina, and to " Eaſt and Weſt Florida, there being little or no " wheat raiſed in theſe provinces. The river *Ohio* " ſeems kindly deſigned by Nature as the channel " through which the two *Floridas* may be ſupplied " with flour, not only for their own conſump- " tion, but for the carrying on an extenſive com- " merce with *Jamaica*, (the Floridas were then in " the poſſeſſion of England) and the *Spaniſh* ſet- " tlements in the *Bay of Mexico*. *Millſtones* in " abundance are to be obtained in the hills near the " Ohio, and the country is every where well wa- " tered with large, and conſtant ſprings, and

in deſpair at the ſacrifice ſhe had made; and I endeavoured to diſcover, in her features and

H 4 looks,

“ ſtreams for griſt and other mills. The paſſage from Philadelphia to Penſacola is ſeldom made in leſs than a month, and ſixty ſhillings ſterling per *ton* freight (conſiſting of ſixteen barrels) is uſually paid for flour, &c. thither. Boats carrying from 800 to 1000 barrels of flour may go in about the ſame time from the Ohio (even from *Pittſburgh*) as from Philadelphia to Penſacola, and for half the above freight; the *Ohio* merchants would be able to deliver flour, &c. there in much better order than from Philadelphia, and without incurring the damage and delay of the ſea, the charges of inſurance, and riſk in time of war, &c. or from thence to Penſacola. This is not mere ſpeculation; for it is a fact, that about the year 1746, there was a great ſcarcity of proviſions at *New Orleans*; and the *French* ſettlements at the *Illinois*, ſmall as they then were, ſent thither, in one winter, upwards of eight hundred thouſand weight of flour.” Mr. *Lewis Evans*, in the Analyſis to his Map of the Middle Colonies of North America, in the year 1755, ſays, that “ Veſſels from 100 to 200 tons burthen, by taking advantage of the ſpring floods, may go from *Pittſburgh* to *the ſea* with *ſafety*, as then the falls, rifts, and ſhoals are covered to an equality with the reſt of the river.” To which Captain *Hutchins*, the preſent *Geographer General to the United States*, adds, “ And though the diſtance is upwards

looks, the ſecret ſentiments of her ſoul. Though ſhe had retired into a little chamber, to make room for us, ſhe frequently came into that where we were; and I ſaw, not without aſtoniſhment, that her natural charms were even embelliſhed by the ſerenity of her mind. She often careſſed her huſband and her child, and appeared to me admirably diſpoſed to fulfil the firſt object of every infant colony—" to increaſe and multiply." Whilſt ſupper was preparing, and we were talking of travels, and examining on the map the road our emigrants were to follow, I recollect that we had as yet an hour's day light, and that it was juſt the time I had ſeen the wood-hens, of which, they aſſured me, there was plenty in the neighbourhood, and that there is a critical moment

" of *two thouſand miles* from *Fort Pitt* to the ſea, " yet as there are *no obſtructions* to prevent veſſels " from proceeding both day and night, I am per- " ſuaded that this extraordinary inland voyage " may be performed, during the ſeaſon of the floods, " by rowing, in *ſixteen* or *ſeventeen* days."——— Here ſurely is a rational and ample field for the well regulated imagination of the philoſopher and politician ! ! ! TRANSLATOR

moment in hunting as well as love. I took my fowling-piece, therefore, and proceeded to the woods; but inſtead of wood-hens, I found only a rabbit, which I wounded; but it rolled down into a bottom, where I loſt ſight of it, till it was diſcovered by Mr. Griſby's dogs, which, accuſtomed to the report of a gun, found it in a hollow tree, to the top of which it would have ſcrambled had its leg not been broken. The rabbits of America differ from thoſe of Europe; they do not burrow, but take refuge in hollow trees, which they climb like cats, and often to a very conſiderable height. Content with my victory, I returned to the houſe, but ſtopped ſome time to hear, at ſunſet, two thruſhes, which ſeemed to challenge each other to the ſong, like the ſhepherds of Theocritus. This bird ought, in my opinion, to be conſidered as the nightingale of America; it reſembles thoſe of Europe in its form, colour, and habits, but is twice as large. Its ſong is ſimilar to that of our thruſh, but ſo varied and ſo much more perfect, that, if we except the uniform plaintive notes of the European night-

nightingale, they might be taken for each other. It is a bird of paſſage, like the mocking-bird, and like it, alſo, ſometimes remains through the winter.

At my return to the houſe, ſupper was the ſole object; about which Mr. and Mrs. Griſby took great pains, whilſt their daughters, about ſixteen or ſeventeen, who were perfect beauties, were laying the cloth. I aſked Mr. Griſby to ſup with us, but he excuſed himſelf, by aſſuring us that he was yet employed in our ſervice; nor was his attention uſeleſs, for we had an excellent ſupper; and though whiſky was our only drink, we contrived to convert it into tolerable toddy. Breakfaſt was ready betimes the next morning, and correſponded with our ſupper. Mr. Griſby, who had nothing to do, ſat down to table with us. He had a horſe ſaddled, that he might accompany us as a guide as far as *Greenly Ferry*, where we were to repaſs the Fluvanna; but I was informed that one of the ſervant's horſes was ſo much wounded in the withers, that it was impoſſible to mount him. This accident was the more inconvenient, as I had already

already been obliged to leave one at Mr. Jefferſon's, ſo that I had no freſh horſe to ſubſtitute. On applying to Mr. Griſby, he told me that the only horſe he had which could anſwer my purpoſe, was the one he generally rode, and which he was going to make uſe of to conduct us, but that he would willingly oblige me with it, and take mine in its place. On my aſſuring him that I would give him any thing he thought proper in return, he went to look at my horſe, and when he came back told me, that when cured, he thought he might be worth his own, and that he left the difference entirely to myſelf. As each of them might be worth ten or twelve guineas, I gave him two in exchange, and he was perfectly contented. I had juſt before aſked for the bill, and when he declined letting me have it, I gave him four guineas. He received them with ſatisfaction, aſſuring me it was double the ſum he could have charged. At laſt we were obliged to take our leave of this good houſe, but not of Mr. Griſby, who had taken another horſe to accompany us. On the road he ſhewed us two plantations which

which he had occupied ſucceſſively, before he ſettled on the one he at preſent cultivates. He had left them in good condition, and ſold them at the rate of twelve or thirteen ſhillings, Virginia currency, an acre, about ten livres of our money (8s. ¼ Engliſh.) We ſaw ſeveral other ſettlements in the woods, all of which were ſituated on the banks of ſome ſtream, whoſe ſource was not far diſtant. The peach-trees, which they take care to plant, and the Judas-tree (or *ſiliquaſtrum*, but different from that which produces the balm of Mecca) which grows naturally at the water's edge, were both in flower, and made a charming contraſt to the immenſe firs and oaks, in the centre of which were ſituated theſe new plantations.

It was near ten o'clock when we arrived at the ferry, and as we approached, ſtill following the courſe of the river, I ſaw an animal, to which I was a ſtranger, returning from the ſide of the river, and endeavouring to reach the wood. I puſhed my horſe towards it, hoping to frighten and make it climb a tree, for I took it for a racoon; in fact it mounted the neareſt tree, but very ſlowly

ſlowly and aukwardly. I had not great difficulty in killing it, for it did not even endeavour to hide itſelf, like the ſquirrel, behind the large branches. When I had taken it from the dogs, among which it ſtruggled hard, and had bitten them pretty ſharply; on examining it with attention, I diſcovered it to be the *monax*, or the *marmoſet* of America. In its form, fur, and colour it reſembled very much the muſk rat; but it is larger, and differs eſſentially in the tail, which is ſhort and rough. Like the muſk rat, however, its ribs are ſo ſhort and flexible, that they might be miſtaken for griſtles; ſo that though it is much bulkier than a hare, it can paſs through a hole of not above two inches in diameter.

Greenly Ferry derives its name from the proprietor, and is ſituated between two ſteep banks. We paſſed it in three trips, and parting with Mr. Griſby, depended entirely on our own induſtry to find the road to a very ſteep, but little frequented gap, the only paſſage by which we could get out of the mountains. They told us, at the ferry, that we ſhould find but one houſe, three miles from thence, and at the foot of the very mountain we were to climb. A little path conducted us to this houſe: after aſking new inſtructions, we followed another path, and began to aſcend, not without difficulty; for in general the acclivity was ſo rapid, that we were obliged to ſtop our horſes to give them breath. This aſcent, which formed the road, is at leaſt three miles long, by which you may judge of the height of theſe mountains; for in the ſpace of an hundred miles, this is the leaſt ſteep of any which compoſe what are called the *Blue Ridges*. Arrived at the ſummit, we enjoyed the reward generally beſtowed on ſuch labours. A magnificent, but ſavage proſpect, preſented itſelf to our eyes; we ſaw the mountains which form the *North Ridge*, and thoſe which, croſſing from one chain to the other, ſometimes unite the Blue Ridges. In one of theſe traverſes of mountains, the *Natural Bridge* is placed. It is to be obſerved, that I ſpeak here only of the view to the north, for we had not the advantage of enjoying the double proſpect; ſome neighbouring ſummits, and the height of of trees, prevented us from extending our view to the ſouthward. The deſcent was not leſs rapid than the aſcent; its length was alſo three miles. We judged it neceſſary, for the relief of our horſes and our own ſafety, to alight and walk; though the ſtones, which rolled under our feet, rendered it very incommodious. The dogs, which were not ſo fatigued by this inconvenience as ourſelves, beat the woods, while we walked ſlowly on, and two hundred paces from us they ſprang five wild turkies; but as theſe birds directed their flight towards a ſteep hill behind us, we did not think proper to follow them. We were almoſt at the bottom of the mountain when we began to perceive the horizon; but this horizon diſcovered nothing but woods and mountains, far leſs elevated than thoſe we were leaving, if we except three ſummits known by the name of the *Peaks* of *Otter*, which are very lofty, and advance from the Blue Ridges as a kind of counter-guard. In general, all the country from the Blue Ridges to the ſources of the *Apamatock*, may be conſidered as a *glacis* compoſed of little mountains, beginning

at

at the foot of the Blue Ridges, and continually diminiſhing. Of this the beſt charts of Virginia give not the leaſt indication, ſo that it is impoſſible, by the inſpection of them, to form a juſt idea of the nature of this country.

It was half paſt one o'clock, and we had rode ſixteen miles in very bad roads, when we arrived at the firſt houſe at the foot of the gap; but as it was an indifferent hut we were obliged to proceed two miles further, to a planter's of the name of *Lambert*, who received us with every mark of politeneſs. He gave us cakes and milk, for he had neither bread nor biſcuit; and, whilſt our horſes were feeding, he entertained us with gay, joyous converſation. Mr. Lambert is a kind of phænomenon in America, where longevity is very rare; he is eighty-three years of age, and ſcarcely appears to be fifty-five; he is well known in the country, for there is hardly a trade he has not followed, nor a part of it he has not lived in. He is now a huſbandman, and reſides at a very fine plantation, which he has cleared, at the foot of the mountains. His wife, who is only

only ſixty-five, looks much older than he does; his ſons are yet young; one is a Captain in the Virginia Legion, and formed his company himſelf in the beginning of the war. It was then compoſed of ſixty-three men, all enliſted in the neighbourhood; and at the end of ſix campaigns all the ſixty-three are living, ſome few of them only having been wounded. At five we mounted again to proceed ten miles further, to the houſe of a Captain *Muller*, who, like Mr. Lambert, does not keep a public-houſe, but willingly receives the few travellers who paſs by this unfrequented road. Although they aſſured us we could not poſſibly miſs the road, they would more properly have ſaid it was impoſſible to find it; for we deemed it very fortunate to loſe ourſelves but twice, and at length, after dark, we arrived at Mr. Muller's. He is a man about ſixty, ſix feet high, and bulky in proportion, very loquacious, but a good kind of man, attached to his country, and a great newſmonger. He told us he would do his beſt to give us ſomething for ſupper, but that he could offer us no other lodging than the room in which he received us, where he would order them to place our beds. The room was ſpacious and clean, but already occupied by a ſick perſon, whom he could not diſturb, and whom he begged us to leave in the little corner he poſſeſſed. This was an unfortunate old man of eighty, who, two days before, travelling in the neighbourhood, had been half devoured by a great bitch, whoſe whelps he had imprudently approached; ſhe had lacerated one of his arms and thighs. Mr. Muller beſtowed on him every poſſible care, and Mrs. Muller herſelf dreſſed his wounds. This poor man ſlept all the evening, but in the night he complained much, and ſometimes awakened us. On my aſking him the next morning, how he found himſelf, he anſwered, *mighty* weak *. Before we went away I deſired to have the bill, but Mr. Muller not chuſing to preſent any, I begged him to accept of a couple of guineas, deſiring, at the ſame time, to know if it was enough. " Too much, replied he, you come from France to my country to ſupport and defend it; I ought

* Mighty little, mighty few, mighty weak, &c. are favourite expreſſions in America. TRANSLATOR.

ought to receive you better and take nothing; but I am only a poor countryman, and not in a condition to demonſtrate my gratitude. If I were not ill, (and indeed he was aſthmatic) I would mount my horſe and attend you to the field of battle."

The little reſource we had found in this houſe, and the neceſſity of dividing the long journey we had to make, determined us to ſet out very early, and breakfaſt at *New London*, a little town, two miles from hence. The difficulty of finding the road ſtill remaining, I luckily met a man in the court-yard, juſt ready to mount, who relieved us from this anxiety. He was an old captain of the Virginia Legion, whom I had ſeen arrive in the evening in company with two tall young ladies, in huge gauze bonnets, covered with ribbands, and dreſſed in ſuch a manner, as formed a perfect contraſt to the ſimplicity of the houſe in which they were *. Theſe, I underſtood,

* The rage for dreſs amongſt the women in America, in the very height of the miſeries of war, was beyond all bounds; nor was it confined to the great towns, it prevailed equally on the ſea-coaſts, and

were Mr. Muller's daughters, returned from ſupping in the neighbourhood; but I was careful not to ſpeak to them, as I doubted not but we had taken poſſeſſion of the beds deſtined for theſe fine ladies and their company, and was in great terror leſt French

in the woods and ſolitudes of the vaſt extent of country, from Florida to New Hampſhire. In travelling into the interior parts of Virginia I ſpent a delicious day at an inn, at the ferry of *Shenandoah*, or the Cataſton Mountains, with the moſt enchanting, accompliſhed, and voluptuous girls, the daughters of the landlord, a native of Boſton, tranſplanted thither; who, with all the gifts of Nature, poſſeſſed the arts of dreſs not unworthy of Pariſian milliners, and went regularly three times a week to the diſtance of ſeven miles, to attend the leſſons of one *de Grace*, a French dancing-maſter, who was making a fortune in the country. In one of my journies, too, I met with a young Frenchman, who was travelling on the buſineſs of the celebrated M. de *Beaumarchais*, and was uncommonly ſucceſsful in his amours, of which I ſpeak from perſonal knowledge. On my enquiring the ſecret of his ſucceſs, he aſſured me, and put it beyond a doubt, that his *paſſe-par-tout*, or maſter-key, conſiſted in a faſhionable aſſortment of ribbands, and other ſmall articles contained in a little box, from which, in difficult caſes, he opened an irreſiſtible and never-failing battery. TRANSLATOR.

French gallantry ſhould compel us to reſign them. I know not how they managed, but they appeared again in the morning, and were far from handſome.

The Captain had been to ſleep a mile from hence, at a ſiſter's of Mr. Muller, and was mounting his horſe to return to *New London*, whither he offered to conduct us, and to provide our breakfaſt, as he kept a tavern. I accepted both his propoſals, and we travelled the diſtance of ten miles very agreeably; the country, like that through which we paſſed the preceding evening, being diverſified with very pretty plantations. New London, where we arrived at ten in the morning, is an infant town, but already pretty conſiderable, for there are at leaſt ſeventy or eighty houſes. There is likewiſe a military magazine eſtabliſhed here, and ſeveral workſhops for repairing arms. Its ſituation, in the middle of the woods, far diſtant from the ſeat of war, as well as commerce, does not require it ſhould be fortified, but Nature has prepared every thing to make it a ſtrong place. Situated upon a little platform, ſurrounded by a glacis, the declivity of which is exactly what could be wished, this little town might be fortified at a small expence, and defended by a trifling garrison; we left it about twelve o'clock, and had twenty-four miles to go to the only house where we could find a good lodging. It was not a tavern, but the proprietor, Mr. *Hunter*, received strangers with pleasure. The difference between a real tavern, and a hospitable house of reception, is greatly to the advantage of the traveller; for in America, as in England, publicans pay heavy taxes, and indemnify themselves by their exorbitant charges. Mr. Hunter received us well, and in a very clean house. We set out early the next morning, and after riding eight miles, always in dry, arid woods, we stopped to breakfast at Mr. *Pattison*'s. He is a fat man, about forty-five, disabled in his legs since he was two years old; and so helpless that he cannot transport himself from one place to another, but by pushing his chair. One would hardly think than a man afflicted with such an infirmity, should choose to live in the midst of woods, where

where he has no company but one white man ſervant, and negroes of each ſex. I believe him impotent in more than one reſpect, for he has lived in a conſtant ſtate of celibacy, and his oſtenſible imbecility would have been no obſtacle in a country where every body marries.

After we had proceeded twenty miles farther, we ſtopped, at four o'clock, at a Scotſman's of the name of *Johnſon*, who is the moſt ridiculous perſonage imaginable. He pronounces Engliſh in ſo unintelligible a manner, that Mr. *Dillon* aſked him, very ingenuouſly, what language he was ſpeaking. As Mr. Johnſon was an ill-tempered fellow, and a little drunk, I foreſaw that this queſtion could not ſucceed, and would turn out to our diſadvantage, on quitting this ſort of tavern. It happened as I imagined; for after a ſtay of only three quarters of an hour, he was not aſhamed to aſk *ſeven dollars* for about twenty pounds weight of the leaves of Indian corn for our horſes, and two bowls of toddy for the ſervants. I conſoled myſelf, like Monſieur de *Pourceaugnac* in Moliere, with the ſatisfaction only, on paying him, of telling him my ſentiments of his behaviour, and went twelve miles further to ſeek hoſpitality at another Scotſman's, where we arrived at the cloſe of day. But this was a very different character from the other. He was an old man of ſeventy-two, called *Hodnett*, who had been eſtabliſhed in America above forty years, though but lately fixed in the plantation where he now lives. He was eager to pleaſe, polite, and even inclined to compliment, proud of being born in Europe, and having paſt ſome time at Cork, where he miſſed, he told me, a fine opportunity of learning French; for he had lived with ſeveral French merchants, whoſe names he yet remembered, although it was upwards of fifty years ago. He enquired at leaſt twenty times of me if I knew them, and brought me an old book, the only one he had in the houſe, which was a bad treatiſe of geography. It was doubled in at the article of *Cork*, and one might ſee that he often read this chapter, as the paper was more thumbed there than elſewhere. Whilſt he preſented me with this book,

book, he obſerved, with an air of importance, that in his opinion it was the beſt geographical work exiſting, nor was it difficult to perceive that it was the only one he ever heard of. I amuſed myſelf however with aſſuring him that he poſſeſſed a real treaſure, and that he ought carefully to preſerve it. He went immediately to lock it up, and returned with a ſcrap of illuminated paper, which repreſented the arms and mottoes of the family of the *Hodnetts*. I made him happy by declaring they were known all over Europe, and ſurely it was not paying too dear for a good ſupper and good beds; for the next morning he would not give us any bill. I thought proper, however, to pay him handſomely; hoping, at the ſame time, that the family of the Hodnetts would know nothing of it, nor think themſelves under the neceſſity of adding the ſign of an ale-houſe to their armorial bearings.

It was on the 23d, but the heat was already very troubleſome, when we arrived to breakfaſt at nine o'clok at *Cumberland Court-houſe*. This is the chief manor-houſe

of

of a very conſiderable country; it is ſituated in a plain of about a mile diameter, ſixteen miles from *Hodnett*'s. Beſides the court-houſe, and a large tavern, its neceſſary appendage, there are ſeven or eight houſes inhabited by gentlemen of fortune. I found the tavern full of people, and underſtood that the judges were aſſembled to hold *a court of claims*; that is to ſay, to hear and regiſter the claims of ſundry perſons, who had furniſhed proviſions for the army. We know that in general, but particularly in unexpected invaſions, the American troops had no eſtabliſhed magazines; and as it was neceſſary to have ſubſiſtence for them, proviſions and forage were indiſcriminately laid hold of, on giving the owners a receipt, which they called a *certificate*. During the campaign, whilſt the enemy was at hand, little attention was given to this ſort of loans, which accumulated inceſſantly, without the ſum total being known, or any means taken to aſcertain the proofs. Virginia being at length loaded with theſe certificates, it became neceſſary, ſooner or later, to liquidate theſe ac-

counts.

counts. The laſt aſſembly of the State of Virginia, had accordingly thought proper to paſs a bill, authorizing the Juſtices of each county to take cognizance of theſe certificates, to authenticate their validity, and to regiſter them, ſpecifying the value of the proviſions in money, according to the eſtabliſhed tariff. I had the curioſity to go to the court-houſe, to ſee how this affair was tranſacted, and ſaw it was performed with great order and ſimplicity. The Judges wore their common clothes, but were ſeated on an elevated tribunal, as at London in the Court of King's Bench or Common Pleas. One of them ſeeing me ſtanding at the door of the hall, deſcended from the bench, and invited me to go and take ſome refreſhment at his houſe, where the family would entertain me till the ſeſſions were finiſhed. I told him I was obliged to proceed on my journey; and really we had no time to loſe, for there yet remained twenty-eight miles to travel, and on a road ſo unprovided with every neceſſary for travellers, that though we intended giving our horſes another bait, we could not find forage nearer than

than at a ſmith's ſhop, at twenty miles diſtance. As I intended therefore ſtaying only half an hour at moſt, I ſeated myſelf under ſome trees; but Monſieur *D'Oyré* having gone into the houſe, returned and told me there was a company of four or five young girls, all pretty and very well dreſſed. Curioſity inducing me to ſee them, my attention was ſoon fixed upon a young woman of eighteen, who was ſuckling her child. Her features were ſo regular, and there was ſuch decency and modeſty in her behaviour, that ſhe recalled to my mind thoſe beautiful virgins of Raphael, the model, or example of the *beau ideal*. As I no longer permit myſelf to conſider beauty but with a philoſophic eye *, I ſhall here make

* The reader will here, doubtleſs, be apt to picture to himſelf the Author as a grey-headed worn-out veteran, or an unimpaſſioned, ſtoical member of the French academy, barely remembering "the days when he was young;" but it is my duty to undeceive him; the *Marquis de Chaſtellux* is a well-made, handſome man, of about four and forty, with eyes full of intelligence and fire, the carriage and deportment of a man of rank, and with a diſpoſition extremely remote from an indifference to beauty.

TRANSLATOR.

make an obſervation which has occurred to me in foreign countries, particularly in England and America; it is, that the beauty of forms and of features, the beauty independant of grace, motion, and expreſſion, is oftener found amongſt the people of the North, or amongſt their deſcendants, than in France, or towards the South. If I were to aſſign the cauſe of this difference, I ſhould ſay, that from ſome unaccountable reaſon, unconnected, doubtleſs, with the temperature of the climate, the youth of both ſexes are more forward, and more ripe, amongſt them than with us; from which it reſults, that young people, particularly young girls of twelve or thirteen, unite that roundneſs of form, freſhneſs of complexion, and regularity of features, before they are modified by paſſions and habits.

In France it is quite different; children are there very pretty to the age of ſeven or eight years; but it is ſeldom that girls preſerve their beauty to the age of puberty. This is the epoch, however, when we muſt form our opinion of what they may be; but even theſe prognoſticks are often deceit-

ful.

ful. This period is a kind of chryſalis, a ſtate of probation, in which the handſome become ugly, and the ugly handſome. It is from the age of twenty to twenty-five that the features develop and declare themſelves, and that Nature compleats her work, if not diverted from her courſe by ſickneſs, but eſpecially by the moral and natural conſequences of marriage. On the other hand, our women, this danger once over, retain their beauty longer than in any other country. It appears as if their very ſouls were identified in their features, and watched over their preſervation; not a movement without a grace, no grace without expreſſion; the deſire of pleaſing improves and perpetuates the means; and Nature, rather aided than counteracted by Art, is never abſolutely abandoned to a domeſtic life, nor laviſhed by an unlimited fecundity*. Thus uſeful trees may

* It is certain that population is not the main object of marriage in France amongſt the higher claſſes. Amongſt the nobility, in particular, the parties are generally contracted, when very young, by their reſpective parents, who bring them together to make an heir or two for the family; which object,

may ſerve to decorate our gardens, if the too great quantity of fruit does not prevent the re-production of their bloſſoms. Theſe reflections prove, that the French women have no reaſon to envy ſtrangers; that their beauty, in fact, though longer in coming to maturity, and leſs perfect, is more bewitching and more durable; that if others furniſh better models for the painter, they will ſtand the teſt of a longer examination; and that, in ſhort, if they are not always thoſe we moſt admire, they are certainly thoſe we muſt love the moſt and the longeſt.

But let me return from this dangerous excurſion, and reſume my journey. We had

once compleated, they part with as little affection as when they met, but with leſs paſſion, and paſs the remainder of their lives in perfect freedom. Whilſt family duty is performing for family purpoſes, their conduct is dictated, in general, by the niceſt honour, and their noble blood is tranſmitted tolerably pure and free from contamination; but "unlimited fecundity," as it is checked by ſome on principles of œconomy and prudence, is deemed *vulgar* and *barbarous* by all, except the lower claſſes, who are ſtrangers to this ſyſtem of refinement. TRANSLATOR.

had rode forty-four miles, and night was closing faſt upon us, when we arrived at *PowhatanCourt-houſe*; this is a more recent, and more ruſtic ſettlement than that of Cumberland. It conſiſts only of two mean huts, one for the purpoſe of holding the ſeſſions, the other by way of publick houſe; but which hitherto is ſcarcely fit for the reception of travellers. It is kept by a young man who has juſt ſettled here; his wife is a tall, handſome woman, his ſiſter-in-law not quite ſo pretty. We had a good ſupper and good beds, but our horſes were obliged to do without forage. The county of Powhatan takes its name from a King of the Savages, famous in the hiſtory of Virginia, who reigned at the commencement of the laſt century; when the colony formed its firſt eſtabliſhment at *James Town*, it was often neceſſary to treat, and ſometimes to wage war with him. He is repreſented as a profound, but perfidious, politician. He had conquered all the country betwixt the Apamatock and Bay of Cheſapeak, and was dreaded by the neighbouring nations.

We

We left Powhatan the 24th, early in the morning, and, after having ſtopped twice, the firſt time to breakfaſt in a poor little houſe, eight miles from Powhatan, and the laſt, twenty-four miles further, at a place called *Cheſterfield Court-houſe*, where we ſaw the ruins of the barracks formerly occupied by Baron Stuben, ſince burnt by the Engliſh, arrived in good time at *Peterſburg*. This day's journey was alſo forty-four miles. The town of Peterſburg is ſituated on the right bank of the *Apamatock*; there are ſome houſes on the oppoſite ſhore, but this kind of ſuburb is a diſtrict independent of Peterſburg, and called *Pocahunta*. We paſſed the river in a ferry-boat, and were conducted to a little public houſe about thirty ſteps from thence, which had an indifferent appearance; but, on entering, we found an apartment very neatly furniſhed; a tall woman, handſomely dreſſed, and of a genteel figure, who gave the neceſſary orders for our reception, and a young lady, equally tall, and very elegant, at work. I enquired their names, which I found were not leſs entitled to reſpect than their appearance.

 The

The miſtreſs of the houſe, already twice a widow, was called *Spencer*, and her daughter, by her firſt huſband, *Miſs Saunders*. I was ſhewn my bedchamber; and the firſt thing which ſtruck me was a large magnificent harpſicord, on which lay alſo a guitar. Theſe muſical inſtruments belonged to Miſs Saunders, who knew very well how to uſe them; but as we ſtood more in need of a good ſupper than a concert, I was apprehenſive at firſt of finding our landladies too good company, and that we ſhould have fewer orders to give than compliments to make. Mrs. Spencer, however, happened to be the beſt woman in the world; a gay, cheerful creature, no common diſpoſition in America; and her daughter, amidſt the elegance of her appearance, was mild, polite, and eaſy in converſation. But to hungry travellers all this could, at the beſt, be conſidered but as a good omen for the ſupper, for which we had not long to wait; for ſcarcely had we time to admire the neatneſs and beauty of the table-cloth, before it was covered with plenty of good diſhes, particularly ſome very large and excellent fiſh. We were very good friends with our charming landladies before we went to bed, and breakfaſted with them the next morning. We were juſt going out to take a walk, when we received a viſit from Mr. *Victor*, whom I had ſeen at Williamſburgh; he is a Pruſſian, who had formerly been in the army, and, after having travelled a great deal in Europe, came and ſettled in this country, where, by his talents, he firſt made his fortune; and, like every body elſe, finiſhed by turning planter. He is an excellent muſician, and plays every kind of inſtrument, which makes his company in great requeſt by the whole neighbourhood. He told us he was come to paſs a few days with Mrs. *Bowling*, one of the greateſt landholders in Virginia, and proprietor of half the town of Peterſburg. He added, that ſhe had heard of our arrival, and hoped we would come and dine with her; which invitation we accepted, and put ourſelves under the guidance of Mr. Victor, who firſt took us to the warehouſes or magazines of tobacco. Theſe warehouſes, of which there are numbers in Virginia, though unfortunately, great part of them has been burned by the Engliſh, are under the direction of public authority. There are inſpectors nominated to prove the quality of the tobacco brought by the planters, and if found good, they give a receipt for the quantity. The tobacco may then be conſidered as ſold, theſe authentic receipts circulating as ready money in the country. For example: ſuppoſe I have depoſited twenty hogſheads of tobacco at Peterſburg, I may go fifty leagues thence to Alexandria or Frederickſburg, and buy horſes, cloths, or any other article, with theſe receipts, which circulate through a number of hands before they reach the merchant who purchaſes the tobacco for exportation. This is an excellent inſtitution, for by this means tobacco becomes not only a ſort of bank-ſtock, but current coin. You often hear the inhabitants ſay, "This watch coſt me ten hogſheads of tobacco; this horſe fifteen hogſheads; or, I have been offered twenty, &c." It is true that the price of this article, which ſeldom varies in peace, is ſubject to fluctuations in time of war: but then,

then, he who receives it in payment, makes a free bargain, calculates the riſks and expectations, and runs the hazard; in ſhort, we may look on this as a very uſeful eſtabliſhment; it gives to commodities value and circulation, as ſoon as they are manufactured, and, in ſome meaſure, renders the planter independent of the merchant.

The warehouſes at Peterſburg belong to Mrs. Bowling. They were ſpared by the Engliſh, either becauſe the Generals Phillips and Arnold, who lodged with her, had ſome reſpect for her property, or becauſe they wiſhed to preſerve the tobacco contained in them in expectation of ſelling it for their profit. Phillips died in Mrs. Bowling's houſe, by which event the ſupreme command devolved upon Arnold; and I heard it ſaid, that Lord Cornwallis, on his arrival, found him at great variance with the navy, who pretended that the booty belonged to them. Lord Cornwallis terminated the diſpute, by burning the tobacco; but not before Mrs. Bowling, by her intereſt, had time ſufficient to get it removed from her warehouſes. She was lucky

 enough,

enough, alſo, to ſave her valuable property in the ſame town, conſiſting of a mill, which turns ſuch a number of mill-ſtones, bolting machines, cribbles, &c. and, in ſo ſimple and eaſy a manner, that it produces above £.800 a year ſterling. I paſſed upwards of an hour in examining its various parts, and admiring the carpenter's work, and the conſtruction. It is turned by the waters of the Apamatock, which are conveyed to it by a canal excavated in the rock. Having continued our walk in the town, where we ſaw a number of ſhops, many of which were well ſtocked, we thought it time to pay our reſpects to Mrs. Bowling, and begged Mr. Victor to conduct us to her. Her houſe, or rather houſes, for ſhe has two on the ſame line reſembling each other, which ſhe propoſes to join together, are ſituated on the ſummit of a conſiderable ſlope, which riſes from the level of the town of Peterſburg, and correſponds ſo exactly with the courſe of the river, that there is no doubt of its having formerly formed one of its banks. This ſlope, and the vaſt platform on which the houſe is built,

built, are covered with graſs, which afford excellent paſturage, and are alſo her property. It was formerly ſurrounded with rails, and ſhe raiſed a number of fine horſes there; but the Engliſh burned the fences, and carried away a great number of the horſes. On our arrival we were ſaluted by Miſs Bowling, a young lady of fifteen, poſſeſſing all the freſhneſs of her age; ſhe was followed by her mother, brother, and ſiſter-in-law. The mother, a lady of fifty, has but little reſemblance to her country-women; ſhe is lively, active, and intelligent; knows perfectly well how to manage her immenſe fortune, and what is yet more rare, knows how to make good uſe of it. Her ſon and daughter-in-law I had already ſeen at Williamſburgh. The young gentleman appears mild and polite, but his wife, of only ſeventeen years of age, is a moſt intereſting acquaintance, not only from her face and form, which are exquiſitely delicate, and quite European, but from her being alſo deſcended from the Indian Princeſs *Pocahunta*, daughter of King *Powhatan*, of whom I have already ſpoken. We may presume that it is rather the disposition of that amiable American woman, than her exterior beauty, which Mrs. Bowling inherits.

Perhaps they who are not particularly acquainted with the history of Virginia, may be ignorant, that Pocahunta was the protectress of the English, and often screened them from the cruelty of her father. She was but twelve years old when Captain *Smith*, the bravest, the most intelligent, and the most humane of the first colonists, fell into the hands of the savages; he already understood their language, and traded with them several times, and often appeased the quarrels between the Europeans and them; often had he been obliged also to fight them, and to punish their perfidy. At length, however, under the pretext of commerce, he was drawn into an ambush, and the only two companions who accompanied him, fell before his eyes; but, though alone, by his dexterity he extricated himself from the troop which surrounded him, until, unfortunately, imagining he could save himself by crossing a morass, he stuck fast, so that the

the ſavages, againſt whom he had no means of defending himſelf, at laſt took and bound him, and conducted him to Powhatan. The King was ſo proud of having Captain Smith in his power, that he ſent him in triumph to all the tributary Princes, and ordered that he ſhould be ſplendidly treated, till he returned to ſuffer that death which was prepared for him *.

The

* *Dr. Robertſon*, *Mr. Adair*, and a number of writers have given an account of the cruel mode by which the Indians torture their priſoners of war, before they put them to death. During my reſidence near Alexandria, in Virginia, in 1782, I had the following relation of their barbarous treatment, from a gentleman who had juſt eſcaped out of the hands of theſe infernal furies. *Colonel Crawford*, and his ſon, two great land ſurveyors, and moſt reſpectable planters in Virginia, in heading a party againſt the Indians and Tories, aided by ſome light horſe from the Britiſh frontiers, who had ſpread horror and devaſtation through the infant back ſettlements of the United States, were defeated and made priſoners. The gentleman, from whom I had this account, was ſurgeon to the party, and was conducted, with Mr. Crawford and his ſon, to be ſacrificed in his turn, at one of the Indian villages, to the manes of their people ſlain in battle. The bloody buſineſs commenced with Mr. Crawford, the father, who was deli-

The fatal moment at last arrived, Captain Smith was laid upon the hearth of the savage

vered over to *the women*, and being fastened to a stake, in the center of a circle formed by the savages *and their allies*, the female furies, after the preamble of a war song, began by tearing out the nails of his toes and fingers, then proceeded, at considerable intervals, to cut off his nose and ears; after which they stuck his lacerated body full of pitch pines, large pieces of which they inserted, horrid to relate! into his private parts; to all of which they set fire, and which continued burning, amidst the inconceivable tortures of the unhappy man, for a considerable time. After thus glutting their revenge, by arts of barbarity, the success of which was repeatedly applauded by the surrounding demons, they cut off his genitals, and rushing in upon him, finished his misery with their tomohawks, and hacked his body limb from limb. This dreadful scene passed in the presence of the son of the unhappy sufferer, and the surgeon, who were to be conveyed to different villages to undergo the same fate. The next day, accordingly, young Crawford was sacrificed with the same circumstances of horror; after which, the surgeon, being entrusted to the care of four of the savages, who fortunately got drunk with some rum, given them as a recompence by their European friends, escaped from them in the woods, and, bound as he was, wandered for four or five and twenty days, subsisting on leaves and berries, before he reached the neighbourhood of Winchester, whence he got down to

ſavage King, and his head placed upon a large ſtone to receive the ſtroke of death, when Pocahunta, the youngeſt and darling daughter of Pouchatan, threw herſelf upon his body, claſped him in her arms, and declared, that if the cruel ſentence were executed, the firſt blow ſhould fall on her. All *ſavages* (*abſolute ſovereigns* and *tyrants* not

Alexandria. Amongſt theſe wretches was one *Simon Girty*, a native of Virginia, who was formerly well acquainted with Colonel Crawford, and had been employed by the aſſembly of Virginia to conciliate the ſavages, and obtain their neutrality; but who having been detected by the Governor in ſome malverſations of the public money entruſted to him, and his duplicity diſcovered, went over to the Britiſh, and became more mercileſs than the worſt of theſe infernal hell-hounds. Mr. Crawford, in the midſt of his tremendous ſufferings, ſeeing *Girty* ſtanding in the circle, with a gun, called to him by his name, and implored him as an old friend, a chriſtian, and a countryman, to ſhoot him, and by that act of mercy relieve him from his miſery; but the inhuman monſter tauntingly replied, "No, Crawford, I have got *no powder*, your aſſembly did not chuſe to truſt me, and you muſt now pay for it," and continued to feaſt his eyes with the bloody ſacrifice.

TRANSLATOR.

not excepted,) are invariably more affected by the tears of infancy, than the voice of humanity. Powhatan could not resist the tears and prayers of his daughter; Captain Smith obtained his life, on condition of paying for his ransom a certain quantity of muskets, powder and iron utensils; but how were they to be obtained? They would neither permit him to return to James-Town, nor let the English know where he was, lest they should demand him sword in hand. Captain Smith, who was as sensible as courageous, said, that if Powhatan would permit one of his subjects to carry to James-Town a little board which he would give him, he should find under a tree, at the day and hour appointed, all the articles demanded for his ransom. Powhatan consented, but without having much faith in his promises, believing it to be only an artifice of the Captain's to prolong his life. But he had written on the board a few lines sufficient to give an account of his situation. The messenger returned. The King sent to the place fixed upon, and

was

was greatly aſtoniſhed to find every thing which had been demanded. Powhatan could not conceive this mode of tranſmitting thoughts, and Captain Smith was henceforth looked upon as a great magician, to whom they could not ſhew too much reſpect. He left the ſavages in this opinion, and haſtened to return home. Two or three years after, ſome freſh differences ariſing amidſt them and the Engliſh, Powhatan, who no longer thought them ſorcerers, but ſtill feared their power, laid a horrid plan to get rid of them altogether. His project was to attack them in profound peace, and cut the throats of the whole colony. The night of this intended conſpiracy, Pocahunta took advantage of the obſcurity, and in a terrible ſtorm which kept the ſavages in their tents, eſcaped from her father's houſe, adviſed the Engliſh to be upon their guard, but conjured them to ſpare her family, to appear ignorant of the intelligence ſhe had given, and terminate all their differences by a new treaty. It would be tedious to relate all the ſervices which this

this angel of peace rendered to both nations. I ſhall only add, that the Engliſh, I know not from what motives, but certainly againſt all faith and equity, thought proper to carry her off. Long and bitterly did ſhe deplore her fate, and the only conſolation ſhe had was Captain Smith, in whom ſhe found a ſecond father. She was treated with great reſpect, and married to a planter of the name of *Rolle*, who ſoon after took her to England. This was in the reign of *James the Firſt*; and, it is ſaid, that this monarch, pedantic and ridiculous in every point, was ſo infatuated with the prerogatives of royalty, that he expreſſed his diſpleaſure, that one of his ſubjects ſhould dare to marry the daughter even of a ſavage *King*. It will not perhaps be difficult to decide on this occaſion, whether it was the ſavage King who derived honour from finding himſelf placed upon a level with the European prince, or the Engliſh monarch, who by his pride and prejudices reduced himſelf to a level with the chief of the ſavages. Be that as it will, Captain Smith,

Smith, who had returned to London before the arrival of Pocahunta, was extremely happy to ſee her again, but dared not to treat her with the ſame familiarity as at James-Town. As ſoon as ſhe ſaw him, ſhe threw herſelf into his arms, calling him her father; but finding that he neither returned her careſſes with equal warmth, nor the endearing title of daughter, ſhe turned aſide her head and wept bitterly, and it was a long time before they could obtain a ſingle word from her. Captain Smith enquired ſeveral times what could be the cauſe of her affliction.—"What!" ſaid ſhe, "did I "not ſave thy life in America? When I was "torn from the arms of my father, and "conducted amongſt thy friends, didſt "thou not promiſe to be a father to me? "Didſt thou not aſſure me, that if I went "into thy country thou wouldſt be my fa-"ther, and that I ſhould be thy daughter? "Thou haſt deceived me, and behold me, "now here, a ſtranger and an orphan." It was not difficult for the Captain to make his peace with this charming creature, whom he tenderly loved. He preſented her

her to ſeveral people of the firſt quality, but never dared take her to court, from which however ſhe received ſeveral favours. After a reſidence of ſeveral years in England, an example of virtue and piety, and attachment to her huſband, ſhe died, as ſhe was on the point of embarking on her return to America. She left an only ſon, who was married, and left only daughters; theſe daughters, others; and thus, with the female line, the blood of the amiable Pocahunta now flows in the veins of the young and charming Mrs. Bowling.

I hope I ſhall be pardoned this long digreſſion, which may be pleaſing to ſome readers. My viſit to Mrs. Bowling and her family, having convinced me, that I ſhould paſs part of the day with them agreeably, I continued my walk, with a promiſe of returning at two o'clock. Mr. Victor conducted me to the camp formerly occupied by the enemy, and teſtified his regret that I could not take a nearer view of Mr. *Banniſter*'s handſome country-houſe, which was in ſight; there being no other obſtacle however than the diſtance, about a mile a mile and a half, and the noonday heat, we determined that this ſhould not ſtop us; and, walking ſlowly, we reached, without fatigue, this houſe, which is really worth ſeeing. It is decorated rather in the Italian, than the Engliſh or American ſtyle, having three porticoes at the three principal entries, each of them ſupported by four columns *. It was then occupied by an in-

* The Italian architecture, that of porticoes in particular, is admirably adapted to all hot climates, and of courſe to the Southern States of America. The ſame motives therefore, which induced the invention of this mode of building in ancient Greece and Rome, and in general throughout the Eaſtern world, would naturally give riſe to the ſame inventions of convenience in ſimilar climates; and, in fact, though the richer and more poliſhed deſcendants of Britain in the New World, may be ſuppoſed to adopt theſe porticoes from Italy, as the cultivated mind of the Author imagines; the very pooreſt ſettler, nay even the native Indian, invariably attempts ſome kind of ſubſtitute for this neceſſary protection from the ſun and weather. Every tavern or inn is provided with a covered portico for the convenience of its gueſts, and this evidently from the neceſſity of the caſe. We have only to examine the reſources of the ſavage iſlander in the Pacific Ocean, and recur

habitant of Carolina, called *Nelson*, who had been driven from his country by the war, which followed him to Petersburg. He invited me to walk in, and whilst he made me, according to custom, drink a glass of wine, another Carolinian, of the name of *Bull*, arrived to dine with him. The latter was a militia General, and came from General Greene's army, where his time of service was expired. The history of Mr. Bull, which is not long, will give a general idea of the state of the Southern Provinces. Possessed of a great number of negroes, large personal property, particularly in plate, previous to, and during the war, he did not think proper, after the capture of Charles-Town, to expose his wealth to the rapacity of the English. He set off therefore with two hundred negroes, followed by a great number of waggons laden with his effects, and provisions for his little

to the origin of all architecture, from the fluted Corinthian in the hall of empire to the rustic prop of the thatched roof, to discover the natural progress of the human mind, and the similarity of human genius. TRANSLATOR.

little army, and travelled, in this manner, thro' South and North Carolina, and part of Virginia, pitching his camp every evening in the most commodious situations. At length he arrived at *Tukakoe*, on James's River, the seat of his old friend Mr. *Randolph*, a rich planter of Virginia, who gave him a spot of ground near his house, on which his negroes built one for himself. Here he lived in tranquillity, surrounded by his slaves and his flocks, until Arnold and Phillips invaded Virginia, and approached his new asylum. Mr. Bull once more departed with his wealth, his flocks, and negroes, to retire into the upper country near Fredericksburg. On my asking him what he would have done, had we not opportunely arrived to expel the English, who intended to compleat the conquest of Virginia, "I should have retired to Maryland," he replied,—and if they had gone thither?—"I should have proceeded to Pensylvania, and so on, even to New England.' Does not this recall to mind the ancient patriarchs emigrating with their families and flocks, with a certainty of finding every where a country to receive and nourish them *? General Bull was preparing to return to Carolina, in hopes

* I have already said, that I had the happiness of a particular acquaintance with many of the principal gentlemen of South Carolina. The reflexion on the pleasing hours I passed with them in their exiled situation at Philadelphia, and the warm friendship with which they honoured me, whilst it reconciles me to the world, and soothes the memory of past sufferings, touches the tenderest affections of a sensible and grateful heart. My bosom beat high with genuine ardour in the cause for which they sacrificed every personal consideration, but I had frequently the opportunity of appreciating that sacrifice. Seeing what I saw, I want no instances of Greek or Roman virtue to stimulate my feelings, or excite my emulation; and it will ever be matter of congratulation with me, to have witnessed, in the principal inhabitants of Carolina, all the blandishments of civilized society, the love of life and all its blessings, a humanity void of reproach, an hospitality not exceeded in the patriarchal ages, contrary to the paradoxes of systematic writers, blended with the inflexible virtue which distinguished the best and purest ages of the world. From the number, I shall only select the brilliant examples of Major *Pierce Butler*, and Mr. *Arthur Middleton*. Wealth, honour, interest, domestic happiness, their children, were nothing in the eyes of such men, though calculated to enjoy, and to communicate happiness in every sphere,

hopes henceforth of paſſing happier days. After putting many queſtions to him reſpecting affairs to the Southward, which he anſwered with great frankneſs and good ſenſe, I returned to Mrs. Bowling's, where I was not diſappointed in finding a good dinner, the honours of which ſhe did with much cordiality, without reſtraint, or ceremony. After dinner, Miſs Bowling played on the harpſicord, and ſung like an adept in muſic, although her voice was not agreeable; whilſt the deſcendant of Pocahunta touched a guitar, and ſung like a perſon unſkilled in muſic, but with a charming voice. On my return home, I had another concert; Miſs Saunders ſinging ſome airs, which ſhe accompanied ſometimes with the harpſicord, and ſometimes with the guitar.

when put in competition with the great objects of univerſal public happineſs, and ſacred Freedom's holy cauſe. How painful is it to be compelled to add, that ſuch was the cold, ſelfiſh ſpirit of too many of the inhabitants of Philadelphia towards their Carolina brethren, who had every claim upon their ſympathy and good offices, as to merit the indignation of every feeling mind, and to fix an indelible ſtain upon their character as men and citizens.

TRANSLATOR.

Next day we were obliged to quit this good houſe and agreeable company; but before I left Peterſburg, I obſerved that it was already a flouriſhing town, and muſt become more ſo every day, from its favourable ſituation with reſpect to commerce. Firſt, becauſe it is placed immediately below the *Falls*, or Rapids of the Apamatock, and the river can here float veſſels of fifty or ſixty tons burthen. Secondly, becauſe the productions of the Southern part of Virginia have no other outlet, and thoſe even of North Carolina are gradually taking this way, the navigation of the *Roanoke* and Albemarle ſound being by no means ſo commodious as that of the Apamatock and James's River. But theſe advantages are unfortunately balanced by the inſalubrity of the climate; for I have been aſſured, that of all the inhabitants of the three little burghs of Pocahunta, of Blandford and Peterſburg, which may be conſidered as forming one town, not two perſons are to be found who are natives of the country. Commerce and navigation, notwithſtanding, produce a concourſe of ſtrangers. The ſituation, beſides, is agreeable, and

and the climate may probably be rendered more ſalubrious by draining ſome moraſſes in the neighbourhood.

Five miles from Peterſburg, we paſſed the ſmall river of Randolph, over a ſtone bridge; and travelling through a rich and well peopled country, arrived at a fork of roads, where we were unlucky enough precisely to make choice of that which did not lead to Richmond, the place of our deſtination. But we had no reaſon to regret our error, as it was only two miles about; and we ſkirted James river to a charming place called *Warwick*, where a groupe of handſome houſes form a ſort of village, and there are ſeveral ſuperb ones in the neighbourhood; amongſt others, that of Colonel Carey *, on the right bank of the river, and M. *Randolph's* on the oppoſite ſhore. One muſt be fatigued with hearing the name of Randolph mentioned in travelling in Virginia (for it is one of the moſt ancient families in the country) a Randolph being amongſt the firſt ſettlers, and is likewiſe one of the moſt numerous and rich.

* This is the gentleman whoſe fine mills were burnt by Arnold, as mentioned in the London Gazette. TRANSLATOR.

It is divided into ſeven or eight branches, and I am not afraid of exaggerating, when I ſay, that they poſſeſs an income of upwards of a million of livres. It is only twenty-five miles from Peterſburg to Richmond, but as we had loſt our way, and travelled but ſlowly, it was near three o'clock when we reached *Mancheſter*, a ſort of ſuburb to Richmond, on the right bank of the river, where you paſs the ferry. The paſſage was ſhort, there being two boats for the accommodation of travellers. Though Richmond be already an old town, and well ſituated for trade, being built on the ſpot where James' river begins to be navigable, that is, juſt below the Rapids, it was, before the war, one of the leaſt conſiderable in Virginia, where they are all, in general, very ſmall; but the ſeat of government having been removed from Williamſburgh, it is become a real capital, and is augmenting every day. It was neceſſary, doubtleſs, to place the legiſlative body at a diſtance from the ſea-coaſt, where it was expoſed to the rapid and unexpected inroads of the Engliſh; but Williamſburgh had the ſtill farther inconvenience

convenience of being ſituated at the extremity of the ſtate, which obliged a great part of the Delegates to make a long journey to the Aſſembly; beſides, that from its poſition between James and York rivers, it has no port nor communication with them, but by ſmall creeks very difficult for navigation, whilſt veſſels of 200 tons come up to Richmond. This new capital is divided into three parts, one of which is on the edge of the river, and may be conſidered as the port; the two others are built on two eminences, which are ſeparated by a little valley. I was conducted to that on the weſt, where I found a good inn, and my lodgings and dinner ordered by a ſervant whom I had ſent on two days before, with a lame horſe. We were ſerved, therefore, immediately, but with ſuch magnificence and profuſion, that there would have been too much for twenty perſons. Every plate that was brought us produced a burſt of laughter, but not without conſiderable alarm for the bill of the next day; for I had been apprized that the inns at Richmond were uncommonly extravagant. I eſcaped, however,

ever, for ſeven or eight Louis d'ors, which was not enormous, conſidering our expenditure. A ſhort time before, Mr. de Rochambeau had paid five and twenty Louis, at another inn, for ſome horſes which remained there for four or five days, although he neither ate nor ſlept in it himſelf. Mr. *Formicalo*, my landlord, was more honeſt; his only error was the exalted idea he had formed of the manner in which French General Officers muſt be treated. He is a Neapolitan, who came to Virginia with *Lord Dunmore*, as his *Maitre d'Hôtel*, but he had gone rather round about, having been before in Ruſſia. At preſent he has a good houſe, furniture, and ſlaves, and will ſoon become a man of conſequence in his new country. He ſtill, however, recollects his native land with pleaſure, and I have no doubt that my attention in addreſſing him only in Italian, ſaved me a few Louis.

After dinner I went to pay a viſit to Mr. *Harriſon*, then Governor of the State. I found him in a homely, but ſpacious enough houſe, which was fitted up for him. As the Aſſembly was not then ſitting, there

was

was nothing to diſtinguiſh him from other citizens. One of his brothers, who is a Colonel of Artillery, and one of his ſons, who acts as his Secretary, were with him. The converſation was free and agreeable, which he was even deſirous of prolonging; for on my riſing in half an hour, leſt I might interrupt him, he aſſured me that the buſineſs of the day was at an end, and deſired me to reſume my ſeat. We talked much of the firſt Congreſs in America, in which he ſat for two years, and which, as I have already ſaid, was compoſed of every perſon diſtinguiſhed for virtue and capacity on the continent. This ſubject led us naturally to that which is the moſt favourite topic amongſt the Americans, the origin and commencement of the preſent revolution. It is a circumſtance peculiar to Virginia, that the inhabitants of that country were certainly in the beſt ſituation of all the coloniſts under the Engliſh government. The Virginians were planters, rather than merchants, and the objects of their culture were rather valuable than the reſult of induſtry. They poſſeſſed, almoſt excluſively, the privileged

vileged article of tobacco, which the English came in queſt of into the very heart of the country, bringing in exchange every article of utility, and even of luxury. They had a particular regard and predilection for Virginia, and favoured accordingly the peculiar diſpoſition of that country, where cupidity and indolence go hand-in-hand, and ſerve only as boundaries to each other. It was undoubtedly no eaſy matter therefore, to perſuade this people to take up arms, becauſe the town of Boſton did not chuſe to pay a duty upon tea, and was in open rupture with England. To produce this effect, it was neceſſary to ſubſtitute activity for indolence, and foreſight for indifference. That idea was to be awakened at which every man, educated in the principles of the Engliſh conſtitution, ſhudders, the idea of a ſervile ſubmiſſion to a tax to which he has not himſelf conſented. The preciſe caſe however relative to them, had not yet occurred, though every enlightened mind foreſaw that ſuch was the object, and would be the inevitable conſequence of the early meaſures of the government:

vernment: but how were the people to be convinced of this? By what other motive could they be brought to adopt decisive measures, if not be the confidence they reposed in their leaders? Mr. Harrison informed me, that when he was on the point of setting out with Mr. Jefferson and Mr. Lee to attend the first Congress at Philadelphia, a number of respectable, but uninformed inhabitants, waited upon, and addressed them as follows: "You assert that "there is a fixed intention to invade our "rights and privileges; we own that we "do not see this clearly, but since you "assure us that it is so, we believe the fact. "We are about to take a very dangerous "step, but we confide in you, and are ready "to support you in every measure you shall "think proper to adopt." Mr. Harrison added, that he found himself greatly relieved by a speech made by Lord North soon after, in which he could not refrain from avowing, in the clearest manner, the plan of the British Government *. This speech was

* I cannot here resist transcribing a passage from Mr. *Payne*'s celebrated Letter to the *Abbé Raynal*,

was printed in the public papers, and all America rang with its contents. Returning

which merits preſervation, and may ſerve to illuſtrate the ideas of America reſpecting the general views of Britain, in hopes that every reflecting Engliſhman is at length diſpaſſionate enough to bear the obſervation. "I ſhall now take my leave of this "paſſage of the Abbé, with an obſervation, which "until ſomething unfolds itſelf to convince me of "the contrary, I cannot avoid believing to be true; "which is, that it was the fixed determination of "the Britiſh cabinet to quarrel with America at all "events. They (the members who compoſe the "cabinet) had no doubt of ſucceſs, if they could "once bring it to the iſſue of a battle; and they "expected from a conqueſt, what they could nei-"ther propoſe with decency, nor hope for by nego-"tiation. The charters and conſtitutions of the "colonies were become to them matters of offence, "and their rapid progreſs in property and popula-"tion were beheld with diſguſt, as the growing and "natural means of independence. They ſaw no "way to retain them long, but by reducing them "in time. A conqueſt would at once have made "them lords and landlords; and put them in poſ-"ſeſſion both of the revenue and the rental. The "whole trouble of government would have ceaſed "in a victory, and a final end been put to remon-"ſtrance and debate. The experience of the ſtamp-"act had taught them how to quarrel, with the ad-

ing afterwards to Virginia, he ſaw the ſame perſons who had thus addreſſed him on his departure, who now confeſſed that he had not deceived them, and that henceforward they were reſolutely determined upon war.

Theſe

" vantages of cover and convenience, and they had " nothing to do but to renew the ſcene, and put " contention into motion. They hoped for a re- " bellion, and they made one. They expected a " declaration of independence, and they were not " diſappointed. But after this, they looked for " victory, and they obtained a defeat. If this be " taken as the generating cauſe of the conteſt, then " is every part of the conduct of the Britiſh mini- " ſtry conſiſtent, from the commencement of the " diſpute, until the ſigning the treaty of Paris, (the " American and French alliance) after which, con- " queſt becoming doubtful, they had recourſe to ne- " gotiation, and were again defeated. If we take a " review of what part Britain has acted, we ſhall " find every thing which ought to make a nation " bluſh. The moſt vulgar abuſe, accompanied by " that ſpecies of haughtineſs which diſtinguiſhes " the hero of a mob from the character of a gentle- " man; it was as much from her *manners*, as from " her injuſtice, that ſhe loſt the colonies. By the " latter ſhe provoked their principles, by the for- " mer ſhe exhauſted their patience. And it ought " to be held out to the world, to ſhew, how neceſ- " ſary it is to conduct the buſineſs of government " with civility." TRANSLATOR.

Thefe particular details cannot but be ufeful to fuch Europeans as are defirous of forming a juft idea of thofe great events, in which they took fo deep an intereft; for they would be much deceived in imagining that all the Thirteen States of America were invariably animated by the fame fpirit, and affected by the fame fentiments. But they would commit a ftill greater error, did they imagine, that thefe people refemble each other in their forms of government, their manners and opinions. One muft be in the country itfelf; one muft be acquainted with the language, and take a pleafure in converfing, and in liftening, to be qualified to form, and that flowly, a proper opinion and a decifive judgment *.

After

* The fame ingenious author of *Common Senfe*, makes another obfervation, in his anfwer to the very ignorant, or very prejudiced work of the Abbé Raynal on the revolution of America, to which, however it may militate againft the utility of the prefent publication, or the notes of the Tranflator, he cannot avoid perfectly fubfcribing: viz. " I never yet " faw an European defcription of America that was " true, neither can any perfon gain a juft idea of it, " but by coming to it." TRANSLATOR.

After this reflection, the reader will not be ſurprized at the pleaſure I took in converſing with Mr. Harriſon. Beſides that I was particularly happy to form an acquaintance with a man of ſo eſtimable character in every reſpect, and whoſe beſt eulogium it is to ſay, that he is the intimate friend of Dr. Franklin *. He preſſed me to dine

* The illuſtrious and amiable character of Dr. Franklin is far beyond my praiſe. To have known him; to have been a frequent witneſs to the diſtinguiſhed acts of his great mind; to have been in a ſituation to learn, and to admire his comprehenſive views, and benevolent motives; to have heard the profound maxims of wiſe philoſophy and ſound politics, drop from his lips with all the unaffected ſimplicity of the moſt indifferent converſation; to have heard him deviate fiom the depths of reaſon, and adapt his inſtructive diſcourſe to the capacity and temper of the young and gay; to have enjoyed in ſhort, the varied luxuries of his delightful ſociety, is a ſubject of triumph and conſolation, of which nothing can deprive me. He too as well as the envious and intereſted enemies of his tranſcendent merit, muſt drop from off the ſcene, but his name, *ære perennius*, is inſcribed in indelible characters on the immortal roll of philoſophy and freedom; for the *ardentia verba* of the moſt honeſt advocate of freedom

with him next day, and to paſs another day at Richmond; but as there was nothing to excite curioſity in that town, and I was deſirous of ſtopping at Weſtover before I returned to Williamſburgh, where I was anxious to arrive, we ſet out the 27th at eight in the morning, under the eſcort of Colonel Harriſon, who accompanied us to a road from which it was impoſſible to go aſtray. We travelled ſix and twenty miles without halting, in very hot weather, but by a very agreeable road, with magnificent houſes in view at every inſtant; for the banks of James-River form the garden of Virginia. That of Mrs. Bird, to which I was going, ſurpaſſes them all in the magnificence of the buildings, the beauty of its

of the preſent age, the late Serjeant Glynn, on a great occaſion, the action againſt Lord Halifax for the falſe impriſonment of Mr. Wilkes, may with peculiar juſtice be applied to this great man. "*Few men* "*in whole revolving ages can be found, who dare op-* "*poſe themſelves to the force of tyranny, and whoſe ſin-* "*gle breaſts contain the ſpirit of nations.*"

TRANSLATOR.

its ſituation, and the pleaſures of ſociety *.

Mrs. *Bird* is the widow of a Colonel who ſerved in the war of 1756, and was afterwards one of the council under the Britiſh Government. His talents, his perſonal qualities, and his riches, for he poſſeſſed an immenſe territory, rendered him one of the principal perſonages of the country; but being a ſpendthrift and a gambler, he left his affairs, as his death, in very great diſorder. He had four children by his firſt wife, who were already ſettled in the world, and has left eight by his ſecond, of whom

 the

* The moſt perfect eaſe and comfort characterize the mode of receiving ſtrangers in Virginia; but no where are theſe circumſtances more conſpicuous than at the houſe of General Waſhington. Your apartments are your home, the ſervants of the houſe are yours, and whilſt every inducement is held out to bring you into the general ſociety in the drawing-room, or at the table, it reſts with yourſelf to be ſerved or not with every thing in your own chamber. In ſhort, nothing can more reſemble the eaſy reception of gueſts at the country reſidence of the late *Sir Charles Turner* in Yorkſhire, where hoſpitality perhaps was ſtrained farther than conſiſted with a proper aſſortment of company, or even with ſafety.

TRANSLATOR.

the widow takes care. She has preſerved his beautiful houſe, ſituated on James-River, a large perſonal property, a conſiderable number of ſlaves, and ſome plantations which ſhe has rendered valuable. She is about two-and-forty, with an agreeable countenance, and great ſenſe. Four of her eight children are daughters, two of whom are near twenty, and they are all amiable and well educated. Her care and activity have in ſome meaſure repaired the effects of her huſband's diſſipation, and her houſe is ſtill the moſt celebrated, and the moſt agreeable of the neighbourhood. She has experienced however freſh misfortunes; three times have the Engliſh landed at Weſtover, under Arnold and Cornwallis; and though theſe viſits coſt her dear, her huſband's former attachment to England, where his eldeſt ſon is now ſerving in the army, her relationſhip with Arnold, whoſe couſin german ſhe is, and perhaps too, the jealouſy of her neighbours, have given birth to ſuſpicions, that war alone was not the object which induced the Engliſh always to make their deſcents at her habitation. She has

has been accuſed even of connivance with them, and the government have once put their ſeal upon her papers; but ſhe has braved the tempeſt, and defended herſelf with firmneſs; and though her affair be not yet terminated, it does not appear as if ſhe was likely to ſuffer any other inconvenience than that of being diſturbed and ſuſpected. Her two eldeſt daughters paſſed the laſt winter at Williamſburgh, where they were greatly complimented by M. de Rochambeau and the whole army *. I had

 alſo

* The prudent conduct of the French officers, and the ſtrict diſcipline of their troops in a country with different manners, language, and religion, full of inveterate prejudices, and wherein they had very lately been regarded as natural enemies, muſt ever be conſidered as an epocha and a phænomenon in the hiſtory of policy and ſubordination. Whilſt all ranks of officers were making it their ſtudy ſucceſsfully to conciliate the good opinion of the higher claſſes, nothing could exceed the probity and urbanity of the common ſoldiers; not only did they live with the American troops in a harmony, hitherto unknown to allied armies, even of kindred language, intereſt, and religion, but their conduct was irreproachable, and even delicate to the inhabitants of the country. They who predicted diſcord on the

alſo received them in the beſt manner I could, and received the thanks of Mrs. Bird, with a preſſing invitation to come and ſee her; I found myſelf in conſequence quite at home. I found here alſo my acquaintance, the young Mrs. Bowling, who was on a viſit to Mr. *Mead*, a friend and neighbour of Mrs. Bird's, who had invited him and his company to dinner. I paſſed this day therefore very agreeably, and Mr. and Mrs. Mead, whom I had alſo known at Williamſburgh, engaged the company to dine with them the next day. The river alone ſeparates the two houſes, which are notwithſtanding, upwards of a mile diſtant from each other; but as there is very little current, the breadth of the water between them does not prevent it from being ſoon paſſed. Mr. Mead's houſe is by no means

introduction of a French army, had reaſon and experience on their ſide; but the ſpirit of policy and wiſdom which preſided in the French councils had gone forth, and diffuſed itſelf through every ſubordinate claſs of men, perſuaded even the meaneſt actors in the war, and baffled foreſight. Nor was this one of the leaſt extraordinary circumſtances of this wonderful revolution. TRANSLATOR.

means ſo handſome as that of Weſtover, but it is extremely well fitted up within, and ſtands on a charming ſituation; for it is directly oppoſite to Mrs. Bird's, which, with its ſurrounding appendages, has the appearance of a ſmall town, and forms a moſt delightful proſpect. Mr. Mead's garden, like that of Weſtover, is in the nature of a terrace on the bank of the river, and is capable of being made ſtill more beautiful, if Mr. Mead preſerves his houſe, and gives ſome attention to it; for he is a philoſopher of a very amiable but ſingular turn of mind, and ſuch as is particularly uncommon in Virginia, ſince he rarely attends to affairs of intereſt, and cannot prevail upon himſelf to make his negroes work †. He is even ſo diſguſted with a

* Whilſt the Tranſlator was employed in this paſſage, he read in the public prints, the exultation of a friend to his fellow-creatures, that a Mr. Pleaſants, a quaker on James-River in Virginia, had liberated his ſlaves, and made a ſacrifice of 3000l. ſterling to this noble act of humanity. The Tranſlator knows the country too well not to feel the force of the Author's ſubſequent reaſoning on the difficulty and danger of a general emancipation of the negroes,

culture wherein it is neceſſary to make uſe of ſlaves, that he tempted to ſell his poſ-ſeſſions in Virginia, and remove to New England. Mrs. Bird, who has a numerous family to provide for, cannot carry her philoſophy ſo far; but ſhe takes great care of her negroes, makes them as happy as their ſituation will admit, and ſerves them herſelf as a doctor in time of ſickneſs. She has even made ſome intereſting diſcoveries on the diſorders incident to them, and diſcovered a very ſalutary method of treating a ſort of putrid fever which carries them off commonly in a few days, and againſt which the phyſicians of the country have exerted themſelves without ſucceſs.

The 29th, the whole of which day I ſpent at Weſtover, furniſhes nothing intereſting in this journal, except ſome information I had the opportunity of acquiring reſpecting two ſorts of animals, of very different

nor after mature reflection now, and on the ſpot, is he able to overcome his objections. But God, in his Divine Providence, forbid that ſo ſplendid an example of active virtue, ſhould claſh with the unavoidable policy, or the neceſſary welfare of ſociety!

TRANSLATOR.

ferent ſpecies, the *ſturgeon* and the *humming-bird*. As I was walking by the river-ſide, I ſaw two negroes carrying an immenſe ſturgeon, and on my aſking them how they had taken it, they told me that at this ſeaſon, they were ſo common as to be taken eaſily in a ſean (a ſort of fiſhing-net), and that fifteen or twenty were found ſometimes in the net; but that there was a much more ſimple method of taking them, which they had juſt been uſing. This ſpecies of monſters, which are ſo active in the evening as to be perpetually leaping to a great height above the ſurface of the water, uſually ſleep profoundly at mid-day †.

Two

† From General Waſhington's houſe, which ſtands on the lofty banks of the Potowmack, in a ſituation more magnificent than I can paint to an European imagination, I have ſeen for ſeveral hours together in a ſummer's evening, hundreds, perhaps I might ſay thouſands of ſturgeon, at a great height from the water at the ſame inſtant, ſo that the quantity in the river muſt have been inconceivably great; but notwithſtanding the rivers in Virginia abound with fiſh, they are by no means plentiful at table, ſuch is the indolence of the inhabitants!

Mr.

Two or three negroes then proceed in a little boat, furnished with a long cord, at the

Mr. *Lund Washington*, a relation of the General's, and who managed all his affairs during his *nine years* absence with the army, informed me that an English frigate having come up the Potowmack, a party was landed who set fire to and destroyed some gentlemen's houses on the Maryland side in sight of *Mount Vernon* the General's house, after which the Captain, (I think Captain *Graves* of the Actæon) sent a boat on shore to the General's, demanding a large supply of provisions, &c. with a menace of burning it likewise in case of a refusal. To this message Mr. Lund Washington replied, "that when the General engaged in the contest he had put all to stake, and was well aware of the exposed situation of his house and property, in consequence of which he had given him orders by no means to comply with any such demands, for that he would make no unworthy compromise with the enemy, and was ready to meet the fate of his neighbours." The Captain was highly incensed on receiving this answer, and removed his frigate to the Virginia shore; but before he commenced his operations, he sent another message to the same purport, offering likewise a passport to Mr. Washington to come of board: he returned accordingly in the boat, carrying with him a small present of poultry, of which he begged the Captain's acceptance. His presence produced the best effect, he was hospitably received notwith-

the end of which is a ſharp iron crook, which they hold ſuſpended like a log line. As ſoon as they find this line ſtopped by ſome obſtacle, they draw it forcibly towards them, ſo as to ſtrike the hook into the ſturgeon, which they either drag out of the water, or which, after ſome ſtrug-

gling,

ſtanding he repeated the ſame ſentiments with the ſame firmneſs. The Captain expreſſed his perſonal reſpect for the character of the General, commending the conduct of Mr. Lund Waſhington, and aſſured him nothing but his having miſconceived the terms of the firſt anſwer could have induced him for a moment to entertain the idea of taking the ſmalleſt meaſure offenſive to ſo illuſtrious a character as the General, explaining at the ſame time the real or ſuppoſed provocations which had compelled his ſeverity on the other ſide of the river. Mr. Waſhington, after ſpending ſome time in perfect harmony on board, returned, and inſtantly diſpatched ſheep, hogs, and an abundant ſupply of other articles as a preſent to the Engliſh frigate. The Tranſlator hopes that in the *preſent ſtate* of men and meaſures in England, Mr. Graves, or whoever the Captain of that frigate was, will neither be offended at this anecdote, nor be afraid to own himſelf the actor in this generous tranſaction. Henry IVth ſupplied Paris with proviſions whilſt he was blockading it! TRANSLATOR.

gling, and losing all its blood, floats at length upon the surface, and is easily taken.

As for the humming-birds, I saw them for the first time, and was never tired of beholding them. The walls of the garden and the house were covered with honey-suckles, which afforded an ample harvest for these charming little animals. I saw them perpetually flying over the flowers, on which they feed without ever alighting, for it is by supporting themselves on the wings that they insinuate their beaks into the calix of the flowers. Sometimes they perch, but it is only for a moment; it is then only one has an opportunity of admiring the beauty of their plumage, especially when opposite to the sun, and when in removing their heads, they display the brilliant enamel of their red necks, which almost rival the splendor of the ruby or the diamond. It is not true that they are naturally passionate, and that they tear to pieces the flowers in which they find no honey. I have never observed any such circumstance myself, either at Westover or Williamsburgh; and the inhabitants of the country assure me, that they had never made any such observation. These birds

appear

appear only with the flowers, with which likewiſe they diſappear, and no perſon can tell what becomes of them. Some are of opinion that they hide themſelves, and remain torpid the remainder of the year. In fact, it is difficult to conceive how their wings, which are ſo ſlight and ſlender as to be imperceptible if not in motion, could poſſibly reſiſt the winds, and tranſport them to diſtant climates. They are not intractable, for I have ſeen one of them, which was taken a few days before, in no wiſe frightened at the perſons who looked at it, but flew about the room, as in a garden, and ſucked the flowers which they preſented to it; but it did not live above a week. Theſe birds are ſo fond of motion, that it is impoſſible for them to live without the enjoyment of the moſt unreſtrained liberty. It is difficult even to catch them, unleſs they happen, as was the caſe with that I am ſpeaking of, to fly into the chamber, or be driven there by the wind. An inhabitant of the country, who amuſed himſelf in preſerving them for his cabinet, has diſcovered a very ingenious method of killing, without disfiguring them. This is a very difficult

difficult undertaking; for a ſingle grain of ſmall ſhot is a cannon bullet for ſo ſmall a creature. This method is to load his gun with a bladder filled with water. The exploſion of this water is ſufficient to knock down the humming-bird, and deprive it of motion.

The reader will certainly not accuſe me of playing the orator, and reſerving objects of the greateſt magnitude for the end of my diſcourſe; for I ſhall here conclude my journal. It is unneceſſary to ſpeak of my return to Williamſburgh, unleſs it be worthy of remark, that the *Chickahoming*, which is only a ſecondary river, ſince it falls into that of James, is yet ſo wide, ſix miles from its conflux, that I was three quarters of an hour in paſſing it. But if he will ſtill favour me with his attention, I ſhall terminate this long narrative of a ſhort journey, by ſome obſervations on a country I have travelled through, and inhabited long enough to know it thoroughly.

The Virginians differ eſſentially from the inhabitants to the north and eaſtward of the Bay, (of Cheſapeak) not only in the nature of their climate, that of their ſoil,

and

and the objects of cultivation peculiar to it, but in that indelible character which is imprinted on every nation at the moment of its origin, and which by perpetuating itself from generation to generation, justifies the following great principles, that *every thing which is, partakes of that which has been.* The discovery of Virginia dates from the end of the sixteenth century, and the settlement of the colony took place at the commencement of the seventeenth. These events passed in the reigns of Elizabeth and James the first. The republican and democratical spirit was not then common in England; that of commerce and navigation was scarcely in its infancy; and the long wars with France and Spain had perpetuated, under another form, the same military cast given to the nation by William the Conqueror, Richard, Coeur de Lion, Edward the third, and the Black Prince. There were no longer any Knights Errant, as in the time of the Croisades, but in their place arose a number of adventurers who served indifferently their own country, and foreign powers; and gentlemen, who disdaining agriculture and commerce, had no other profession but that of of arms; for at that period the military ſpirit maintained the prejudices favourable to that nobility, from which it was long inſeparable; beſides that the dignity of the peerage, from being leſs common in England, gave more eclat and more conſiſtence to thoſe who poſſeſſed it by hereditary right. The firſt coloniſts of Virginia were compoſed, in great meaſure, of ſuch ſoldiers, and ſuch gentlemen, ſome of whom went in ſearch of fortune, and others, of adventures. And in fact, if the eſtabliſhment of a colony requires all the induſtry of the merchant and the cultivator, the diſcovery, and conqueſt of unknown countries ſeems more peculiarly adapted to the ideas of the warlike and romantic. Accordingly the firſt company which obtained the excluſive property of Virginia, was principally compoſed of men the moſt diſtinguiſhed by their rank or birth; and though all theſe illuſtrious proprietors did not actually become coloniſts, ſeveral of them were not afraid to paſs the ſeas; and a *Lord Delawarr* was amongſt the firſt Governors of Virginia. It was natural therefore for theſe new coloniſts, who were filled with military principles,

ciples, and the prejudices of nobility, to carry them into the midſt even of the ſavages whoſe lands they were uſurping; and of all our European ideas, theſe were what the unpoliſhed tribes moſt readily conceived. I know that there now remains but an inconſiderable number of theſe ancient families; but they have retained a great eſtimation, and the firſt impulſe once given, it is not in the power of any legiſlator, nor even of time itſelf, wholly to deſtroy its effect. The government may become democratic, as it is at the preſent moment; but the national character, the ſpirit of the government itſelf, will be always ariſtocratic. Nor can this be doubted, when we take into conſideration another cauſe, co-operating with the former; I mean to ſpeak of ſlavery; not that it is any mark of diſtinction, or peculiar privilege to poſſeſs negroes, but becauſe the empire men exerciſe over them cheriſhes vanity and ſloth, two vices which accord wonderfully with the already eſtabliſhed prejudices. It will, doubtleſs, be aſked, how theſe prejudices have been brought to coincide with a revolution founded on ſuch different principles. I ſhall anſwer, that they have even perhaps contributed to produce it. That whilſt the revolt of New England was the reſult of reaſon and calculation, pride poſſibly had no inconſiderable ſhare in dictating the meaſures of Virginia. I ſhall add, what I have above hinted, that in the beginning, even the indolence of this people may have been uſeful to them, as it obliged them to rely upon a ſmall number of virtuous and enlightened citizens, who led them farther than they would have proceeded, without a guide, had they conſulted only their own diſpoſitions. For it muſt be allowed, that Virginia ſtepped forth with a good grace, at the very commencement of the troubles; that ſhe was the firſt to offer ſuccours to the Boſtonians, and the firſt alſo to ſet on foot a conſiderable body of troops. But it may likewiſe be obſerved, that as ſoon as the new legiſlature was eſtabliſhed, and when, inſtead of leaders, ſhe had a government, the maſs of citizens was taking part in that government, the national character prevailed, and every thing went worse and worse. Thus states, like individuals, are born with a particular complexion, the bad effects of which may be corrected by regimen and habits, but can never be entirely changed. Thus legislators, like physicians, ought never to flatter themselves that they can bestow, at pleasure, a particular temperament on bodies politic, but strive to discover what they already have, and thence study to remedy the inconveniencies, and multiply the advantages resulting from it. A general glance at the different States of America will serve to justify this opinion. The people of New England had no other motive for settling in the New World, than to escape from the arbitrary power of their monarchs, who, at once, sovereigns of the state, and heads of the church, exercised at that period the double tyranny of despotism and intolerance. They were not adventurers, they were men who wished to live in peace, and who laboured for their subsistence. Their principles taught them equality, and disposed them to induſtrious purſuits. The ſoil, naturally barren, affording them but ſcanty reſources, they attached themſelves to fiſhing and navigation; and at this hour, they are ſtill friends to equality and induſtry; they are fiſhermen and navigators. The ſtates of New-York, and the Jerſeys, were peopled by neceſſitous Dutchmen who wanted land in their own country, and occupied themſelves more about domeſtic œconomy than the public government. Theſe people have preſerved the ſame character; their intereſts, their efforts, ſo to ſpeak, are perſonal; their views are concentered in their families, and it is only from neceſſity that theſe families are formed into a State. Accordingly, when General Burgoyne was on his march to Albany, the New Englandmen chiefly contributed to impede his progreſs; and, if the inhabitants of the State of New-York and of the Jerſeys have often taken arms, and diſplayed courage, it is becauſe the former were animated by an inveterate hatred againſt the

ſavages,

ſavages, which generally preceded the Engliſh armies *, and the latter were excited

to

* The employing the Indians, independent of the meaſure, it is now pretty generally admitted, produced conſequences directly oppoſite to the intereſt of Great-Britain; uniting the inhabitants of all the countries liable to their incurſions as one man againſt them and their allies, and producing ſuch bloody ſcenes of inveterate animoſity and vengeance as make human nature ſhudder. The following narrative will prove how far men of all caſts, colours, and religions, reſemble each other in ſimilar ſituations; and to what lengths even the chriſtians of an enlightened age can go, when compelled to act under the guidance of the worſt paſſions. The inhabitants of the back frontiers of Penſylvania, goaded to fury by the ravages committed on them by the Indians, and by the murder of their families and kindred, collected the militia in the beginning of 1782, and took the field againſt the ſavage intruders. In one of their excurſions they fell in with a ſmall tribe of chriſtian Indians, called the *Muſkingums*, who being ſuſpected of attachment to the Americans, had been for ſome time confined at Detroit, and were releaſed only on condition of obſerving a ſtrict neutrality, ſince they could not be perſuaded to take arms. Theſe unhappy wretches, to the number of about two hundred, returning to their habitations, were employed in putting their ſeed-corn into the ground, when they were ſurpriſed by the American militia. In vain did they urge

to take perſonal vengeance for the exceſſes committed by the troops of the enemy, when

their ſituation, and their ſufferings from the Britiſh; they were *Indians*, and their captors, men who had loſt ſons, brothers, fathers, wives or children in this horrid war; no other plea was neceſſary to palliate their meditated vengeance. The Indians were ſhut up in a barn, and ordered to prepare for death; but with this barbarous conſolation, that, as they were converted chriſtians, they ſhould be allowed a reſpite till the next morning. The innocent victims ſpent the night in ſinging Moravian hymns, and in other acts of chriſtian devotion; and in the morning were led, men, women, and children, to the ſlaughter, and butchered by their fellow worſhippers of the meek Jeſus! The Moravians at Bethlehem and Nazareth, whoſe miſſionaries had converted them, made ſtrong repreſentations to Congreſs on the ſubject. I was at Philadelphia when the news arrived; and it is but juſtice to ſay, that horror was painted on every countenance, and every mind was at work to deviſe expedients for avenging this atrocious murder; but after various efforts, both Congreſs and the Aſſembly of the State were found unequal to the puniſhment of theſe aſſaſſins, who were armed, diſtant from the ſeat of government, the only ſafeguard and protection of the frontiers, and from their own ſavage nature alone fit to cope with the dreadful enemy brought into action by the Britiſh.

when they over-ran the country *. If you go further to the ſouth, and paſs the Delaware, you will find that the government of Penſylvania, in its origin, was founded on two very oppoſite principles; it was a government of property, a government in itſelf feodal, or, if you will, patriarchal, but the ſpirit of which was the greateſt toleration, and the moſt compleat liberty. *Penn's* family at firſt formed the vain project of eſtabliſhing a ſort of *Utopia*, or perfect government, and afterwards of deriving the greateſt poſſible advantage from their immenſe property, by attracting foreigners from all parts. Here it ariſes that the people of Penſylvania have no characteriſtic aſſimilation, that they are intermingled and confounded, and more actuated to individual, than to public liberty, more inclined to anar-

* The murder committed on *Mrs. Maxwell*, the wife of a reſpectable and popular clergyman in the Jerſeys, and afterwards on himſelf, with ſimilar acts of cruelty perpetrated by a licentious ſoldiery, and unprincipled refugees, inflamed the minds of a great body of the inhabitants, particularly of the Dutch

chy than to democracy*. Maryland, subjected in the first instance to a proprietary government,

and their descendants, who, as the Marquis observes, were certainly disposed at least to a neutrality.

TRANSLATOR.

* The Irish and the Germans form the most numerous part of the inhabitants of Pensylvania. The latter, if I am not mistaken, constitutes a fifth, if not a fourth, of the whole number, and are a most useful, industrious body of men, well versed in the mechanic arts and agriculture. I have travelled several days in the interior parts of that state, and heard scarcely any other language than German; the acts of Congress and the State, are promulgated in that language, German Gazettes are published at Philadelphia, and in general they proved themselves true friends to the revolution. Congress availing themselves of this circumstance, very politically encamped the Brunswick, and other German troops taken with Burgoyne, near the town of Reading, where I saw them. The neighbourhood abounding with their countrymen, the men had permission to work at harvest, and other trades, and soon formed connexions with the females of the country. Calculating their market price, and the obligation they lay under to restore them, or their prime cost, they took every measure to prevent them from remaining in the country; for which purpose, they transmitted but small sums at a time by their commissaries from New-York, taking care to keep large arrears in their hands, as a

vernment, and confidered only as a private domain, remained long in a ftate of the moft abfolute dependence. This is the firft time fhe merits to be regarded as a ftate; but this ftate feems to be forming under good aufpices; fhe may become of great weight after the prefent revolution, becaufe fhe was formerly of no fignificance. The two Carolinas and Georgia are next to be confidered; but I am not fufficiently acquainted with thefe three ftates to hazard on them any obfervations, which may not be fo juft in fact as they appear to me; but which are at leaft of a delicate nature, and require more than a fuperficial examination. I only know, that North Carolina, peopled by Scotfmen, brought thither by poverty, rather than by induftry, is a prey to acts of pillage, and to internal diffen-

temptation for their return. But all thefe precautions were, as may naturally be imagined, but of a partial effect, with men habituated to a country of freedom, wherein they felt themfelves reftored to their natural rights, and animated by the example of their countrymen, enjoying the full comforts of their honeft induftry; contrafted too with the degraded ftate of a wretched mercenary, held up to fale by his arbitrary mafter. TRANSLATOR.

dissensions *: that South Carolina, possessing a commerce, wholly of exportation, owes

* It is true that a great number of Scotsmen are settled in North Carolina, but that they were not even the majority of the inhabitants is very apparent from the events of the late revolution; for the Scots, though loyalists nearly to a man, were repeatedly defeated, and finally crushed by the militia of the country. Notwithstanding her efforts appeared less concentered, and more vaguely directed, owing to the local circumstances of the province, and the dispersed state of the inhabitants, rather than disinclination to the cause, North Carolina rendered most essential services by her exertions in the field, and the Delegates she sent to Congress. Her constitution of government, contracted as it is, is not perhaps inferior to many in the confederacy, and bespeaks the wisdom of "the enlightened few," to which the Marquis attributes the wise councils of Virginia. It was the North Carolina militia which gave the first turn to the ruined affairs of America to the southward, by their spirited attack and defeat of Colonel Ferguson at King's Mountain. The Translator, who was then in England, received, by a private channel, the first intelligence of that important event, which he communicated to the public; but the circumstances of the surprise of a large body of British troops, flushed with the capture of Charlestown, and the victory at Camden, by a body

owes its exiſtence to its ſea-ports, eſpecially to that of Charleſtown, which has rapidly increaſed,

of 1600 *horſeman*, from the back country of North Carolina, appeared ſo extraordinary, that he could not obtain credit for the fact, either with the friends to America, or the miniſterial party in that country. The Miniſters had no intelligence of the matter, and the eaſterly winds then happening to prevail for a period of ſix weeks, it was treated as a fiction, both in and out of Parliament, and the Tranſlator as an enthuſiaſt or a fabricator of falſe news. Time, however, verified the fact, which he knew to be authentic, to its full extent, viz. that Colonel Ferguſſon, with eight hundred Britiſh troops, had been ſurpriſed; himſelf ſlain, and his whole force defeated by ſixteen hundred Carolina militia, mounted on horſeback, haſtily collected, and commanded by a few militia Colonels! This ſpirited and ſucceſsful enterpriſe, with its conſequences, merits certainly a conſpicuous place in the hiſtory of this great revolution; for, like the ſurpriſe at Trenton, it changed the whole face of affairs, and reſtored energy to the friends of America in that important ſeat of war.

North Carolina is a very fine country, beautifully diverſified with pleaſant hills, large vallies, and noble rivers, though none of them is navigable for veſſels above 80 tons, except the rivers Fear and Clarendon; yet as they interſect the country in every direction, they are admirably calculated for inland navigation. There are, for this reaſon, no large towns,

creased, and is become a commercial town, in which strangers abound, as at Marseilles and Amsterdam*: that the manners there are consequently polished and easy: that the inhabitants love pleasure, the arts, and society; and that this country is more European in its manners than any in America.

Now, if there be any accuracy in this sketch, let me desire the reader to compare the spirit of the American States with their present government. I desire him to form

but from the various produce of this state, and the rapid increase of population, the white inhabitants, now amounting to near two hundred thousand; there is every reason to believe that it will become not one of the least considerable on the continent, nor will the philosopher view the circumstances which forbid the formation of large towns, as an evil, either in this country or in Virginia. TRANSLATOR.

* The author here refers to the former situation of the province; but, as I have already mentioned, the interior of this extensive state is daily peopling with a race of healthy, industrious planters, and is highly susceptible of every species of improvement. As for sea-ports, there are none worth mentioning but Charlestown; and as for Georgia, its position is in every respect similar to that of South Carolina.

TRANSLATOR.

form the comparifon at the prefent moment, in twenty, or in fifty years hence, and I am perfuaded, that fince all thefe governments refemble each other, as they are all democratical, he will ftill difcover the traces of that original character, of that fpirit which prefides at the formation of people, and at the eftablifhment of nations.

Virginia will retain this difcriminating character longer than the other States; whether it be that prejudices are more durable, the more abfurd, and the more frivolous they are, or that thofe which injure a part only of the human race, are more fubject to remark than thofe which affect all mankind. In the prefent revolution, the ancient families have feen, with pain, new men occupying diftinguifhed fituations in the army, and in the magiftracy; and the Tories have even hence drawn advantages, to cool the ardour of the lefs zealous of the Whigs. But the popular party have maintained their ground, and it is only to be regretted that they have not difplayed the fame activity in combating the Englifh, as in difputing precedences. It is to be apprehended, ed, however, that circumſtances becoming leſs favourable to them, on a peace, they may be obliged entirely to give way, or to ſupport themſelves by factions, which muſt neceſſarily diſturb the order of ſociety. But if Reaſon ought to bluſh at beholding ſuch prejudices ſo ſtrongly eſtabliſhed amongſt a new people, Humanity has ſtill more to ſuffer from the ſtate of poverty, in which a great number of white people live in Virginia. It is in this country that I ſaw poor perſons, for the firſt time, after I paſſed the ſea; for, in the midſt of thoſe rich plantations, where the negro alone is wretched, miſerable huts are often to be met with, inhabited by whites, whoſe wan looks and ragged garments beſpeak poverty. At firſt I was puzzled to explain to myſelf, how, in a country where there is ſtill ſo much land to clear, men who do not refuſe to work, ſhould remain in miſery; but I have ſince learned, that all theſe uſeleſs territories, theſe immenſe eſtates, with which Virginia is covered, have their proprietors. Nothing is more common than to ſee ſome of them poſſeſſing five or ſix thouſand acres of land,

land, who clear out only as much as their negroes can cultivate; yet they will not give, nor even ſell the ſmalleſt portion of them, becauſe they form a part of their poſſeſſions, and they are in hopes of one day augmenting the number of their negroes. Theſe white men, without fortune, and frequently without induſtry, are ſtraitened, therefore, on every ſide, and reduced to the ſmall number of acres they are able to acquire. Now, the land not being good in general in America *, eſpecially in Virginia, a conſiderable number of them is neceſſary, in

* The land, *within the mountains*, in the hitherto ſettled parts of North America, are not in general very good, and it is of theſe only that the Marquis ſpeaks; but as the authors of the *Nouvelle Encyclopedie* obſerve, in their *new article* of the *United States*, this muſt have been the caſe in almoſt every new country, the ſoil of Europe having been meliorated by the progreſs of population, the quantity of manure, and the means by which the earth is protected from the effects of heavy rains, &c. by care and cultivation. Abbé Raynal's remarks on this ſubject, in his laſt work, called the Revolution of America, diſcover ſo much ignorance as ſcarcely to merit the elaborate diſcuſſion beſtowed on them by the ingenious authors of the *Encyclopedie*, who have

in order to clear it with ſucceſs, becauſe they are the cattle from which the cultivator derives his aid and his ſubſiſtence. To the eaſtward are a great number of cleared grounds, but the portions of land which are eaſily purchaſed there, and for almoſt nothing, conſiſt always of at leaſt two hundred acres; beſides, that to the ſouthward, the climate is leſs healthy, and the new ſettlers, without partaking of the wealth of Virginia, ſhare all the inconveniencies of the climate, and even the indolence it inſpires *.

Beneath

likewiſe tranſcribed from him ſeveral important paſſages, which have been ably and fully refuted by Mr. Payne. TRANSLATOR.

* The indolence and diſſipation of the middling and lower claſſes of white inhabitants of Virginia, are ſuch as to give pain to every reflecting mind. Horſe-racing, cock-fighting, and boxing-matches, are ſtanding amuſements, for which they neglect all buſineſs; and in the latter of which they conduct themſelves with a barbarity worthy of their ſavage neighbours. The ferocious practice of ſtage-boxing in England, is urbanity, compared with the Virginian mode of fighting. In their combats, unleſs ſpecially precluded, they are admitted (to uſe their own term) "to bite, b-ll-ck, and goudge;" which operations, when the firſt onſet with fiſts is over, conſiſts in faſtening

Beneath this claſs of inhabitants, we muſt place the negroes, whoſe ſituation would be ſtill

on the noſe or ears of their adverſaries with their teeth, ſeizing him by the genitals, and dexterouſly ſcooping out an eye; on which account it is no uncommon circumſtance to meet men in the prime of youth, deprived of one of thoſe organs. This is no traveller's exaggeration, I ſpeak from knowledge and obſervation. In the ſummer months it is very common to make a party on horſeback to a limeſtone ſpring, near which there is uſually ſome little hut with ſpirituous liquors, if the party are not themſelves provided, where their debauch frequently terminates in a boxing-match, a horſe-race, or perhaps both. During a day's reſidence at Leeſburg, I was myſelf accidentally drawn into one of theſe parties, where I ſoon experienced the ſtrength of the liquor, which was concealed by the refreſhing coolneſs of the water. While we were ſeated round the ſpring, at the edge of a delightful wood, four or five countrymen arrived, headed by a veteran cyclops, the terror of the neighbourhood, ready on every occaſion to riſk his remaining eye. We ſoon found ourſelves under the neceſſity of relinquiſhing our poſts, and making our eſcape from theſe fellows, who evidently ſought to provoke a quarrel. On our return home, whilſt I was rejoicing at our good fortune, and admiring the moderation of my company, we arrived at a plain ſpot of ground by a wood ſide, on which my horſe no ſooner ſet foot, than taking the bit between his teeth, off he went at full ſpeed, at-

ſtill more lamentable, did not their natural inſenſibility extenuate, in ſome degree, the ſufferings annexed to ſlavery. On ſeeing them ill lodged, ill clothed, and often oppreſſed with labour, I concluded that their treatment was as rigorous as elſewhere. I have been aſſured, however, that it is extremely mild, in compariſon with what they ſuffer in the ſugar colonies; and, in truth, you do not uſually hear, as at Saint Domingo,

tended by the hoops and hallowings of my companions. An Engliſhman is not eaſily thrown off his guard on horſeback; but at the end of half a mile my horſe ſtopped ſhort, as if he had been ſhot, and threw me with conſiderable violence over his head; my buckle, for I was without boots, entangled me in the ſtirrup, but fortunately broke into twenty pieces. The company rode up, delighted with the adventure; and it was then, for the firſt time, I diſcovered that I had been purpoſely induced, by one of my *friends*, to change horſes with him for the afternoon; that his horſe had been accuſtomed to ſimilar exploits on the ſame *race ground*; that the whole of the buſineſs was neither more nor leſs than a Virginian piece of pleaſantry; and that my friends thought they had exhibited great moderation in not expoſing me, at the ſpring, to the effects of "*biting*, *b-ll--king*, and *goudging*."

TRANSLATOR.

Domingo, and Jamaica, the ſound of whips, and the cries of the unhappy wretches whoſe bodies they are tearing to pieces *. This ariſes from the general character of the

 Virginians,

* During the Tranſlator's reſidence in the Weſt Indies, he took conſiderable pains to inform himſelf of the different modes of treatment of the negroes, by the principal European nations, poſſeſſing colonies in that quarter of the globe, the reſult of which was, that the Dutch are the moſt cruel; the Engliſh more humane; the French ſtill more ſo; and the Spaniards the moſt indulgent maſters. He was greatly ſtruck with this gradation, the truth of which ſeemed to be confirmed by his own obſervations; but he leaves it to others to decide what influence the various forms of government, and the religious principles or prejudices of each of theſe nations, may have in the operation of this ſeeming paradox. A lover of truth will never ſhrink from the diſcuſſion of any queſtion intereſting to humanity, whatever be his political or religious bias. The Tranſlator, from impulſe, and from reaſon, is a ſtrenuous aſſertor of the rights and original equality of mankind; but it is an old remark, that Republicans are the worſt maſters; a poſition which purſued through the above ſucceſſion, ſeems in ſome meaſure to receive a confirmation: yet to him appears unaccountable from any given principles, unleſs it be the ariſtocratic principles, which, to the misfortune of mankind, have hitherto uniformly taken poſſeſſion of all

Virginians, which is more mild than that of the inhabitants of the ſugar iſlands, who conſiſt almoſt entirely of rapacious men, eager and preſſing to make fortunes to return to Europe. Another reaſon is, that the produce of their culture not being of ſo much value, labour is not urged on them with ſo much ſeverity; and, to do juſtice to both, it is becauſe the negroes, on their ſide, are not ſo much addicted to cheating and thieving as in the iſlands. For the propagation of the black ſpecies being very rapid, and very conſiderable here, the greateſt part of the negroes are born in the country; and it is remarked that they are generally leſs depraved than thoſe imported from Africa. I muſt likewiſe do the Virginians the juſtice to declare, that many of them treat their negroes with great humanity. I muſt add likewiſe, a ſtill more honourable teſtimony,

the republican governments, and baffled the foreſight of the virtuous and good. But there is reaſon to hope that the democracies of America will form a brilliant and conſoling exception to the triumphant reproaches of the idolaters of regal power.

TRANSLATOR.

ny, that in general they ſeem afflicted to have any ſlavery, and are conſtantly talking of aboliſhing it, and of contriving ſome other means of cultivating their eſtates. It is true that this opinion, which is almoſt generally received, is inſpired by different motives. The philoſophers, and the young men, who are almoſt all educated in the principles of a ſound philoſophy *, regard nothing but juſtice, and the rights of humanity. The fathers of families, and ſuch as are principally occupied with ſchemes of intereſt, complain that the maintenance of their negroes is very expenſive; that their labour is neither ſo productive nor ſo cheap, as that of day labourers, or white ſervants; and, laſtly, that epidemical diſorders, which are very common, render both their property and their revenue extremely precari-

* The truth is, that the prevalent religion of the principal inhabitants in America, and particularly to the Southward, is *pure deiſm*, called by the name of Philoſophy in Europe; a ſpirit which has contributed in no ſmall degree to the revolution, and produced their unfettered conſtitutions of freedom and toleration. TRANSLATOR.

ous. However this may be, it is fortunate that different motives concur in disgusting men with that tyranny which they exercise upon their fellow-creatures at least, if not people entirely of the same species; for the more we regard the negroes, the more must we be persuaded that the difference between them and us, consists in something more than complexion. As for the rest, it cannot be denied that it is a very delicate point to abolish slavery in America. The negroes in Virginia amount to two hundred thousand. They equal at least, if they do not exceed, the number of white men. Necessarily united by interest, by the conformity of their situation, and the similarity of colour, they would unquestionably form a distinct people, from whom neither succour, virtue, nor labour, could be expected. Sufficient attention has not been paid to the difference between slavery, such as it exists in our colonies, and the slavery which was generally established among the ancients. A white slave had no other cause of humiliation, than his actual state; on his being freed, he mixed immediately with free men, and became their equal. Hence that emulation among the ſlaves to obtain their liberty, either as a favour, or to purchaſe it with the fruit of their labour. There were two advantages in this; the poſſibility of enfranchiſing them without danger, and that ambition which almoſt generally took place among them, and turned to the advantage of morals, and of induſtry. But in the preſent caſe, it is not only the ſlave who is beneath his maſter, it is the negro who is beneath the white man. No act of enfranchiſement can efface this unfortunate diſtinction; accordingly we do not ſee the negroes very anxious to obtain their freedom, nor much pleaſed when they have obtained it. The free negroes continue to live with the negro ſlaves, and never with the white men; inſomuch that intereſt alone makes them deſirous of quitting ſlavery, when they are endowed with a particular induſtry, of which they wiſh to reap the profits. It appears, therefore, that there is no other method of aboliſhing ſlavery, than by getting rid of the negroes, a meaſure which muſt be very gradually adopted. The beſt expedient would be to export a great number of males, and to encourage the marriage of white men with the females. For this purpoſe the law muſt be abrogated which tranſmits ſlavery by the ſide of the mother; or it might be enacted, that every female ſlave ſhall become, *ipſo facto*, free, by marrying a free man. From reſpect to property, perhaps it might be juſt to require of the latter, a compenſation to be fixed by law, to be paid either in labour or in money, as an indemnity to the proprietors of the negreſs; but it is certain, at all events, that ſuch a law, aided by the illicit, but already well eſtabliſhed commerce between the white men and negreſſes, could not fail of giving birth to a race of mulattoes, which would produce another of *Quarterons*, and ſo on until the colour ſhould be totally effaced.

But I have enlarged ſufficiently on this ſubject, which has not eſcaped the policy and philoſophy of the preſent age. I have only to apologize for not having treated it with *declamation*; but it has always been my opinion, that eloquence can influence only the reſolutions of the moment, and

that

that every thing which can only be effected by time alone, must be the result of reason; it is not difficult, however, to add ten or a dozen pages to these reflections, which are to be considered as a symphony composed only of the principal parts, *con corni ad libitum*.

We have seen the inconveniencies of slavery, and of the too extensive possession of territory in Virginia; let us now examine the inconsiderable number of advantages arising from them. The Virginians have the reputation, and with reason, of living nobly in their houses, and of being hospitable; they give strangers not only a willing, but a liberal reception. This arises, on one hand, from their having no large towns, where they may assemble, by which means they are little acquainted with society, except from the visits they make; and, on the other, their lands and their negroes furnishing them with every article of consumption, and the necessary service, this renowned hospitality costs them very little. Their houses are spacious, and ornamented, but their apartments are not commo-

commodious; they make no ceremony of putting three or four perſons into the ſame room*; nor do theſe make any objection to their being thus heaped together; for being in general ignorant of the comfort of reading and writing, they want nothing in the whole houſe but a bed, a dining-room, and a drawing-room for company. The chief magnificence of the Virginians conſiſts in furniture, linen, and plate; in which they reſemble our anceſtors, who had neither cabinets nor wardrobes in their caſtles, but contented themſelves with a well-ſtored cellar, and a handſome buffet. If they ſometimes diſſipate their fortunes, it is by gaming, hunting, and horſe-races†; but the

* Throughout America, in private houſes, as well as in the inns, ſeveral people are crowded together in the ſame room; and in the latter it very commonly happens, that after you have been ſome time in bed, a ſtranger of any condition, (for there is little diſtinction) comes into the room, pulls off his clothes, and places himſelf, without ceremony, between your ſheets.

TRANSLATOR.

† I have already ſpoken of horſe-races, but it is with regret I add, that the general ſpirit of gaming is prevalent in this as well as in all the United States,

the latter are of ſome utility, inaſmuch as they encourage the breed of horſes, which are really very handſome in Virginia. We ſee that the women have little ſhare in the amuſements of the men; beauty here ſerves only to procure them huſbands; for the moſt wealthy planters, giving but a ſmall fortune with their daughters, their fate is uſually decided by their figure. The conſequence of this is, that they are often pert and coquettiſh before, and ſorrowful helpmates after marriage. The luxury of being ſerved by ſlaves ſtill farthur augments their natural indolence; they are always ſurrounded by a great number of them, for their own ſervice, and that of their children, whom they content themſelves with ſuckling only. They, as well as their huſbands, pay attention to them when young, and neglect them when grown up. We may ſay in general of the Americans, as of the Engliſh, that they are very

but more particularly throughout the ſouthern ones, which has already been attended with ſuicide, and all its baneful conſequences. TRANSLATOR.

very fond of their *infants*, and care little for their *children*. It would be a delicate discussion, perhaps, to enquire, whether this be really a natural sentiment; and whether our conduct, which is very different, be not the result of self-love, or of ambition; but we may safely affirm, that the care we take of ours, is a means of attaching ourselves to them, and of ensuring their reciprocal attachment; a sentiment the nobleness and utility of which cannot be contested *.

I was desirous of celebrating the virtues peculiar to the Virginians, and in spite of my wishes, I am obliged to limit myself to their magnificence and hospitality. It is not in my power to add generosity; for they are strongly attached to their interests; and their great riches, joined to their pretensions, gives more deformity to this vice. I ought,

* I confess myself at a loss to discover from what source of observation the author has derived the fact on which he reasons so ingeniously. Perhaps it is the secret spirit of natural prejudice that has led me, who was born an Englishman, to reverse the remark, as applied to the two countries of France and England; but I leave the fact and the discussion to more acute observers. TRANSLATOR.

ought, in the firſt inſtance, to have treated of the article of religion; but there is nothing remarkable reſpecting it in this country, except the facility with which they diſpenſe with it. The eſtabliſhed religion, previous to the Revolution, was that of the Church of England, which we know requires Epiſcopacy, and that every Prieſt muſt be ordained by a Biſhop. Before the war, perſons deſtined to the Church, went to England, to ſtudy and to be ordained. It is impoſſible, therefore, in the preſent circumſtances, to ſupply the vacancies of the Paſtors who drop off. What has been the conſequence of this? That the churches have remained ſhut; the people have done without a Paſtor, and not a thought has been employed towards any ſettlement of an Engliſh church, independent of England *. The moſt complete toleration is eſtabliſhed; but the other communions have

* During the war there was a great ſcarcity of Miniſters of the Epiſcopal Church, on account of the numbers of that body who attached themſelves to England, which was pretty generally the caſe; but after the peace, many young Americans, diſtin-

have made no acquisition from the losses of the former; each sect has remained in its original situation; and this sort of religious interregnum, has been productive of no disorder. The clergy have besides received a severe check in the new constitution, which excludes them from all share in the government, even from the right of voting at elections.

guished for the gown, finding a repugnance on the part of the English Bishops, got ordained by the Nonjuring Bishops in Scotland. An act has at length passed, however, to authorize the ordination of Foreign Clergy by the English Bishops, which is evidently intended to promote the cause of the Hierarchy in the United States. I shall here take the opportunity of mentioning, that on account of the great scarcity of Bibles, a new edition was published by one Aikin, a printer, of Philiadelphia, by order of Congress, under the inspection of the Reverend Mr. White, brother-in-law to Mr. Morris, and the other Chaplain to that body; but such are ancient prejudices, that very few of the zealous followers either of Luther or of Calvin, could be brought to look upon it as the genuine old book. The wary devotees, dreaded, no doubt, similar errors to that for which the Company of Stationers were mulcted in the time of King Charles; the omission of the *negative* in one of the Commandments, by printing "Thou *shalt* do murder." TRANSLATOR.

elections. It is true, that the judges and lawyers are ſubjected to the ſame excluſion, but that is from another motive; to prevent the public intereſt from falling into competition with that of individuals. The legiſlator dreaded the re-action of theſe intereſts; it has been thought proper, in ſhort, to form a ſort of ſeparate body in the State, under the name of the Judicial Body. Theſe general views are perhaps ſalutary in themſelves; but they are attended with an inconvenience at the preſent moment; for the lawyers, who are certainly the moſt enlightened part of the community, are removed from the civil councils, and the adminiſtration is entruſted either to ignorant, or to the leaſt ſkilful men. This is the principal objection made in the country to the preſent form of government, which to me appears excellent in many reſpects. It is every where in print, and eaſily to be procured; bnt I ſhall endeavour to give a ſketch of it in a few words. It is compoſed, 1ſt, Of the Aſſembly of Deputies, named by the cities and counties, a body correſponding with the Houſe of Commons. 2dly, Of a

Senate,

Senate, the members of which are elected by several united counties, in a greater or less number, according to the population of the counties, which answers to the House of Peers. 3dly, Of an Executive Council, of which the Governor is president, and the members chosen by the two Chambers; a substitute for the executive power of the King in England*.

It is not by accident that I have postponed the consideration of every thing respecting the progress of the Arts and Sciences in this country, until the conclusion of my reflections on Virginia; I have done it expressly, because the mind, after bestowing its attention on the variety of human institutions, reposes itself with pleasure on those which tend to the perfection of the understanding, and the progress of information; and above all, because having found myself under the necessity of speaking less advantageously

* See the Constitutions of the different States, republished in England by the Reverend Mr. Jackson, and the excellent translation from the original, with notes, published in Paris by the *Duke de la Rochefoucault*. TRANSLATOR.

tageously of this State than I wished to have done, I am happy to conclude with an article, which is wholly in their commendation. The College of William and Mary, whose founders are announced by the very name, is a noble establishment which embellishes Williamsburg, and does honour to Virginia. The beauty of the edifice is surpassed by the richness of its library, and that, still farther, by the distinguished merit of several of the Professors, such as the Doctors *Maddison*, *Wythe*, *Bellini*, &c. &c. who may be regarded as living books, at once affording precepts and examples. I must likewise add, that the zeal of these Professors has been crowned with the most distinguished success, and that they have already formed many distinguished characters, ready to serve their country in the various departments of government. Amongst these, it is with pleasure I mention Mr. *Short*, with whom I was particularly connected. After doing justice to the exertions of the *University* of Williamsburg, for such is the College of William and Mary; if it be neceſſary for its further glory to cite miracles, I ſhall only obſerve that they created me a Doctor of Laws.

Williamſburg,
1ſt of May 1782.

A Journey

A Journey into New Hampſhire, the State of Maſſachuſets, and Upper Penſylvania.

THE Baron de Viomenil having joined the army in the beginning of October, I ought to have reſigned to him of courſe the command of the firſt diviſion; ſo that I had now no neceſſary occupation, unleſs I had choſen to take the command of the ſecond diviſion; in which caſe I muſt have ſuperſeded the Comte de Viomenil, which was far from my intention; it depended upon myſelf, therefore, to return to Philadelphia, to wait for M. de Rochambeau, who was expected there, after marching his troops to the eaſtward; but my departure would have too plainly diſcovered the intention of embarking them, which it was wiſhed to keep a ſecret, at leaſt until they had reached Hartford. The Comte de Viomenil, on the other hand, being deſirous of viſiting Saratoga, the Baron de Viomenil requeſted me to retain the command of the firſt, whilſt he took that of the ſecond diviſion. I conſented, therefore, to ſacrifice another liſtleſs and fatiguing fortnight, and marched with the troops to Hartford *. I ſubmitted alſo

* The Tranſlator attended the French army on their march, nearly the whole way, from Alexandria to the North River, and was a witneſs to their ſtrict diſcipline, and the ſurprizing harmony between them and the people of the country, to whom they gave not the ſlighteſt reaſon of complaint. He inſiſts the more on this fact, as it appears to him no leſs ſingular than intereſting. On their arrival at their quarters on the march, the whole country came to ſee them, and it was a general ſcene of gaiety and good humour. When they encamped at Alexandria, on the ground formerly occupied by Braddock, the moſt elegant and handſome young ladies of the neighbourhood danced with the officers on the turf, in the middle of the camp, to the ſound of military muſic; and, (a circumſtance which will appear ſingular to European ideas,) the circle was in a great meaſure compoſed of ſoldiers, who, from the heat of the weather, had diſengaged themſelves from their clothes, retaining not an article of dreſs except their ſhirts, which in general were neither extremely long, nor in the beſt condition; nor did this occaſion the leaſt embarraſſment to the ladies, many of whom were of highly poliſhed manners, and the moſt exquiſite delicacy; or to their friends or parents; ſo whimſical and arbitrary are manners.

TRANSLATOR.

also not to return to the southward, before Mr. de Rochambeau, and to accompany him thither after seeing them embarked. I determined, however, to avail myself of these circumstances to visit the upper part of the State of Massachussets, and New Hampshire, which I had not yet seen. With this view I set out from Hartford the 4th of November, the very day the Comte de Rochambeau marched with the first division to encamp at Bolton *. It was two in the afternoon when I got on horseback; my companions were Messieurs Lynch, de Montesquieu, the Baron de Taleyrand, and Mr. de Vaudreuil. We followed the Bolton route to a cross road, about three miles be-

* The French army, at the time the Marquis speaks of, had been for some time encamped at Crompont, near Cortland's manor, a few miles from that of General Washington's, and between which there was a daily intercourse. The Translator dined, in October 1782, in General Washington's tent, with the Marquis de Laval, the Baron de Viomenil, and several French officers, within hearing of the British guns, which were at that period happily become a *brutum fulmen*.

TRANSLATOR.

yond the Meeting-houſe, where there is a ſtone for the traveller's direction. We here took to the left, to reach Mr. Kendal's tavern, in the townſhip of *Coventry*, ſeventeen miles from Bolton, and four from the croſs roads. In a quarter of an hour we met Mr. Kendal, who was on horſeback, carrying letters to Mr. de Rochambeau, from the Marquis de Vaudreuil, our Admiral; for this route, which is the ſhorteſt between Bolton and Hartford, was preferred for the chain of expreſſes between the fleet, the army, and Philadelphia. Mr. de Monteſquieu returned with him to Bolton, to know whether theſe letters contained any intereſting intelligence. As we travelled ſlowly, he joined us in half an hour, and informed us, that they were only anſwers to thoſe he had received from the army, with the ſtate of the troops to be embarked. Before we reached Mr. Kendal's, we paſſed a hut which ſcarcely merited the name of a *boghouſe*, and was only half covered, but which was inhabited by a man who accoſted us in French; he was a labourer from Canada, who had frequently changed

changed habitations, and had ſeven children. We were well lodged and treated at Mr. Kendal's, who is above the common claſs, and is more occupied in commerce than in farming; he ſat down to table with us, and we were pleaſed with his converſation.

We ſet out at half paſt eight in the morning of the 5th, and travelled through a very agreeable and variegated country, preſenting us every moment with the view of handſome habitations. The face of the country is unequal, but the hills are neither high nor ſteep. We ſtopped to bait our horſes at Mr. Clark's tavern, in *Aſhford* townſhip, by the ſide of the rivulet of *Mounthope*, on this ſide of a river marked in the chart by the name of *Monchoas*, and of a branch of that river called *Bigſlack*. We left this place at two o'clock, the country ſtill continuing to be pleaſant. I was particularly ſtruck with the poſition of *Woodſtock* meeting, which is placed on an eminence, commanding a very gay and well-peopled country. There are ſeveral inns around this meeting, but we went three miles and a half further, to Mrs. Chandler's. Our journey, this day, was thirty-three miles, it being ſeventeen from *Clark*'s to *Chandler*'s *tavern*. This houſe is kept by a widow, who was from home; and Mr. Lynch, who had preceded us, was very ill received by an old ſervant maid. We found him in great diſtreſs, becauſe ſhe would make no preparation of even killing a few chickens, before ſhe received the orders of her miſtreſs. Fortunately, however, the latter arrived in a quarter of an hour, in a ſort of ſingle horſe chaiſe, and we found her very polite and obliging, ſhe gave us a tolerable ſupper, and we were neatly lodged*.

The 6th we ſet out at ten o'clock, having been apprized that on reaching *Oxford*, it would be neceſſary to enquire the road at a tavern kept by Mr. *Lord*, at twelve miles diſtance; but the weather being bad when we got there, we determined to ſtop a couple of hours until the rain ceaſed, which had continued the whole morning. We had two roads to chuſe; that which goes through

* This is one of the beſt houſes I met with in America. TRANSLATOR.

through *Shrewſbury* would have led us more directly to *Portſmouth*; but I preferred that by *Grafton*, which leads to *Concord*; that celebrated ſpot, where the firſt blood was ſhed, which commenced the civil war. The rain abating a little, we reſumed our journey at two, and paſſed through *Salton*, a pretty enough place, where there are ſeveral well-built houſes; but the rain redoubling, we were obliged to halt ſeven miles farther on, at *Baron*'s tavern, where we were well received. We dried ourſelves by a good fire, in a very handſome apartment, adorned with good prints, and handſome mahogany furniture; and finding the uſeful correſpond with the agreeable in this houſe, we reconciled ourſelves to the bad weather, which had forced us into ſuch good quarters.

We left this place at nine the next morning, the road leading us through Grafton, after which we paſſed *Blackſtone* river, and arrived at *Gale*'s tavern, fifteen miles from Baron's, after a journey through a very pleaſant country. I remarked that the meadows, of which there are a great number,

number, were in general interſected and watered by trenches cut on purpoſe. Mr. Gales informed me, that theſe meadows were worth from ten to twenty dollars an acre; from one of which, in his poſſeſſion, he reaped four tons of hay an acre. The after-graſs is for the cattle, to produce butter and cheeſe, principally of this country. The price of meat is here about two-pence halfpenny the pound of fourteen ounces. After baiting our horſes, we continued our journey by *Marlborough*, where there are handſome houſes, and more collected than in the other towns or townſhips. We at length entered a wood, which conducted us to the river of Concord, or *Billerika*, over which we paſſed by a bridge about a mile from the Meeting, and at the ſame diſtance from Mr. *John*'s, where it was near nine o'clock before we arrived. This is an excellent inn, kept by a moſt determined Whig, who acted his part in the affair of Concord *. Major *Pitcairn*, who commanded the Engliſh on this occaſion, had lodged

* It took place on the 19th of April 1775. General Gage had detached from Boſton all his grenadiers, light infantry, and ſome other troops,

lodged frequently at his houſe, in travelling through the country in diſguiſe; a method he had ſometimes taken, though very dangerous, of gaining information to communicate to General Gage. The day on which he headed the Engliſh troops to Concord, he arrived at ſeven in the morning, followed by a company of grenadiers, and went immediately to Mr. John's tavern, the door of which being ſhut, he knocked ſeveral times, and on the refuſal to open it, ordered his grenadiers to force it. Entering it himſelf the firſt, he puſhed Mr. John with ſuch violence

amounting together to 900 men, under the orders of Lieutenant Colonel Smith, and Major Pitcairn. At Lexington they fell in with a company of Militia, whom they found under arms. The Engliſh, in a haughty tone, ordered the Americans to diſperſe, which they refuſed; and whilſt the converſation was confined to words, the Engliſh fired without giving notice, and at that diſcharge killed ſeven or eight Americans, who had made no diſpoſition to ſhelter themſelves from the fire; they were compelled to give way to numbers. The Engliſh advanced to Concord, where they paid dearly for their violence; and this firſt act of hoſtility, for which they were alone reſponſible, coſt them near 300 men. Major Pitcairn was ſlain at the battle of Bunker's Hill, a ſhort time after the affair of Concord.

violence as to throw him down, and afterwards placed a guard over him, frequently insisting on his pointing out the magazines of the rebels. The Americans had, in fact, collected some cannon and warlike stores at Concord, but having received timely notice in the night, they had removed every thing into the woods, except three twenty-four pounders, which remained in the prison-yard, of which Mr. John was the keeper. Major Pitcairn carrying his violence so far as to clap a pistol to his throat, Mr. John, who had himself been in a passion, grew calm, and tried to pacify the English commander. He assured him that there were only the above three pieces at Concord, and that he should see them if he would follow him. He conducted him to the prison, where the English entered, he says, in a rage, at seeing the *Yankees* so expert in mounting cannon, and in providing themselves with every thing necessary for the service of artillery, such as spunges, rammers, &c. Major Pitcairn made his men destroy the carriages, and break the trunnions; then ordered the prison to be set open,

open, where he found two prisoners, one of whom, being a Tory, he released.

The first moments of trouble and vivacity being over, Major Pitcairn returned to Mr. John's, where he breakfasted, and paid for it. The latter resumed his station of innkeeper; numbers of the English came to ask for rum, which he measured out as usual, and made them pay exactly. In the mean time, the Americans, who had passed the river in their retreat, began to rally, and to unite with those, who, apprized by the alarum bells, and various expresses, were coming to their assistance. The disposition Major Pitcairn had to make for his security, whilst he was employed in searching for, and destroying the ammunition, was by no means difficult; it was only necessary to place strong guards at the two bridges to the North and South, which he had done. Towards ten o'clock in the morning, the firing of musquetry was heard at the North Bridge, on which the English rallied at the place appointed, on a height, in a church-yard situated to the right of the road, and opposite the town-house. Three hundred Americans, who were aſſembled on the other ſide of the river, deſcended from the heights by a winding road which leads obliquely to the bridge, but which, at ſixty paces from the river, turns to the left, and comes ſtraight upon it. Until they had reached this angle, they had their flank covered by a ſmall ſtone wall; but when they came to this point, they marched up boldly to the bridge, which they found the enemy employed in breaking down. The latter fired the firſt, but the Americans fell upon them, and they eaſily gave way, which appears rather extraordinary. Mr. John affirms, that the Engliſh at firſt imagined the Americans had no ball, but that they ſoon found their error, on ſeeing ſeveral of their ſoldiers wounded. They even ſpeak here of an officer, who informed his men that they had nothing to fear, for that *the Americans fired only with powder*; but a drummer who was near him receiving at the moment a muſquet ſhot, replied, *Take care of that powder, Captain.* The Engliſh had three men killed here, and ſeveral wounded, two of them were officers.

The Americans now paſſed the bridge, and formed immediately on a ſmall eminence, to the left of the road, as they were ſituated, and a ſhort cannon ſhot from that on which the Engliſh were collected. There they remained ſome time watching each other; but the ſight of ſome houſes on fire irritated the Americans, and determined them to march towards the Engliſh, who then retreated by the Lexington road, which forming an elbow, the Americans, who knew the country, took the ſtring of the bow, and got up with them before they advanced a mile. It was here the retreating fight began, of which every body has ſeen the accounts, and which continued to Lexington, where the Engliſh were joined by the reinforcement under the command of *Earl Percy*.

It was on the morning of the 8th that I examined the field of battle at Concord, which took me up till half paſt ten, when I reſumed my journey. Ten miles from Concord is *Bellerika*, a pretty conſiderable townſhip; the country here was leſs fertile, and the road rather ſtony. We halted at

South

South Andover, five miles beyond Billerika, at a bad inn, kept by one Forſter; his wife had ſome beautiful children, but ſhe appeared diſordered, and I thought her rather drunk. She ſhewed me, with much importance, a book her eldeſt daughter was reading, and I found it, to my no ſmall ſurprize, to be a book of prayers in Italian. This daughter, who was about ſeventeen, repeated alſo a prayer in the Indian language, of which ſhe underſtood not a word, having learnt it accidentally from an Indian ſervant; but her mother thought all this admirable. We contented ourſelves with baiting our horſes in this wretched alehouſe, and ſet out at half paſt one, travelled through *South* and *North Andover*. *North-Pariſh*, or, North Andover, is a charming place, where there are a great number of very handſome houſes, a quantity of meadows, and fine cattle. Almoſt on quitting this long townſhip, you enter *Bradford*, where night overtook us, and we travelled two or three miles in the dark before we reached *Haverhill* ferry. It was half paſt ſix before we had croſſed it, and got to Mr. Harward's ward's inn, where we had a good ſupper, and good lodgings. At Haverhill, the *Merimack* is only fit for veſſels of thirty tons, but much larger ones are built here, which are floated down empty to Newbury. Three miles above Haverhill are falls, and higher up the river is only navigable for boats. The trade of this town formerly conſiſted in timber for ſhip-building, which has been ſuſpended ſince the war. It is pretty conſiderable, and tolerably well built; and its ſituation, in the form of an amphitheatre on the left ſhore of the Merimack, gives it many agreeable aſpects.

We left this place the 9th, at nine in the morning, our road lying through *Plaſtow*, a pretty conſiderable townſhip; after which we met with woods, and a wild and horrid country. We ſaw a great number of pines and epicias; there are alſo ſeveral large lakes, ſome of which are traced upon the chart. Since we quitted the confines of Connecticut, I have in general obſerved a great number of theſe ponds, which contributed to increaſe the reſemblance between this country and that of the *Bour-*

bonnois, and the *Nivernois*, in France. Twelve miles from Haverhill is *Kingſton*, a townſhip inferior to thoſe we had obſerved upon the route; and at the end of eighteen miles is *Exeter*, at preſent the capital of New Hampſhire, that is to ſay, the place where the Preſident or Governor reſides, and the members of the ſtate aſſemble. It is rather a handſome town, and is a ſort of port; for veſſels of ſeventy tons can come up, and others as large as three or four hundred tons are built here, which are floated down Exeter river into the bay of that name, and thence to *Piſcataqua*. We ſtopped at a very handſome inn kept by Mr. Ruſpert, which we quitted at half paſt two; and though we rode very faſt, night was coming on when we reached Portſmouth. The road from Exeter is very hilly. We paſſed through *Greenland*, a very populous townſhip, compoſed of well built houſes. Cattle here are abundant, but not ſo handſome as in Connecticut, and the State of Maſſachuſſets. They are diſperſed over fine meadows, and it is a beatiful ſight to ſee them collected near their hovels in the evening.

evening. This country preſents, in every reſpect, the picture of Abundance and of Happineſs. The road from Greenland to Portſmouth is wide and beautiful, interſperſed with habitations, ſo that theſe two townſhips almoſt touch. I alighted at Mr. *Brooſter's*, where I was well lodged; he ſeemed to me a reſpectable man, and much attached to his country.

In the morning of the 10th I went to pay a viſit to Mr. Albert de Rioms, Captain of the *Pluton* *, who had a houſe on ſhore, where he reſided for his health; he invited me to dinner, which he adviſed me to accept, as the Comte de Vaudreuil was in great confuſion on board his ſhip, the mizen maſt of which had been ſtruck by lightning five days before, and which penetrated to his firſt battery; but he offered me his boat to

 carry

* The Marquis de Vaudreuil's ſquadron was then at Boſton, and ſome of his ſhips were refitting, and taking in maſts at Portſmouth. M. de Albert de Rioms is the officer who commanded the evolutions of the French ſquadron, on the late viſit of the King to Cherbourg. TRANSLATOR.

carry me on board the *Auguste*. In returning for my cloak, I happened to pass by the meeting, precisely at the time of service, and had the curiosity to enter, where I remained above half an hour, that I might not interrupt the preacher, and to shew my respect for the assembly; the audience were not numerous on account of the severe cold, but I saw some handsome women, elegantly dressed. Mr. *Barkminster*, a young minister, spoke with a great deal of grace, and reasonably enough for a preacher. I could not help admiring the address with which he introduced politics into his sermon, by comparing the Christians redeemed by the blood of Jesus Christ, but still compelled to fight against the flesh and sin, to the Thirteen United States, who, notwithstanding they have acquired liberty and independence, are under the necessity of employing all their force to combat a formidable power, and to preserve those invaluable treasures. It was near twelve when I embarked in Mr. Albert's boat, and saw on the left, near the little Island of *Rising Castle*,

Castle, the *America* *, (the ship given by Congress to the King of France) which

had

* The America is the vessel given by Congress to the King of France, to replace the *Magnifique*, lost on Lovel's island in Boston harbour, when the French fleet entered that port some months after the defeat of the Comte de Grasse. This ship was designed for the well known *Paul Jones*, who by his command of the little squadron on the coasts of England, had acquired the title of Commodore, and was sighing after that of Admiral of America, which Congress, no bad appreciators of merit, thought proper to refuse him. The Translator met him at a public table at Boston, on his return from Portsmouth, where he told the company, that notwithstanding the reason he had to be discontented, he had given his advice in the construction and launching of the vessel; in which latter operation, however, the ship struck fast on the slip, but without any material damage. This accident is not intended by any means as an imputation on Mr. Jones, who certainly was fortunate enough, at one time, to render considerable service to America. He is said to have acquired a considerable property by the prizes he made in that cruize, but his officers and crews complain (the Translator does not say with what justice) that there has never been any distribution of the prize money; and that numbers of his maimed and mutilated sailors were reduced to beg for a subsistence in France, and elsewhere, to the discredit of Ame-

had been juſt launched, and appeared to me a fine ſhip. I left on the right the Iſle of Waſhington, on which ſtands a fort of that name. It is built in the form of a ſtar, the parapets of which are ſupported by ſtakes, and was not finiſhed. Then leaving *Newcaſtle* on the right, and *Bittery* on the left, we arrived at the anchoring ground, within the firſt paſs. I found Mr. Vaudreuil on board, who preſented me to the officers of his ſhip, and afterwards to thoſe of the detachment of the army, among whom were three officers of my former regiment of Guienne, at preſent called Viennois. He then took me to ſee the ravages made by the lightning, of which M. de Biré, who then commanded the ſhip, M. de Vaudreuil having ſlept on ſhore, gave me the following account: At half paſt two in the morning, in the midſt of very

rica. Mr. Jones read ſome pretty enough verſes in his own honour to the ſame company, at Brackett's tavern in Boſton, extracted from a London newſpaper, and ſaid to be written by Lady Craven. The America is now at Breſt, and is eſteemed one of the handſomeſt ſhips in the French navy.

TRANSLATOR.

very violent rain, a dreadful explosion was heard suddenly, and the centinel, who was in the gallery, came in a panic into the council chamber, where he met with M. Biré, who had leaped to the foot of his bed, and they were both struck with a strong sulphureous smell. The bell was immediately rung, and the ship examined, when it was found that the mizen mast was cut short in two, four feet from the forecastle; that it had been lifted in the air, and fallen perpendicularly on the quarter-deck, through which it had penetrated, as well as the second battery. Two sailors were crushed by its fall, two others, who never could be found, had doubtless been thrown into the sea by the commotion, and several were wounded.

At one o'clock we returned on shore to dine with Mr. Albert de Rioms, and our fellow guests were M. de Biré, who acted as Flag Captain, though but a Lieutenant; M. de Mortegues, who formerly commanded the *Magnifique* (lost at the same period on Lovel's island in Boston harbour) and was destined to the command of the

America; M. de Siber, Lieutenant *en pied* of the Pluton; M. d'Hizeures, Captain of the regiment of Viennois, &c. after dinner we went to drink tea with Mr. *Langdon*. He is a handſome man, and of a noble carriage; he has been a member of Congreſs, and is now one of the firſt people of the country; his houſe is elegant and well furniſhed, and the apartments admirably well wainſcoted; he has a good manuſcript chart of the harbour of Portſmouth. Mrs. Langdon, his wife, is young, fair, and tolerably handſome; but I converſed leſs with her than with her huſband, in whoſe favour I was prejudiced, from knowing that he had diſplayed great courage and patriotiſm at the time of Burgoyne's expedition. For repairing to the council chamber, of which he was a member, and perceiving that they were about to diſcuſs ſome affairs of little conſequence, he addreſſed them as follows: "Gentlemen, you may talk as long as you "pleaſe, but I know that the enemy is on "our frontiers, and that I am going to "take my piſtols, and mount my horſe, "to combat with my fellow citizens;"

the

the greatest part of the members of the council and assembly followed him, and joined General Gates at Saratoga. As he was marching day and night, reposing himself only in the woods, a negro servant who attended him, says to him, "Master, you "are hurting yourself, but no matter, you "are going to fight for Liberty; I should "suffer also patiently if I had Liberty to "defend." "Don't let that stop you," replied Mr. Langdon, "from this moment "you are free." The negro followed him, behaved with courage, and has never quitted him. On leaving Mr. Langdon's, we went to pay a visit to Colonel *Wentworth*, who is respected in this country, not only from his being of the same family with Lord Rockingham, but from his general acknowledged character for probity and talents. He conducted the naval department at Portsmouth, and our officers are never weary in his commendation. From Mr. Wentworth's, M. de Vaudreuil and M. de Rioms took me to Mrs. *Whipple*'s, a widow lady, who is, I believe, sister-in-law to *General Whipple*; she is neither young nor hand-

handſome, but appeared to me to have a good underſtanding, and gaiety. She is educating one of her nieces, only fourteen years old, who is already charming. Mrs. Whipple's houſe, as well as that of Mr. Wentworth's, and all thoſe I ſaw at Portſmouth, are very handſome and well furniſhed.

I propoſed, on the morning of the 11th, to make a tour amongſt the iſlands in the harbour, but ſome ſnow having fallen, and the weather being by no means inviting, I contented myſelf with paying viſits to ſome officers of the navy, and amongſt others to the Comte de Vaudreuil, who had ſlept on ſhore the preceding night; after which we again met at dinner at Mr. Albert's, a point of union which was always agreeable. M. d'Hizeure had ordered the muſic of the regiment of Vennois to attend, and I found with pleaſure, that the taſte for muſic, which I had inſpired into that corps, ſtill ſubſiſted, and that the ancient muſicians had been judiciouſly replaced *. After dinner,

* The Marquis de Chaſtellux, amongſt his various accompliſhments, is diſtinguiſhed not only in the character of an *amateur*, but for his ſcientific knowledge of muſic. TRANSLATOR.

ner, we again drank tea at Mr. Langdon's, and then paid a viſit to Dr. *Brackett*, an eſteemed phyſician of the country, and afterwards to Mr. *Thompſon*. The latter was born in England; he is a good ſeaman, and an excellent ſhip-builder, and is beſides a ſenſible man, greatly attached to his new country, which it is only fifteen years ſince he adopted. His wife is an American, and pleaſes by her countenance, but ſtill more by her amiable and polite behaviour. We finiſhed the evening at Mr. Wentworth's, where the Comte de Vaudreuil lodged; he gave us a very handſome ſupper, without ceremony, during which the converſation was gay and agreeable.

The 12th I ſet out, after taking leave of M. de Vaudreuil, whom I met as he was coming to call on me, and it was certainly with the greateſt ſincerity that I teſtified to him my ſenſe of the polite manner in which I had been received by him, and by the officers under his command.

The following are the ideas which I had an opportunity of acquiring relative to the town of Portſmouth. It was in a pretty flouriſhing

flouriſhing ſtate before the war, and carried on the trade of ſhip timber, and ſalt fiſh. It is eaſy to conceive that this commerce muſt have greatly ſuffered ſince the commencement of the troubles, but notwithſtanding, Portſmouth is, perhaps, of all the American towns, that which will gain the moſt by the preſent war. There is every appearance of its becoming to *New* England, what the other Portſmouth is to the *Old*; that is to ſay, that this place will be made choice of as the depôt of the continental marine. The acceſs to the harbour is eaſy, the road immenſe, and there are ſeven fathoms water as far up as two miles above the town; add to this, that notwithſtanding its northern ſituation, the harbour of Portſmouth is never frozen, an advantage ariſing from the rapidity of the current. This circumſtance, joined to its proximity to the timber for ſhip-building, eſpecially for maſts, which can only be balanced by the harbour of Rhode Iſland, will doubtleſs determine the choice of Congreſs. But if a naval eſtabliſhment be thought neceſſary at Portſmouth, the quays, the rope-walks, the

the arſenals, &c. muſt be placed in the iſlands, and not on the continent; for it would be eaſy for an enemy's army to land there, and take poſſeſſion of the town, the local ſituation of which would require too conſiderable a develòpement of fortification to ſhelter it from inſult. I imagine however, that a good entrenched camp might be formed between the two creeks, but I am only able to judge of that from a ſlight obſervation, and from charts.

It has happened in New Hampſhire, as in the State of Maſſachuſſets, that the loſſes of commerce have turned to the advantage of agriculture; the capitals of the rich, and the induſtry of the people having flowed back from the coaſts towards the interior of the country, which has profited rapidly by the reflux. It is certain that this country has a very flouriſhing appearance, and that new houſes are building, and new farms are ſettling every day.

New Hampſhire hitherto has no permanent conſtitution, and its preſent government is no more than a ſimple convention; it much reſembles that of Penſylvania, for

it

it consists of one legislative body, composed of the representatives of the people, and the executive council, which has for its chief, a President, instead of Governor. But during my stay at Portsmouth, I learnt that there was an assembly at Exeter for the purpose of establishing a constitution, the principal articles of which were already agreed on. This constitution will be founded on the same principles as those of New-York and Massachussets. There will be, as in the former, an executive power vested in the hands of the Governor, the Chancellor and the Chief Justices; the latter of whom will be perpetual, at least *quam diu se bene gesserint*, during good behaviour, but the members of the senate will be annually changed, and the requisite qualification of a senator, very inconsiderable, which I think is a great inconvenience *. Mr. Langdon observes, and perhaps with reason, that the country is as yet too young, and the materials wanting to give this senate all

* A new form of government has been established since the peace. TRANSLATOR.

all the weight and confiftence it ought to have, as in Maryland, where the fenators are elected for three years, and muft poffefs at leaft five hundred pounds.

At Portfmouth I was told of a new fect, which could not fail of making fome noife in the country. An individual, I think, of the name of *Andrews*, thinks proper to preach a doctrine called that of the *Univerfalifts*. He pretends that Jefus Chrift having redeemed all men, no man can be damned; for were it otherwife, his miffion would be ufelefs, at leaft in a great meafure. If this opinion be not novel, it is certainly very commodious; but it forms rather a fubject of converfation, and even of pleafantry, than matter of difpute.

When I was at Portfmouth the neceffaries of life were very dear, owing to the great drought of the preceding fummer. Corn cofts two dollars a bufhel, (of fixty pounds weight) oats almoft as much, and Indian corn was extremely fcarce. I fhall hardly be believed when I fay, that I paid eight livres ten fols (about feven fhillings and three-pence) a day for each horfe.

Butcher's

Butcher's meat only was cheap, ſelling at two-pence halfpenny a pound. That part of New Hampſhire bordering on the coaſt is not fertile; there are good lands at forty or fifty miles diſtance from the ſea, but the expence of carriage greatly augments the price of articles, when ſold in the more inhabited parts. As for the value of landed property it is dear enough for ſo new a country. Mr. Ruſpert, my landlord, paid ſeventy pounds currency per annum, (at eighteen livres, or fifteen ſhillings the pound) for his inn. Lands ſell at from ten to ſixteen dollars an acre. The country produces little fruit, and the cyder is indifferent.

The road from Portſmouth to *Newbury* paſſes through a barren country. *Hampton* is the only townſhip you meet with, and there are not ſuch handſome houſes there as at Greenland. As we had only twenty miles to go, I was unwilling to ſtop, and deſired the Vicomte de Vaudreuil only, to go on a little before us to dinner. It was two o'clock when we reached Merimack ferry, and from the ſhore we ſaw the openings

ings of the harbour, the channel of which paſſes near the northern extremity of *Plumb Iſland,* on which is a ſmall fort, with a few cannon and mortars. Its ſituation appears to me well choſen, at leaſt as far as I was capable of judging from a diſtance. At the entrance of the harbour is a bar, on which there are only eighteen feet water in the higheſt tides, ſo that although it be a very commercial place, it has always been reſpected by the Engliſh. Several frigates had been built here; amongſt others, the *Charles-Town*, and the *Alliance* *. The har-

 bour

* The privateers which ſo greatly moleſted the Britiſh trade were chiefly from the ports of Newbury, Beverley, and Salem, in which places large fortunes were made by this means; and ſuch muſt ever be the caſe in any future war, from the peculiarity of their poſition, whence they may run out at any ſeaſon of the year, and commit depredations on any of the maritime powers to which America is hoſtile, with little fear of retaliation. Newfoundland, Nova Scotia, the Gulphs of St. Lawrence, and of Florida, and the whole trade of the Weſt-Indian Archipelago, are in a manner at their doors. However Great-Britain may affect to deſpiſe America, ſhe is perhaps, even in her preſent infant

bour is extensive, and well sheltered. After passing the ferry in little flat boats, which held

state, from various circumstances, the most formidable enemy she can have to cope with, in case of a rupture; for, as nations ought collectively to be dispassionate, though individuals are not, it behoves her to reflect, where, and in what manner she can return the blow. Mr. *Jefferson*, the present Minister of the United States at Versailles, amongst other excellent observations on this subject has the following, which I extract with pleasure from his *Notes on Virginia*, a most interesting work, with which I have just privately been favoured. "The sea is the field "on which we should meet an European enemy, "on that element it is necessary we should possess "some power. To aim at such a navy as the "greater nations of Europe possess would be a "foolish and wicked waste of the energies of our "countrymen. It would be to pull on our heads "that load of military expence which makes the "European labourer go supperless to bed, and moi-"stens his bread with the sweat of his brow. It "will be enough if we enable ourselves to prevent "insult from those nations of Europe which are "weak on the sea, because *circumstances exist which* "*render even the stronger ones weak as to us. Provi-*"*dence has placed their richest and most defenceless pos-*"*sessions at our door; has obliged their most precious* "*commerce to pass as it were in review before us.* "To protect this, or to assail us, *a small part*

held only five horſes each, we went to Mr. *Davenport*'s inn, where we found a good

" only of their naval force will ever be riſqued " acroſs the Atlantic. The dangers to which the " elements expoſe them here are too well known, " and the greater danger to which they would be " expoſed at home, were any general calamity to " involve their whole fleet. They can attack us " by *detachment only*; and it will ſuffice to make our- " ſelves equal to what they may detach. Even a " ſmaller force than they may detach will be ren- " dered equal or ſuperior *by the quickneſs with which* " *any check may be repaired with us*, while loſſes with " them will be irreparable till too late. A ſmall " naval force then is neceſſary for us, and a ſmall " one is neceſſary. What this ſhould be I will not " undertake to ſay. I will only ſay it ſhould by no " means be ſo great as we are able to make it. Sup- " poſing the million of dollars, or £300,000 ſterl. " which Virginia would annually ſpare without diſ- " treſs, be applied to the creating a navy. A ſingle " year's contribution would build, equip, man, and " ſend to ſea a force which ſhould carry 300 guns. " The reſt of the confederacy exerting themſelves " in the ſame proportion would equip 1500 guns " more. So that one year's contribution would ſet " up a navy of 1800 guns. The Britiſh ſhips of the " line average 76 guns; their frigates 38. 1800 " guns then would form a fleet of 30 ſhips, 18

dinner ready. I had letters from Mr. Wentworth to Mr. *John Tracy*, the moſt conſiderable merchant in the place; but, before I had time to ſend them, he had heard of my arrival, and, as I was ariſing from table, entered the room, and very politely invited me to paſs the evening with him. He was accompanied by a Colonel, whoſe name is too difficult for me to write, having never been able to catch the manner of pronouncing it; but it was ſomething like *Wigſleps*. This Colonel remained with me till Mr. Tracy finiſhed his buſineſs, when he came with two handſome carriages, well equipped, and conducted me and my Aide de Campe to his country-houſe. This houſe ſtands a mile from the town, in a very beautiful ſituation; but of this I could myſelf

" of which might be of the line, and 12 frigates. " Allowing eight men, the Britiſh average, for every " gun, their annual expence, including ſubſiſtence, " clothing, pay, and ordinary repairs, would be " about 1280 dollars for every gun, or 2,304,000 " dollars for the whole. I ſtate this only as one " year's poſſible exertion, without deciding whe- " ther more or leſs than a year's exertion ſhould " be thus applied." TRANSLATOR.

ſelf form no judgment, as it was already night. I went however, by moonlight, to ſee the garden, which is compoſed of different terraces. There is likewiſe a hot-houſe and a number of young trees. The houſe is very handſome and well finiſhed, and every thing breathes that air of magnificence accompanied with ſimplicity, which is only to be found amongſt merchants. The evening paſſed rapidly by the aid of agreeable converſation and a few glaſſes of punch. The ladies we found aſſembled were Mrs. Tracy, her two ſiſters, and their couſin, Miſs *Lee*. Mrs. Tracy has an agreeable and a ſenſible countenance, and her manners correſpond with her appearance. At ten o'clock an excellent ſupper was ſerved, we drank good wine, Miſs Lee ſung, and prevailed on Meſſieurs de Vaudreuil and Taleyrand to ſing alſo : towards midnight the ladies withdrew, but we continued drinking Maderia and Xery. Mr. Tracy, according to the cuſtom of the country, offered us pipes, which were accepted by M. de Taleyrand, and M. de Monteſquieu, the conſequence of which was that they become intoxicated, and were led home, where they were happy to get to bed. As to myſelf, I remained perfectly cool, and continued to converſe on trade and politics with Mr. Tracy, who intereſted me greatly with an account of all the viciſſitudes of his fortune ſince the beginning of the war. At the end of 1777, his brother and he had loſt one and forty ſhips, and with regard to himſelf, he had not a ray of hope but in a ſingle letter of marque of eight guns, of which he had received no news. As he was walking one day with his brother, and they were reaſoning together on the means of ſubſiſting their families (for they were both married) they perceived a ſail making for the harbour. He immediately interrupted the converſation, ſaying to his brother, "Perhaps it is a prize for me." The latter laughed at him, but he immediately took a boat, went to meet the ſhip, and found that it was in fact a prize belonging to him, worth five and twenty thouſand pounds ſterling. Since that period, he has been almoſt always fortunate, and he is at preſent

ſent thought to be worth near £120,000 ſterling. He has my warmeſt wiſhes for his proſperity; for he is a ſenſible polite man, and a good patriot. He has always aſſiſted his country in time of need, and in 1781 lent five thouſand pounds to the State of Maſſachuſſets for the clothing of their troops, and that only on the receipt of the Treaſurer, yet his quota of taxes in that very year amounted to *ſix thouſand pounds*. One can hardly conceive how a ſimple individual can be burthened ſo far; but it muſt be underſtood, that beſides the duty of 5 per cent. on importation, requir-ed by Congreſs, the State impoſed another tax of the ſame value on the ſale of every article, in the nature of an exciſe, on rum, ſugar, coffee, &c. Theſe taxes are levied with great rigour: a merchant who re-ceives a veſſel is obliged to declare the car-go, and nothing can go out of the ſhip or warehouſe without paying the duty. The conſequence of this reſtraint is, that the merchants, in order to obtain free uſe of their property, are obliged themſelves to turn retailers, and pay the whole duty, the value of which they muſt recover from thoſe to whom they ſell. Without this, they could neither draw from their ſtores what is neceſſary for their own conſumption, nor the ſmall articles, which they are in the way of ſelling, at the firſt hand; they are conſequently obliged to take out *licences*, like tavern-keepers and retailers, thus ſupporting the whole weight of the impoſt both as merchants and as ſhop-keepers. Patriot as he is, Mr. Tracy cannot help blaming the rigour with which commerce is treated; a rigour ariſing from the preponderance of the farmers or landholders, and alſo from the neceſſity which the government is under of finding money where it can; for the farmers eaſily evade the taxes; *certificates*, *receipts*, *alledged grievances*, reduce them almoſt to nothing. Thus has a State, yet in its infancy, all the infirmities of age, and taxation attaches itſelf to the very ſource of wealth, at the riſk of drying up its channels. [This obſervation appears rather forced, as applied generally, the Marquis admitting that theſe impoſitions

impositions were the result of a critical and immediate want. *Translator.*]

I left *Newbury Port*, the 13th at ten in the morning, and often stopped before I lost sight of this pretty little town, for I had great pleasure in enjoying the different aspects it presents. It is in general well built, and is daily increasing in new buildings. The warehouses of the merchants, which are near their own houses, serve by way of ornament, and in point of architecture resemble not a little our large greenhouses. You cannot see the ocean from the road to *Ipswich*; and the country to the eastward is dry and rocky. Toward the west it is more fertile; but in general the land throughout the country, bordering on the sea, is not fruitful. At the end of twelve miles is Ipswich, where we stopped to bait our horses, and were surprized to find a town between Newbury and Salem, at least as populous as these two sea-ports, though indeed much less opulent. But mounting an eminence near the tavern, I saw that Ipswich was also a sea-port. I was told however that the entrance was difficult,

difficult, and that at ſome times of the year there were not five feet upon the bar. From this eminence you ſee Cape Anne, and the ſouth ſide of Plumb iſland, as well as a part of the north. The bearing of the coaſt, which trends to the eaſtward, ſeems to me badly laid down in the charts; this coaſt trends more ſoutherly above Ipſwich, and forms a ſort of bay. Ipſwich at preſent has but little trade, and its fiſhery is alſo on the decline; but the ground in the neighbourhood is pretty good, and abounds in paſturage, ſo that the ſeamen having turned farmers, they have been in no want of ſubſiſtence *, which may account likewiſe for

* The activity and enterprize of the inhabitants of the Eaſtern States are unremitted. The ſeaman when on ſhore immediately applies himſelf to ſome handicraft occupation, or to huſbandry, and is always ready at a moment's warning to accompany the captain his neighbour, who is likewiſe frequently a mechanic, to the fiſheries. Weſt-India voyages are the moſt perilous expeditions, ſo that it is no uncommon circumſtance to find in a crew of excellent New-England mariners, not a ſingle ſeaman, ſo to ſpeak, by profeſſion. Hence ariſe that zeal, ſobriety, induſtry, œconomy and attachment for

for the very conſiderable population of this place where you meet with upwards of two

which they are ſo juſtly celebrated, and which cannot fail of giving them, ſooner or later, a decided ſuperiority at leaſt in the ſeas of the New World. This education and theſe manners, are the operative cauſes of that wonderful ſpirit of enterprize and perſeverance, ſo admirably painted by Mr. Edmund Burke, in his wiſe, eloquent, and immortal ſpeech of March 22, 1775, on his motion for conciliation with the colonies. " Pray, Sir, ſays he, " what in the world is equal to it? Paſs by the " other parts (of America,) and look at the manner " in which the people of New England have of late " carried on the whale fiſhery. Whilſt we follow " them among the tumbling mountains of ice, and " behold them penetrating into the deepeſt receſ- " ſes of Hudſon's Bay, and Davis's Streights, whilſt " we are looking for them beneath the arctic circle, " we hear that they have pierced into the oppoſite " region of polar cold, that they are at the antipodes, " and engaged under the frozen ſerpent of the " ſouth. Falkland's Iſland which ſeemed too re- " mote and romantic an object for the graſp of na- " tional ambition, is but a ſtage and reſting-place " in the progreſs of their victorious induſtry. Nor " is the equinoctial heat more diſcouraging to them " than the accumulated winter of both the poles. " We know that whilſt ſome of them draw the

two hundred houſes, in about two miles ſquare. Before you arrive at Salem, is a handſome riſing town called *Beverley*. This is a new eſtabliſhment produced by commerce, on the left ſhore of the creek which bathes the town of Salem on the north ſide. One cannot but be aſtoniſhed to ſee beautiful houſes, large warehouſes, &c. ſpringing up in great numbers, at ſo ſmall a diſtance from a commercial town, the proſperity of which is not diminiſhed by it *. The

"line and ſtrike the harpoon on the coaſt of Africa, "others run the longitude, and purſue their gi- "gantic game along the coaſt of Brazil. No ſea "but what is vexed by their fiſheries. No cli- "mate that is not witneſs to their toils. Neither "the perſeverance of Holland, nor the activity of "France, nor the dextrous and firm ſagacity of "Engliſh enterprize, ever carried this moſt peri- "lous mode of hardy induſtry to the extent to which "it has been puſhed by this recent people; a people "who are ſtill, as it were, but in the griſtle, and "not yet hardened into the bone of manhood."

TRANSLATOR.

* The town of Beverley began to flouriſh greatly towards the concluſion of the war by the extraordinary ſpirit of enterprize, and great ſucceſs of the Meſſieurs

The rain overtook us juſt as we were paſſing near the lake which is three miles from Beverley. We croſſed the creek in two flat-bottomed boats, containing each ſix horſes. It is near a mile wide; and in croſſing, we could very plainly diſtinguiſh the opening of the harbour, and a caſtle ſituated on the extremity of the neck, which defends the entrance. This neck is a tongue of land running to the eaſtward and connected with Salem only by a very narrow ſort of cauſeway. On the other ſide of the neck, and of the cauſeway, is the creek that forms the true port of Salem, which has no other defence than the extreme difficulty of entering without a good practical pilot. The view of theſe two ports, which are confounded together to

Meſſieurs *Cobbets*, gentlemen of ſtrong underſtandings and the moſt liberal minds, well adapted to the moſt enlarged commercial undertakings, and the buſineſs of government. Two of their privateers had the good fortune to capture in the European ſeas, a few weeks previous to the peace, ſeveral Weſt-Indiamen to the value of at leaſt £100,000 ſterling. TRANSLATOR.

I

to the ſight; that of the town of Salem, which is embraced by two creeks, or rather arms of the ſea, the ſhips and edifices which appear intermingled, form a very beautiful picture, which I regret not having ſeen at a better ſeaſon of the year. As I had no letters for any inhabitants of Salem, I alighted at *Goodhue's* tavern, now kept by Mr. *Robinſon*, which I found very good, and was ſoon ſerved with an excellent ſupper. In this inn was a ſort of club of merchants, two or three of whom came to viſit me; and amongſt others, Mr. *de la Fille*, a merchant of Bourdeaux, who had been eſtabliſhed five years at Boſton; he appeared a ſenſible man, and pretty well informed reſpecting the commerce of the country, the language of which he ſpeaks well *.

The 14th in the morning, Mr. de la Fille called upon me to conduct me to ſee the port

* The Tranſlator, who was reſiding at this time at Salem, regretted exceedingly his accidental abſence on the day the Marquis ſpent there, which he learnt, to his great mortification, on his return to the inn which the Marquis had juſt quitted.

TRANSLATOR.

port and ſome of the warehouſes. I found the harbour commodious for commerce, as veſſels may unload and take in their lading at the quays; there were about twenty in the port, ſeveral of which were ready to ſail, and others which had juſt arrived. In general, this place has a rich and animated appearance. At my return to the inn I found ſeveral merchants who came to teſtify their regret at not having been apprized more early of my arrival, and at not having it in their power to do the honours of the town. At eleven, I got on horſeback, and taking the road to Boſton, was ſurpriſed to ſee the town, or ſuburb of Salem, extending near a mile in length to the weſtward. On the whole it is difficult to conceive the ſtate of increaſe, and the proſperity of this country, after ſo long, and ſo calamitous a war. The road from Salem to Boſton paſſes through an arid and rocky country, always within three or four miles of the ſea, without having a ſight of it; at length, however, after paſſing *Lynn* *, and Lynn Creek, you get a view of it, and find yourſelf in a bay formed by *Nahant*'s *Point*, and *Pulling*'s *Point*. I got upon the rocks to the right of the roads, in order to embrace more of the country, and form a better judgment. I could diſtinguiſh not only the whole bay, but ſeveral of the iſlands in Boſton road, and part of the peninſula of *Nantucket*, near which I diſcovered the maſts of our ſhips of war. From hence to *Winiſimmet* ferry, you travel over diſagreeable roads, ſometimes at the foot of rocks, at others acroſs ſalt marſhes. It is juſt eighteen miles from Salem to the ferry, where we embarked in a large *ſcow*, containing twenty horſes; and the wind, which was rather contrary, becoming more ſo, we made ſeven tacks, and were near an hour in paſſing. The landing is to the northward of the port, and to the eaſt of *Charles-Town* ferry. Altho'

* Lynn is a very populous little place, and is celebrated for the manufacture of women's ſhoes, which they ſend to all parts of the continent. The town is almoſt wholly inhabited by ſhoemakers.

TRANSLATOR.

I knew that Mr. *Dumas* had prepared me a lodging. I found it more convenient to alight at Mr. *Brackett*'s, the *Cromwell*'s head, where I dined *. After dinner I went to the lodgings prepared for me at Mr. Colſon's, a glover in the main ſtreet. As I was dreſſing to wait on the Marquis de Vaudreuil, he called upon me, and after permitting me to finiſh the buſineſs of the toilet, we went together to *Dr. Cooper*'s, and thence to the aſſociation ball, where I was received by my old acquaintance Mr. *Brick*, who was one of the managers. Here I remained till ten o'clock; the Marquis de Vaudreuil opened the ball

* This is a moſt excellent inn, and Mr. Brackett a ſhrewd and active friend to the true principles of the revolution. His ſign of *Cromwell*'s *head* gave great umbrage to the Britiſh under General Gage, who would not ſuffer it to remain. This circumſtance alone could have induced Mr. Brackett to reſtore it after they were expelled the town, as reflection might have convinced him, that in the actual poſition of America, there was much more to be apprehended from a Cromwell than a Charles.

TRANSLATOR.

with Mrs. *Temple* *. M. de l'Aiguille the elder, and M. Trueguet danced alſo, each of

* The reader will obſerve that the author in ſpeaking of this lady, of Mr. Bowdoin, her father, and the reſt of the family, diſdains to mention her huſband, Mr. *John Temple*, ſo celebrated for political duplicity on both ſides of the water. This gentleman was, however, at this very time at Boſton, abuſing Gov. Hancock, Dr. Cooper, and the moſt tried friends to America, in the public prints, and endeavouring to ſow diſſenſions amongſt the people. Every newſpaper into which he could obtain admiſſion, was ſtuffed with diſguſting encomiums on Mr. *John Temple*, whom Mr. John Temple himſelf held forth as the paragon of American patriotiſm, as the moſt active and inveterate enemy to England, and a victim to Britiſh vengeance; which he endeavoured to prove by inſtances taken from the Engliſh prints, of his treachery to England, and by boaſting of his dexterity in outwitting the Miniſter of that country. Yet no ſooner did peace take place, than to the aſtoniſhment of every ſenſible and honeſt man in Europe and America, this very perſon, equally deteſted by, and obnoxious to, both countries, was diſpatched as the ſole repreſentative of England to that country, of which he is alſo a ſworn citizen, and whoſe father-in-law is the preſent Governor of Maſſachuſſets. It is impoſſible to add to the folly and infamy of ſuch a nomination. The choice of an Ambaſſodor to Congreſs would have

of them a minuet, and did honour to the French nation, by their noble and eaſy manner; but I am ſorry to ſay, that the contraſt was conſiderable between them and the Americans, who are in general very aukward, particularly in the minuet. The prettieſt women dancers were Mrs. *Jarvis*, her ſiſter, Miſs *Betſy Broom*, and Mrs. *Whitmore*. The ladies were all well dreſſed, but with leſs elegance and refinement than at Philadelphia *. The aſſembly room is

fallen with more propriety on *Arnold*. His was a bold and ſingle act of treachery; the whole *political* life of Mr. Temple has been one continued violation of good faith. For further particulars of this gentleman's conduct, *ſee* the *Political Magazine* for 1780, p. 691, and 740, but volumes might be written on this ſubject. The Tranſlator is ſorry to add, that whilſt he lives and flouriſhes, the virtuous, the amiable Dr. Cooper is in his grave, and Mr. Hancock, that illuſtrious citizen, he fears, not far removed from it. TRANSLATOR.

* The Tranſlator was preſent at this aſſembly at Boſton, which was truly elegant, where we ſaw Mr. J. Temple ſtanding behind the croud, eyeing, like Milton's Devil, the perfect harmony and good humour ſubſiſting between the French officers and the inhabitants, not as a friend to Britain, for that would

ſuperb, in a good ſtyle of architecture, well decorated, and well lighted; it is admirably well calculated for the *coup d'œil*, and there is good order, and every neceſſary refreſhment. This aſſembly is much ſuperior to that of the City Tavern at Philadelphia.

The 15th, in the morning, M. de Vaudreuil, and M. le Tombes, the French Conſul, called on me the moment I was going out to viſit them. After ſome converſation, we went firſt to wait on Governor Hancock *, who was ill of the gout, and unable to receive us; thence we went to

have been pardonable, but to diſcord, for he was at this very inſtant boaſting of his inveteracy to Britain.
TRANSLATOR.

* I had ſeen Mr. Hancock eighteen months before, on my former journey to Boſton, and had a long converſation with him, in which I eaſily diſcovered that energy of character which had enabled him to act ſo diſtinguiſhed a part in the preſent revolution. He formerly poſſeſſed a large fortune, which he has almoſt entirely ſacrificed in the defence of his country, and which contributed not a little to maintain its credit. Though yet a young man, for he is not yet fifty, he is unfortunately very ſubject to the gout, and is ſometimes, for whole months, unable to ſee company.

to Mr. *Bowdoin*'s, Mr. *Brick*'s, and Mr. *Cuſhing*'s, the Deputy Governor. I dined with the Marquis de Vaudreuil, and after dinner drank tea at Mr. Bowdoin's, who engaged us to ſupper, only allowing M. de Vaudreuil and myſelf half an hour to pay a viſit to Mrs. Cuſhing. The evening was ſpent agreeably, in a company of about twenty perſons, among whom was Mrs. Whitmore, and young Mrs. Bowdoin, who was a new acquaintance for me, not having ſeen her at Boſton when I was there the preceding year. She has a mild and agreeable countenance, and a character correſponding with her appearance.

The next morning I went with the Marquis de Vaudreuil to pay ſome other viſits, and dined with Mr. Brick, where were upwards of thirty perſons, and amongſt others Mrs. *Tudor*, Mrs. *Morton*, Mrs. *Swan*, &c. The two former underſtood French; Mrs. Tudor in particular knows it perfectly, and ſpeaks it tolerably well. I was very intimate with her during my ſtay at Boſton, and found her poſſeſſed, not only of underſtanding, but of grace and delicacy, in her mind and manners. After dinner, tea was ſerved, which being over, Mr. Brick in ſome ſort inſiſted, but very politely, on our ſtaying ſupper. This ſupper was on table exactly four hours after we roſe from dinner; it may be imagined therefore that we did not eat much, but the Americans paid ſome little compliments to it; for, in general, they eat leſs than we do, at their repaſts, but as often as you chooſe, which is in my opinion a very bad method. Their aliments behave with their ſtomachs, as we do in France on paying viſits; they never depart, until they ſee others enter. In other reſpects we paſſed the day very agreeably. Mr. Brick is an amiable man, and does the honours of his table extremely well; and there reigned in this ſociety a *ton* of eaſe and freedom, which is pretty general at Boſton, and cannot fail of being pleaſing to the French.

The day following I waited at home for M. de Vaudreuil, who called on me to conduct me to dinner on board the *Souverain*. This ſhip, as well as the *Hercule*, was at anchor about a mile from the port. The officer who com-

commanded her, gave us a great and excellent dinner, the honours of which he did, both to the French and Americans, with that noble and benevolent ſpirit which characterizes him. Among the latter was a young man of eighteen, of the name of *Barrel*, who had been two months on board, that by living continually with the French, he might accuſtom himſelf to ſpeak their language, which cannot fail of being one day uſeful to him *. For this is far from being a common qualification in America, nor can it be conceived to what a degree it has hitherto been neglected; the importance of it however begins to be felt, nor can it be too much encouraged for the benefit of both nations. It is ſaid, and certainly with great truth, that not only individuals, but even nations, only quarrel for want of a proper underſtanding; but it may be af-

* This is a very amiable young gentleman, and his father a great connoiſſeur in prints and paintings. He was happy to have the opportunity of purchaſing a compleat collection of *Hogarth's* prints from the Tranſlator, then on his return to Europe.

TRANSLATOR.

firmed in a more direct and positive sense, that mankind in general are not disposed to love those to whom they cannot easily communicate their ideas and impressions. Not only does their vivacity suffer, and their impatience become inflamed, but self-love is offended as often as they speak without being understood; instead of which, a man experiences a real satisfaction in enjoying an advantage not possessed by others, and of which he is authorized constantly to avail himself. I have remarked during my residence in America, that those amongst our officers, who spoke English, were much more disposed to like the inhabitants of the country, than the others who were not able to familiarize themselves with the language. Such is in fact the procedure of the human mind, to impute to others the contrarieties we ourselves experience; and such, possibly, is the true origin of that disposition we call *humeur*, which must be considered as a discontent of which we cannot complain; an interior dissatisfaction which torments us, without giving us the right of attributing the cause of it to any other

other perſon. *Humeur*, or *peeviſhneſs*, ſeems to be to anger, what melancholy is to grief; both one and the other are of longer duration, becauſe they have no fixed object, and do not carry, ſo to ſpeak, their *complement* with them; ſo that never attaining that exceſs, that *maximum* of ſenſibility, which brings on that repoſe, or change of ſituation which nature wills, they can neither be completely gratified, nor exhale themſelves entirely. As for the Americans, they teſtify more ſurprize than peeviſhneſs, at meeting with a foreigner who did not underſtand Engliſh. But if they are indebted for this opinion to a prejudice of education, a ſort of national pride, that pride ſuffered not a little from the reflection, which frequently occurred, of the language of the country being that of their oppreſſors. Accordingly they avoided theſe expreſſions, *you ſpeak Engliſh*; *you underſtand Engliſh well*; and I have often heard them ſay—*you ſpeak American well*; *the American is not difficult to learn*. Nay, they have carried it even ſo far, as ſeriouſly to propoſe introducing a new language; and

ſome

ſome perſons were deſirous, for the convenience of the public, that the *Hebrew* ſhould be ſubſtituted for the Engliſh. The propoſal was, that it ſhould be taught in the ſchools, and made uſe of in all public acts. We may imagine that this project went no farther; but we may conclude from the mere ſuggeſtion, that the Americans could not expreſs in a more energetic manner, their averſion for the Engliſh.

This digreſſion has led me far from the *Souverain*, where I would return, however, with pleaſure, were it not to take leave of the Commandeur de Glanderes, and to experience a thick fog, which compelled me to renounce an excurſion I propoſe making in the harbour, and to get back to Boſton as faſt as poſſible, without viſiting *Caſtle Iſland*, and *Fort William*. On landing, the Marquis de Vaudreuil and I went to drink tea at Mr. Cuſhing's, who is Lieutenant Governor of the State; whence we went to Mr. Tudor's, and ſpent a very agreeable evening. M. de Parois, nephew of M. de Vaudreuil, had brought his harp, which he accom-

accompanied with great taſte and ſkill; this was the firſt time, however, for three years, that I had heard truly vocal and national muſic. It was the firſt time that my ear had been ſtruck with thoſe airs, and thoſe words, which reminded me of the pleaſures, and agreeable ſentiments, which employed the beſt æra of my life. I thought myſelf in Heaven, or which is the ſame thing, I thought myſelf returned to my country, and once more ſurrounded by the objects of my affection.

On the 17th, I breakfaſted with ſeveral artillery officers, who had arrived with their troop; that corps having greatly preceded the reſt of the infantry, in order to have time to embark their cannon, and other ſtores. At eleven I mounted my horſe, and went to *Cambridge*, to pay a viſit to Mr. *Willard*, the Preſident of that Univerſity. My route, though ſhort, it being ſcarce two leagues from Boſton to Cambridge, required me to travel both by ſea and land, and to paſs through a field of battle, and an intrenched camp. It has been long ſaid that the route to Parnaſſus is difficult, but the obſtacle we have there to

encounter,

encounter, are rarely of the ſame nature with thoſe which were in my way. A view of the chart of the road, and town of Boſton, will explain this better than the moſt elaborate deſcription. The reader will ſee that this town, one of the moſt ancient in America, and which contains from twenty to five and twenty thouſand inhabitants, is built upon a peninſula in the bottom of a large bay, the entrance of which is difficult, and in which lie diſperſed a number of iſlands, that ſerve ſtill further for its defence; it is only acceſſible one way on the land ſide, by a long neck or tongue of land, ſurrounded by the ſea on each ſide, forming a ſort of cauſeway. To the Northward of the town is another peninſula, which adheres to the oppoſite ſhore by a very ſhort rock, and on this peninſula is an eminence called *Bunker's-hill*, at the foot of which are the remains of the little town of *Charles-town*. Cambridge is ſituated to the North-weſt, about two miles from Boſton; but to go there in a right line, you muſt croſs a pretty conſiderable arm of the ſea, in which are dangerous ſhoals, and, upon the coaſt, moraſſes

moraſſes difficult to paſs; ſo that the only communication between the whole northern part of the Continent, and the town of Boſton, is by the ferry of *Charleſtown*, or that of *Winiſſimet*. The road to Cambridge lies through the field of battle of Bunker's-hill. After an attentive examination of that poſt, I could find nothing formidable in it *; for the Americans had ſcarcely time to form a breaſtwork, that is, a ſlight retrenchment without a ditch, which ſhelters the men from muſquet ſhot, as high as the breaſt. Their obſtinate reſiſtance therefore, and the prodigious loſs ſuſtained by the Engliſh on this occaſion, muſt be attributed ſolely to their valour. The Britiſh troops were repulſed on all ſides, and put in ſuch diſorder, that Gen. Howe is ſaid to have been at one time left ſingle in the field of battle, until General Clinton arrived with a reinforcement, and turned the left of the American poſition, which

* Bunker's-hill is an eminence neither more ſteep, nor more difficult of acceſs than *Primroſe*-hill near Hampſtead, in the neighbourhood of London.

TRANSLATOR.

which was weaker and more acceſſible on that ſide. It was then that Gen. *Warren*, who was formerly a phyſician, fell, and the Americans quitted the field, leſs perhaps from the ſuperiority of the enemy, than from knowing that they had another poſition as good, behind the neck which leads to Cambridge; for, in fact, that of Bunker's-hill was uſeful only in as much as it commanded Charleſtown ferry*, and allowed them to raiſe batteries againſt the town of Boſton. But was it neceſſary to expoſe themſelves to the deſtruction of their own houſes, and the ſlaughter of their fellow citizens, only that they might haraſs the Engliſh in any aſylum which ſooner or later they muſt abandon? Beſides that, the Americans could only occupy the heights of Bunker's-hill, the ſloops and frigates of the enemy taking them in flank the inſtant they deſcended

* A bridge of 1503 feet in length, and 42 in breadth, is juſt compleated (in 1786) between Boſton and Charleſtown, well lighted at night with 40 lamps. This important work was executed by ſubſcription. The greateſt depth of the water is 46 feet nine inches, and the leaſt is 14 feet. TRANSLATOR.

deſcended from them. Such, however, was the effect of this memorable battle, in every reſpect honourable for our allies, that it is impoſſible to calculate the conſequences of a complete victory*. The Engliſh, who had upwards of eleven hundred men killed and wounded, in which number were ſeventy officers, might poſſibly have loſt as many more in their retreat; for they were under the neceſſity of embarking to return to Boſton, which would have been almoſt impracticable, without the protection of their ſhipping; the little army of Boſton would in that caſe have been almoſt totally deſtroyed, and the town muſt of courſe have been evacuated. But what would have been the reſult of this? Independence was not then declared, and the road to negociation was ſtill open; an accommodation might have taken place between the Mother Country and her Colonies, and animoſities might have

* This attack on Bunker's-hill took place in the time of the hay harveſt, and much execution was done amongſt the Britiſh by ſome field-pieces and muſquetry concealed behind the cocks of hay.

TRANSLATOR.

have ſubſided. The ſeparation not having been compleated, England would not have expended one hundred millions; ſhe would have preſerved Minorca and the Floridas; nor would the balance of Europe, and the liberty of the ſeas have been reſtored. For it muſt in general be admitted, that England alone has reaſon to complain of the manner in which the fate of arms has decided this long quarrel.

Scarcely have you paſſed the neck which joins the peninſula to the Continent, and which is hemmed in on one ſide by the mouth of the *Myſtick*, and on the other by a bay called *Milk Pond*, than you ſee the ground riſing before you, and you diſtinguiſh on ſeveral eminences the principal forts which defended the entrenched camp of Cambridge. The left of this camp was bounded by the river, and the right extended towards the ſea, covering this town which lay in the rear. I examined ſeveral of theſe forts, particularly that of *Proſpect-hill*. All theſe entrenchments ſeemed to me to be executed with intelligence; nor was I ſurprized that the Engliſh reſpected them

them the whole winter of 1776. The American troops, who guarded this poſt, paſſed the winter at their eaſe, in good barracks, well flanked, and well covered; they had at that time abundance of proviſions, whilſt the Engliſh, notwithſtanding their communication with the ſea, were in want of various eſſential articles, particularly fire-wood and freſh meat. Their government, not expecting to find the Americans ſo bold and obſtinate, provided too late for the ſupply of the little army at Boſton. This negligence, however, they endeavoured to repair, and ſpared nothing for that purpoſe, by freighting a great number of veſſels, in which they crowded a vaſt number of ſheep, oxen, hogs, and poultry of every kind; but theſe ſhips, ſailing at a bad ſeaſon of the year, met with gales of wind in going out of port, and were obliged to throw the greateſt part of their cargoes into the ſea; inſomuch that, it is ſaid, the coaſt of Ireland, and the adjoining ocean, were for ſome time covered with herds, which unlike thoſe of Proteus, were neither able to live amidſt the waves, nor gain the ſhore.

 The

The Americans, on the contrary, who had the whole continent at their dispofal, and had neither exhaufted their refources, nor their credit, lived happy and tranquil in their barracks, awaiting the fuccours promifed them in the fpring. Thefe fuccours were offered and furnifhed with much generofity by the Southern Provinces; provinces, with which, under the Englifh Government, they had no connexion whatever, and which were more foreign to them than the mother country. It was already a great mark of confidence, therefore, on the part of the New Englanders, to count upon that aid which was offered by generofity alone*: but who could forefee that a citizen of Virginia, who, for the firft time, vifited thefe northern countries, not only fhould become their liberator, but fhould even know how to erect trophies, to ferve as a bafe to the great

* Surely good policy had fome fhare in the alacrity of thefe proffered fuccours, nor does this fuppofition, whilft it does credit to the difcernment, derogate from the generofity of the Virginians.—— *Tua res agitur, paries cum proximus ardet!*

TRANSLATOR.

great edifice of Liberty? Who could foresee that the enterprize, which failed at Bunker's-hill, at the price even of the blood of the brave Warren, and that of a thousand English sacrificed to his valour, attempted on another side and conducted by General Washington, should be the work only of one night, the effect of a simple manœuvre, of a single combination? Who could foresee, in short, that the English would be compelled to evacuate Boston, and to abandon their whole artillery and all their ammunition, without costing the life of a single soldier?

To attain this important object, it was only necessary to occupy the heights of *Dorchester*, which formed another peninsula, the extremity of which is within cannon shot of Boston, and in a great measure commands the port: but it required the eye of General Washington to appreciate the importance of this post; it required his activity and resolution to undertake to steal a march upon the English, who surrounded it with their shipping, and who could transport troops thither with the greatest facility. But it required ſtill more: nothing ſhort of the power, or rather the great credit he had already acquired in the army, and the diſcipline he had eſtabliſhed, were requiſite to effect a general movement of the troops encamped at Cambridge and at Roxbury, and carry his plan into execution, in one night, with ſuch celerity and ſilence, as that the Engliſh ſhould only be apprized of it, on ſeeing, at the break of day, entrenchments already thrown up, and batteries ready to open upon them. Indeed he had carried his precautions ſo far, as to order the whips to be taken from the waggoners, leſt their impatience, and the difficulty of the roads might induce them to make uſe of them, and occaſion an alarm. It is not eaſy to add to the aſtoniſhment naturally excited by the principal, and above all, by the early events of this memorable war; but I muſt mention, that whilſt General Waſhington was blockading the Engliſh in Boſton, his army was in ſuch want of powder as not to have three rounds a man; and that if a bomb-ketch had not chanced to run on ſhore

ſhore in the road, containing ſome tons of powder, which fell into the hands of the Americans, it would have been impoſſible to attempt the affair of Dorcheſter; as without it, they had not wherewithal to ſerve the batteries propoſed to be erected.

I apprehend that nobody will be diſpleaſed at this digreſſion; but ſhould it be otherwiſe, I muſt obſerve, that in a very ſhort excurſion I had made to Boſton, eighteen months before, having viſited all the retrenchments at Roxbury and Dorcheſter, I thought it unneceſſary to return thither, and I was the leſs diſpoſed to it from the rigour of the ſeaſon, and the ſhort time I had to remain at Boſton. But how is it poſſible to enter into a few details of this ſo juſtly celebrated town, without recalling the principal events which have given it renown? But how, above all, reſiſt the pleaſure of retracing every thing which may contribute to the glory of the Americans, and the reputation of the illuſtrious Chief? Nor is this ſtraying from the temple of the Muſes, to conſider objects which muſt long continue to conſtitute their

 theme

theme. Cambridge is an aſylum worthy of them; it is a little town inhabited only by ſtudents, profeſſors, and the ſmall number of ſervants and workmen whom they employ. The building deſtined for the univerſity is noble and commanding, though it be not yet compleated; it already contains three handſome halls for the claſſes, a cabinet of natural philoſophy, and inſtruments of every kind, as well for aſtronomy, as for the ſciences dependant on mathematics; a vaſt gallery, in which the library is placed, and a chapel correſponding with the grandeur and magnificence of the other parts of the edifice. The library, which is already numerous, and which contains handſome editions of the beſt authors, and well bound books, owes its richneſs to the zeal of ſeveral citizens, who, ſhortly before the war, formed a ſubſcription, by means of which they began to ſend for books from England. But as their fund was very moderate, they availed themſelves of their connexions with the mother country, and, above all, of that generoſity which the Engliſh invariably diſplay whenever

ever the object is, to propagate useful knowledge in any part of the world. These zealous citizens not only wrote to England, but made several voyages thither in search of assistance, which they readily obtained. One individual alone, made them a present to the amouut of £ 500 sterling; I wish I could recollect his name, but it is easy to discover it *. It is inscribed in letters of gold over the compartment containing the books which he bestowed, and which form a particular library. For it is the rule, that

* The Translator is happy in being able to supply this deficiency, by recording the respectful name of the late THOMAS HOLLIS, Esq; a truly eminent citizen of England, who, in every act of his public and private life, did honour to his illustrious name, to his country, and to human nature. One of his ancestors too, of the same name, founded, in this same college, a professorship for the mathematics and natural philosophy, and ten scholarships for students in these and other sciences, with other benefactions, to the amount of little less than £5000 sterling. Public virtue, and private accomplishments seem to be hereditary in this family; Mr. *Thomas Brand Hollis*, the inheritor of this fortune, pursuing the footsteps of his excellent predecessors—*passibus æquis*.

TRANSLATOR.

each donation to the univerſity ſhall remain as it was received, and occupy a place apart; a practice better adapted to encourage the generoſity of benefactors, and to expreſs gratitude, than to facilitate the librarian's labour, or that of the ſtudents. It is probable therefore, that, as the collection is augmenting daily, a more commodious arrangement will be adopted.

The profeſſors of the univerſity live in their own houſes, and the ſtudents board in the town for a moderate price. Mr. *Willard*, who was juſt elected Preſident, is alſo a member of the academy of Boſton, to which he acts as Secretary of the foreign correſpondence. We had already had ſome intercourſe with each other, but it pleaſed me to have the opportunity of forming a more particular acquaintance with him; he unites to great underſtanding and literature, a knowledge of the abſtruſe ſciences, and particularly aſtronomy. I muſt here repeat, what I have obſerved elſewhere, that in comparing our univerſities and our ſtudies in general, with thoſe of the Americans, it would

would not be our intereſt to call for a deciſion of the queſtion, which of the two nations ſhould be conſidered as an infant people.

The ſhort time I remained at Cambridge allowed me to ſee only two of the profeſſors, and as many ſtudents, whom I either met with, or who came to viſit me at Mr. Willard's. I was expected to dine with our Conſul, Mr. de Letombes, and I was obliged to hurry, for they dine earlier at Boſton than at Philadelphia. I found upwards of twenty perſons aſſembled, as well French officers, as American gentlemen, in the number of whom was *Doctor Cooper*, a man juſtly celebrated, and not leſs diſtinguiſhed by the graces of his mind, and the amiableneſs of his character, than by his uncommon eloquence, and patriotic zeal. He has always lived in the ſtricteſt intimacy with Mr. Hancock, and has been uſeful to him on more than one occaſion. Amongſt the Americans attached by political intereſt to France, no one has diſplayed a more marked attention to the French, nor has any man received from Nature a

character

character more analogous to their own. But it was in the ſermon he delivered, at the ſolemn inauguration of the new conſtitution of Maſſachuſſets, that he ſeemed to pour forth his whole ſoul, and develop at once all the reſources of his genius, and every ſentiment of his heart. The French nation, and the monarch who governs it, are there characterized and celebrated with equal grace and delicacy. Never was there ſo happy, and ſo poignant a mixture of religion, politics, philoſophy, morality, and even of literature. This diſcourſe muſt be known at Paris, where I ſent ſeveral copies, which I have no doubt will be eagerly tranſlated. I hope only that it will eſcape the avidity of thoſe haſty writers, who have made a ſort of property of the preſent revolution; nothing, in fact, is more dangerous than theſe precipitate traders in literature, who pluck the fruit the moment they have any hopes of ſelling it, thus depriving us of the pleaſure of enjoying it in its maturity. It is for a Salluſt and a Tacitus alone to tranſmit in their works, the actions and harangues of their contem-

contemporaries; nor did *they* write till after ſome great change in affairs had placed an immenſe interval between the epocha of the hiſtory they tranſmitted, and that in which it was compoſed; the art of printing too, being then unknown, they were enabled to meaſure, and to moderate, at pleaſure, the publicity they thought proper to give to their productions.

Doctor Cooper, whom I never quitted without regret, propoſing to me to drink tea with him, I accepted it without difficulty. He received me in a very ſmall houſe, furniſhed in the ſimpleſt manner, every thing in it bore the character of a modeſty which proved the feeble foundation of thoſe colonies ſo induſtriouſly propagated by the Engliſh, who loſt no occaſion of inſinuating that his zeal for the Congreſs and their allies had a very different motive from patriotiſm and the genuine love of liberty *. A viſit to Mrs. Tudor, where Mr. de Vaudreuil

* Mr. John Temple finding himſelf detected, and ill received at Boſton, was the undoubted author of theſe calumnies againſt Doctor Cooper, who had nobly dared to warn his countrymen againſt his

Vaudreuil and I had again the pleaſure of an agreeable converſation, interrupted from time to time by pleaſing muſic, rapidly brought round the hour for repairing to the club. This aſſembly is held every Tueſday, in rotation, at the houſes of the different members who compoſe it; this was the day for Mr. *Ruſſel* *, an honeſt merchant,

inſidious attempts to diſunite the friends to liberty, under the maſk of zeal and attachment to America. He dared, contrary to the deciſive evidence of a long ſeries of pure diſintereſted public conduct in the hour of danger, when Mr. Temple was a ſkulking, penſioned refugee in England, more than to inſinuate, that Doctor Cooper, and *Mr. Hancock*, that martyr to the public cauſe, were actually in pay of the French court; but if ever there could be a doubt entertained of ſuch characters, founded on the aſſertions of ſuch a man, his ſubſequent conduct has irrefragably proved, that as the calumny was propagated by him, ſo the ſuggeſtion muſt have originated in his own heart. Let not the Anglo-American Conſul General to the United States complain. Hiſtorical juſtice will overtake both him and Arnold. It is a condition in the indenture of their bargain.

TRANSLATOR.

* The Tranſlator had the pleaſure of being acquainted with the ſon of Mr. Ruſſel and his friend *Winthrop*, in France and Holland. He had the good fortune likewiſe to meet with the latter at Boſ-

chant, who gave us an excellent reception. The laws of the club are not ſtraitening, the number of diſhes for ſupper alone are limited, and there muſt be only two of meat, for ſupper is not the American repaſt. Vegetables, pies, and eſpecially good wines, are not ſpared. The hour of aſſembling is after tea, when the company play at cards, converſe, and read the public papers, and ſit down to table between nine and ten. The ſupper was as free as if there had been no ſtrangers, ſongs were given at table, and a Mr. Stewart ſung ſome which were very gay, with a tolerable good voice.

The 19th the weather was very bad, and I went to breakfaſt with Mr. *Broom*, where I remained ſome time, the converſation being always agreeable and unreſtrained. Some officers who called upon me, having taken up the reſt of the morning, I at length joined Mr. de Vaudreuil to go and dine

ton. He takes a pride in mentioning theſe amiable young men, as they cannot fail of becoming valuable members of a riſing country which attracts the attention of the world. TRANSLATOR.

dine with Mr. Cuſhing. The Lieutenant Governor, on this occaſion, perfectly ſupported the juſtly acquired reputation of the inhabitants of Boſton, of being friends to good wine, good cheer, and hoſpitality. After dinner he conducted us into the apartment of his ſon, and his daughter-in-law, with whom we were invited to drink tea. For though they inhabited the ſame houſe with their father, they had a ſeparate houſehold, according to the cuſtom in America; where it is very rare for young people to live with their parents, when they are once ſettled in the world. In a nation which is in a perpetual ſtate of increaſe, every thing ſavours of that general tendency; every thing divides and multiplies. The ſenſible and amiable Mrs. Tudor was once more our centre of union, during the evening, which terminated in a familiar and very agreeable ſupper at young Mrs. Bowdoin's. Mr. de Parois, and Mr. Dumas ſung different airs and duets, and Mrs. Whitmore undertook the pleaſure of the eyes, whilſt they ſupplied the gratification of our ears.

The

The 20th was wholly devoted to ſociety. Mr. Broom gave me an excellent dinner, the honours of which were performed by Mrs. Jarvis and her ſiſter, with as much politeneſs and attention as if they had been old and ugly. I ſupped with Mr. Bowdoin, where I ſtill found more handſome women aſſembled. If I do not place Mrs. Temple, Mr. Bowdoin's daughter in the number, it is not from want of reſpect, but becauſe her figure is ſo diſtinguiſhed as to make it unneceſſary to pronounce her truly beautiful; nor did ſhe ſuffer in the compariſon with a girl of twelve years old, who was formed however to attract attention. This was neither a handſome child nor a pretty woman, but rather an angel in diſguiſe of a young girl; for I am at a loſs otherwiſe to expreſs the idea which young perſons, of that age, convey in England and America; which, as I have already ſaid, is not, amongſt us, the age of Beauty and the Graces. They made me play at whiſt, for the firſt time ſince my arrival in America. The cards were Engliſh, that is, much handſomer and dearer than ours, and we marked our points with Louis-d'ors, or ſix-and-thirties; when the party was finiſhed, the loſs was not difficult to ſettle; for the company was ſtill faithful to that voluntary law eſtabliſhed in ſociety from the commencement of the troubles, which prohibited playing for money during the war. This law however, was not ſcrupulouſly obſerved in the clubs, and parties made by the men amongſt themſelves. The inhabitants of Boſton are fond of high play, and it is fortunate, perhaps, that the war happened when it did, to moderate this paſſion which began to be attended with dangerous conſequences *.

On Thurſday the 21ſt there fell ſo much ſnow as to determine me to defer my departure, and Mr. Brick, who gave a great dinner to Mr. d'Aboville, and the French artillery officers, underſtanding that I was ſtill at Boſton, invited me to dine, whither I went

* It is with real concern the Tranſlator adds, that gaming is a vice but too prevalent in all the great towns, and which has been already attended with the moſt fatal conſequences, and with frequent ſuicide. TRANSLATOR.

went in Mr. de Vaudreuil's carriage. Mr. Barrel came alſo to invite me to tea, where we went after dinner; and, as ſoon as we were diſengaged, haſtened to return to Mrs. Tudor's. Her huſband *, after frequently whiſpering to her, at length communicated to us an excellent piece of pleaſantry of her invention, which was a petition to the Queen, written in French, wherein, under the pretext of complaining of Mr. de Vaudreuil and his ſquadron, ſhe beſtowed on them the moſt delicate and moſt charming eulogium. We paſſed the remainder of the evening with Mr. Brick, who had again invited us to ſupper, where we enjoyed all the pleaſures inſeparable from his ſociety. I had a great deal of converſation with Doctor *Jarvis*, a young phyſician, and alſo a ſurgeon, but what was better, a good whig, with excellent views in politics. When Mr. *D'Eſtaing* left Boſton, the ſick and wounded were intruſted to his care,

 and

* Mr. Tudor is the gentleman who has ſo frequently diſtinguiſhed himſelf by animated orations on the annual commemoration of ſome of the leading events of this civil war. TRANSLATOR.

and he informed me, that the ſick, who were recovering faſt, in general relapſed, on removing them from the town of Boſton, where they enjoyed a good air, to Roxbury, which is an unhealthy ſpot, ſurrounded with marſhes. The phyſicians in America pay much more attention than ours to the qualities of the atmoſphere, and frequently employ change of air as an effectual remedy.

The 22d I ſet out at ten o'clock, after taking leave of Mr. Vaudreuil, and having had reaſon to be ſatisfied with him, and the town of Boſton. It is inconceivable how the ſtay of the ſquadron has contributed to conciliate the two nations, and to ſtrengthen the connections which unite them *. The virtue

* During my ſtay at Boſton, a young Chevalier de Malthe, Monſieur *de l'Epine*, belonging to Mr. de Vaudreuil's ſquadron, died, and I was preſent at his funeral. He was buried with the forms of the Catholic Church, by the firſt Chaplain to the fleet, and his remains were attended to the place of interment, beſides his brother officers, &c. by the members of the ſenate and aſſembly, the principal inhabitants of the town, and the miniſters of *every ſect of religion* in Boſton. The holy candles, and all the

virtue of Mr. de Vaudreuil, his ſplendid example of good morals, as well as the ſimplicity and goodneſs of his manners, an example followed, beyond all hope and belief, by the officers of his ſquadron, have captivated the hearts of a people, who, though now the moſt determined enemies to the Engliſh, had never hitherto been friendly to the French. I have heard it obſerved a hundred times at Boſton, that in the time

Catholic ceremonies were uſed on the occaſion, in a town too, where, a few years before, the hierarchical pomp even of the church of England barely met with toleration; an uſeful leſſon this to Machiavelian rulers, whoſe ſtrength conſiſts in the ſilly diſcord and diviſions of their fellow creatures. The Tranſlator contemplated this intereſting ſcene with a complacent curioſity, which was only interrupted by the ſolitary diſſatisfaction of Mr. John Temple, who, as well as his honeſt coadjutor, the *pious* Arnold, "was ſhocked at ſeeing his countrymen "participating in the rites of a church, againſt "whoſe *antichriſtian* corruptions your pious anceſtors "would have witneſſed with their blood." *See* this zealous *proteſtant's* proclamation, after ſelling himſelf to England, for £7000 3 per cents. and ſacrificing the amiable, unhappy *Major André*.

TRANSLATOR.

even of the greateſt harmony with the mother country, an Engliſh ſhip of war never anchored in the port without ſome violent quarrels between the people and the ſailors; yet the French ſquadron had been there three months without occaſioning the ſlighteſt difference. The officers of our navy were every where received, not only as allies, but brothers; and though they were admitted by the ladies of Boſton to the greateſt familiarity, not a ſingle indiſcretion, not even the moſt diſtant attempt at impertinence ever diſturbed the confidence, or innocent harmony of this pleaſing intercourſe.

The obſervations I have already made on the commerce of New England, render it unneceſſary to enter into any particular details on that of the town of Boſton. I ſhall only mention a vexation exerciſed towards the merchants; a vexation ſtill more odious than that I have ſpoken of relative to Mr. Tracy, and of which I had not the ſmalleſt ſuſpicion, until Mr. Brick gave me a particular account of it. Beſides the exciſe and licenſe duties mentioned above, the merchants are ſubject to a ſort of tax on wealth, which is artibrarily impoſed by twelve aſſeſſors, named indeed by the inhabitants of the town; but as the moſt conſiderable merchant has only one vote any more than the ſmalleſt ſhopkeeper, it may be imagined how the intereſts of the rich are reſpected by this committee. Theſe twelve aſſeſſors having full powers to tax the people according to their ability, they eſtimate, on a view, the buſineſs tranſacted by each merchant, and his probable profits. Mr. Brick, for example, being agent for the French navy, and intereſted beſides in ſeveral branches of commerce, amongſt others in that of inſurance, they calculate how much buſineſs he may be ſuppoſed to do, of which they judge by the bills of exchange he endorſes, and by the policies he underwrites, and according to their valuation, in which neither loſſes nor expences are reckoned, they ſuppoſe him to gain ſo much a day; and he is conſequently ſubjected to a proportionable daily tax. During the year 1781, Mr. Brick paid no leſs than *three guineas and a half per day*. It is evident that nothing short of patriotism, and above all, the hope of a speedy conclusion to the war, could induce men to submit to so odious and arbitrary an impost; nor can the patience with which the commercial interest in general, and Mr. Brick in particular, bear this burthen, be too much commended.

The 22d I went, without stopping, to *Wrentham*, where I slept, and reached Providence to dinner the 23d; where I found our infantry assembled, and waiting till the vessels were ready to receive them. Here I remained six days, during which I made an excursion of four-and-twenty hours to visit my old friends at Newport.

The 30th I left Providence, with Messrs. Lynch, Montesquieu, and de Vaudreuil, and slept at Voluntown. The next day Mr. Lynch returned to Providence *, and we

* Mr. Lynch, who was Aide Major General, and designed to be employed under the orders of the Baron de Viomenil, embarked with the troops. Mr. de Taleyrand was determined to follow them as a simple volunteer, and, assuming the uniform of a soldier in the regiment of Soissonnois,

we ſeparated with mutual regret. The ſame day, the 1ſt of December, we ſtopped at Windham to reſt our horſes, and ſlept at *White*'s tavern at Andover, near Bolton. The 2d I got to breakfaſt at Hartford, where I ſtaid two or three hours, as well to arrange many particulars relative to the departure of my baggage, as to pay a viſit to Mrs. Wadſworth. Mr. Frank Dillon, who had come to me at Providence, where he remained a day longer than me, joined me here. From hence we went to Farmington, where we arrived as night was coming on, and alighted at an inn kept by a Mr. Wadſworth, no relation of the Colonel's; but with whom I had lodged a month before, when on the march with my diviſion. Mrs. Lewis, hearing of my arrival, ſent her ſon to offer me a bed at her houſe, which I declined, with a promiſe of breakfaſting

he marched into Boſton in the ranks of the company of Chaſſeurs. This company embarked in the ſame veſſel with the Comte de Segur, then Colonel *en ſecond* of the Soiſſonnois; and Mr. de Taleyrand remained attached to it till his return to Europe.

with her the next morning; but, in a quarter of an hour, ſhe called on me herſelf, accompanied by a militia Colonel, whoſe name I have forgot, and ſupped with us. The 3d, in the morning, I viſited Mr. *Pitkin* the miniſter, with whom I had lodged the preceding year, when the French army was on its march to join General Waſhington on the North river. He is a man of an extraordinary turn, and rather an original, but is neither deficient in literature nor information. His father was formerly Governor of Connecticut; he profeſſes a great regard for the French, and charged me, half joking, and half in earneſt, to give his compliments to the King, and tell him that there was one Preſbyterian miniſter in America on whoſe prayers he might reckon. I went to breakfaſt with Mrs. Lewis, and at ten ſet out for Litchfield. The roads were very bad, but the country is embelliſhed by new ſettlements, and a conſiderable number of houſes newly built, ſeveral of which were taverns. It was four when we arrived at Litchfield, and took up our quarters at *Shelding*'s *tavern*, a new inn, large, ſpacious

cious and neat, but indifferently provided. We were ſtruck with melancholy on ſeeing Mr. Shelding ſending a negro on horſeback into the neighbourhood to get ſomething for our ſupper, for which however we did not wait long, and it was pretty good.

The 4th we ſet out at half paſt eight, and baited at Waſhington, after admiring a ſecond time the picturеſque proſpect of the two *falls*, and the furnaces, half-way between Litchfield and Waſhington. Nor was it without pleaſure that I obſerved the great change two years had produced in a country at that time wild and deſert. On paſſing through it two years before, there was only one miſerable alehouſe at this place; at preſent we had the choice of four or five inns, all clean and fit to lodge in. *Morgan*'s paſſes for the beſt, but through miſtake we alighted at another, which I think is not inferior to it. Thus has the war, by ſtopping the progreſs of commerce, proved uſeful to the interior of the country; for it has not only obliged ſeveral merchants to quit the coaſts, in ſearch of peaceable habitations

habitations in the mountains, but it has compelled commerce to have recourſe to inland conveyance, by which means many roads are now frequented which formerly were but little uſed. It was five in the afternoon when I arrived at Moorhouſe's tavern. In this journey, I paſſed the river at *Bull's works*, and having again ſtopped to admire the beauty of the landſcape, I had an opportunity of convincing myſelf that my former eulogium is not exaggerated. The river, which was ſwelled by the thaw, rendered the cataract ſtill more ſublime; but a magazine of coals having fallen down, in ſome meaſure deſtroyed the proſpect of the furnaces. On this occaſion I had not much reaſon to boaſt of the tavern. Colonel Moorhouſe, after whom it was named, no longer kept it, but had reſigned it to his ſon, who was abſent, ſo that there were none but women in the houſe. Mr. Dillon, who had gone on a little before, had the greateſt difficulty in the world to perſuade them to kill ſome chickens; our ſupper was but indifferent, and as ſoon as it was over, and we had got near the fire, we ſaw theſe women, to the number of four, take our place

place at table, and eat the remainder of it, with an American dragoon, who was ſtationed there. This gave us ſome uneaſineſs for our ſervants, to whom they left in fact a very trifling portion. On aſking one of them, a girl of ſixteen, and tolerably handſome, ſome queſtions the next morning, I learnt that ſhe, as well as her ſiſter, who was ſomething older, did not belong to the family; but that having been driven by the ſavages from the neighbourhood of *Wyoming*, where they lived, they had taken refuge in this part of the country, where they worked for a livelihood; and that being intimate with Mrs. Moorhouſe, they took a pleaſure in helping her, when there were many travellers; for this road is at preſent much frequented. Obſerving this poor girl's eyes filled with tears in relating her misfortune, I became more intereſted, and on deſiring farther particulars, ſhe told me, that her brother was murdered, almoſt before her eyes, and that ſhe had barely time to ſave herſelf on foot, by running as faſt as ſhe could; that ſhe had travelled in this manner fifty miles, with her feet covered with blood, before ſhe found a horſe. In

other

other respects she was in no want, nor did she experience any misery. That is a burthen almost unknown in America. Strangers and fugitives, these unfortunate sisters had met with succours. Lodgings, and nourishment, are never wanting in this country; clothing is more difficult to procure, from the dearness of all sorts of stuffs; but for this they strive to find a substitute by their own labour. I gave them a Louis to buy some articles of dress with, my Aides de Camp, to whom I communicated the story, made them a present likewise; and this little act of munificence being soon made known to the mistress of the house, obtained us her esteem, and she appeared very penitent for having shewn so much repugnance to kill her chickens.

The 5th we set out at nine, and rode, without stopping, to Fish-kill, where we arrived at half past two, after a four and twenty miles journey through very bad roads. I alighted at *Boerorn*'s tavern, which I knew to be the same I had been at two years before, and kept by Mrs. Egremont. The house was changed for the better, and we made a very good supper. We passed the

the North-river as night came on, and arrived at ſix o clock at *Newburgh*, where I found Mr. and Mrs. Waſhington, Colonel *Tilgham*, Colonel *Humphreys*, and Major *Walker*. The head quarters of Newburgh conſiſt of a ſingle houſe, neither vaſt nor commodious, which is built in the Dutch faſhion. The largeſt room in it (which was the proprietor's parlour for his family, and which General Waſhington has converted into his dining-room) is in truth tolerably ſpacious, but it has ſeven doors, and only one window. The chimney, or rather the chimney back, is againſt the wall; ſo that there is in fact but one vent for the ſmoke, and the fire is in the room itſelf. I found the company aſſembled in a ſmall room which ſerved by way of parlour. At nine ſupper was ſerved, and when the hour of bed-time came, I found that the chamber, to which the General conducted me, was the very parlour I ſpeak of, wherein he had made them place a camp-bed. We aſſembled at breakfaſt the next morning at ten, during which interval my bed was folded up, and my chamber became the ſitting-room for the whole afternoon; for American manners

do

do not admit of a bed in the room in which company is received, eſpecially when there are women. The ſmallneſs of the houſe, and the difficulty to which I ſaw that Mr. and Mrs. Waſhington had put themſelves to receive me, made me apprehenſive leſt Mr. Rochambeau, who was ſet out the day after me, by travelling as faſt, might arrive on the day that I remained there. I reſolved therefore to ſend to Fiſh-kill to meet him, with a requeſt that he would ſtay there that night. Nor was my precaution ſuperfluous, for my expreſs found him already at the *landing*, where he ſlept, and did not join us till the next morning as I was ſetting out. The day I remained at head quarters was paſſed either at table or in converſation. General *Hand*, Adjutant General, Colonel *Reed* of New Hampſhire, and Major *Graham* dined with us. On the 7th I took leave of General Waſhington, nor is it difficult to imagine the pain this ſeparation gave me; but I have too much pleaſure in recollecting the real tenderneſs with which it affected him, not to take a pride in mentioning it. Colonel

Tilghman got on horſeback to ſhew me, in the road, the barracks that ſerve as winter-quarters for the American army, which were not quite finiſhed, though the ſeaſon was already far advanced, and the cold very ſevere. They are ſpacious, healthy, and well built, and conſiſt in a row of log-houſes containing two chambers, each inhabited by eight ſoldiers when compleat, which makes commonly from five to ſix effectives; a ſecond range of barracks is deſtined for the non-commiſſioned officers. Theſe barracks are placed in the middle of the woods, on the ſlope of the hills, and within reach of water, as the great object is a healthy and convenient ſituation; the army are on ſeveral lines, not exactly parallel with each other. But it will appear ſingular in Europe, that theſe barracks ſhould be built without a bit of iron, not even nails, which would render the work tedious and difficult, were not the Americans very expert in putting wood together. After viewing the barracks, I regained the high road; but paſſing before General Gates's houſe, the ſame that General Knox inhabited

bited in 1780, I ſtopped ſome time to make a viſit of politeneſs. The remainder of the day I had very fine weather, and I ſtopped and baited my horſes at an inn in the township of *Cheſter*. In this inn I found nothing but a woman, who appeared good and honeſt, and who had charming children. This route is little peopled, but new ſettlements are forming every day. Before we reached Cheſter we paſſed by a bridge of wood, over a creek, called *Murderers* river, which falls into the North River, above New Windſor, on the other ſide of Cheſter; I ſtill kept ſkirting the ridge of mountains which ſeparates this country from *the Clove*. Warwick, where I ſlept, a pretty large place for ſo wild a country, is twelve miles from Cheſter, and twenty-eight from Newburgh; I lodged here in a very good inn kept by Mr. Smith, the ſame at whoſe houſe I had ſlept two years before at *Ckeat*, which was much inferior to this. The American army having, for two years paſt, had their winter quarters near Weſtpoint, Mr. Smith imagined, with reaſon, that this road would be more frequented than that of Paramus,

and

and he had taken this inn of a Mr. *Beard*, at whoſe houſe we ſtopped next day to breakfaſt. The houſe had been given up to him with ſome furniture, and he had upwards of one hundred and fifty acres of land belonging to it, for the whole of which he paid ſeventy pounds, (currency) making about one hundred piſtoles. I had every reaſon to be content both with my old acquaintance and the new eſtabliſhment.

The next morning, the 7th, we ſet out before breakfaſt, and the ſnow began to fall as ſoon as we got on horſeback, which did not ceaſe till we got to Beard's tavern. This houſe was not near ſo good as the other, but the workmen were buſy in augmenting it. On enquiring of Mr. Beard, who is an Iriſhman, the reaſon of his quitting his good houſe at Warwick to keep this inn, he informed me, that it was a ſettlement he was forming for his ſon-in-law, and that as ſoon as he had put it in order, he ſhould return to his houſe at Warwick. This Mr. Beard had long lived as a merchant at New-York, and even ſold books, which I learnt from obſerving ſome good ones at his houſe, amongſt others, *Human Prudence*, which I purchaſed of him. It ceaſed ſnowing at noon, and the weather moderated; but in the afternoon it returned in blaſts, for which however I was indemnified by the beautiful effect produced by the ſetting-ſun amidſt the clouds, its rays being reflected on the eaſt, and forming a ſort of parhelion. Towards the evening the weather became very cold, and we reached *Suſſex* an hour before dark, and took up our lodgings at Mr. Willis's. The fire being not well lighted in the room intended for me, I ſtepped into the parlour, where I found ſeveral people who appeared to be collected together upon buſineſs; they had, according to cuſtom, drank a good quantity of grog, one of them, called Mr. *Archibald Stewart*, ſmelt pretty ſtrong. A converſation took place among us, and Mr. *Poops*, formerly Aide de Camp to General *Dickinſon*, and at preſent a rich landholder in the Jerſeys, having learnt that I was going to *Bethlehem* *, or imagining

* Bethlehem is a ſort of colony founded by the *Moravian brethren*, frequently called *Herrenhuter*.

gining ſo from the queſtions I aſked about the roads, very obligingly invited me to come the next day and ſleep at his houſe. His houſe is on the banks of the Delaware, twenty-ſix miles from Suſſex, thirteen from Eaſton, and twenty-four from Bethlehem. At firſt I had ſome difficulty in accepting his offer, from the apprehenſion one naturally has of being ſtraitened oneſelf, or of ſtraitening others. He inſiſted however ſo ſtrongly, and aſſured me ſo often that I ſhould find no inn, that I partly promiſed to lie at his houſe the following night. Theſe gentlemen, and he in particular, gave me every neceſſary information: and, as I was deſirous of ſeeing Moravian Mill *, a village ſituated near Eaſton, four miles above Suſſex, he directed me to Mr. *Calver*, who keeps a ſort of an inn there. The company went away, and we paſſed a very

It was to ſee this eſtabliſhment, and the town of *Eaſton* and the *Upper Delaware*, that I quitted the ordinary route, which leads from New Windſor to Philiadelphia.

* This is a property they have purchaſed in the neighbourhood of Bethlehem.

agreeable evening by a good fire, hugging ourſelves at not being expoſed to the ſevere cold we experienced on ſtirring out of the houſe. We were alſo well content with our landlord, Mr. Willis, who ſeemed to be a gallant man, and very converſable. He was born at Elizabeth-town, but has been ſixteen years ſettled at Suſſex. Thus does population advance into the interior parts, and go in ſearch of new countries.

I ſet out the 8th a little before nine, the weather being extremely cold, and the roads covered with ſnow and ice; but on quitting the *Ridge*, and turning towards the weſt, by deſcending from the high mountains to lower ground, we found the temperature more mild, and the earth entirely free. We arrived at half paſt eleven at the *Moravian Mill*, and, on ſtopping at Mr. *Galver*'s, found that Mr. Poops had announced our coming, and that breakfaſt was prepared for us *. This freſh attention on his part, encouraged me to accept his

* The Moravian ſect is pretty generally known in Europe. They are the followers of the famous

his offer for the evening. As ſoon as we had breakfaſted, Mr. Calver, who had treat-

 ed

Count *Zinzendorff* *, whoſe picture they have at Bethlehem; they have ſeveral eſtabliſhments in Europe, ſimilar to thoſe the Marquis is about to ſpeak of; one of which I have ſeen at *Zieſt* near Utrecht, where Louis the XIVth took up his quarters, but America ſeems to be the promiſed land of ſectaries. Even the deſpiſed, ill-treated Jews, are well received in the United States, and begin to be very numerous; many of them were excellent citizens during the ſevere trial of the war, and ſome even loſt their lives as ſoldiers, gallantly fighting for the liberties of their country. One family in particular, I believe of the name of Salvador, at Rhode Iſland, was moſt eminently diſtinguiſhed. What a glorious field is this for unprejudiced philanthropic ſpeculation!

TRANSLATOR.

* The following account of the Moravians is taken from a tranſlation from the German, of an account of that body, by the Reverend B. La Trobe.——" The ſect of the *Unitas Fratrum*, " more commonly known by the names of Herrenhuters and Mo" ravians, was at firſt formed by Nicholas Lewis, Count of Zin" zendorff, at Bartheldorf in Upper Luſatia, in the year 1722. " Finding his followers increaſe, particularly from Moravia, he " built an houſe in a wood near Bartheldorf for their public " meetings: and, before the end of the year 1732, this place grew " into a village, which was called Herrnhuth, and contained " about ſix hundred inhabitants, all of them following Zinzen" dorff, and leading a kind of monaſtic life. From this time " the ſect has ſpread its branches from Germany, through all the

ed us with an anxiety and reſpect, more German than American, ſerved, us by way of conductor, and led us firſt to ſee the ſaw-mill, which is the moſt beautiful, and the beſt contrived I ever ſaw. A ſingle man only is neceſſary to direct the work; the ſame wheels which keep the ſaw in motion, ſerve alſo to convey the trunks of trees from the ſpot where they are depoſited to the work-houſe, a diſtance of twenty-five or thirty toiſes; they are placed on a ſledge, which ſliding on a groove, is drawn by a rope which rolls and unrolls on the axis of the wheel itſelf. Planks are ſold at ſix ſhillings, Penſylvania currency (about three ſhillings and four-pence ſterling) the hundred; if you find the wood, it is only half the money, and the plank in that caſe is ſawed

"Proteſtant ſtates in Europe, made conſiderable eſtabliſhments "on the continent of America, and Weſtern Iſles, and extended "itſelf to the Eaſt-Indies, and into Africa. In England, Mo-"ravian congregations are founded at London, Bedford, Oak-"brook near Derby, Pudſey near Leeds, Dunkerfield in Cheſhire, "Leominſter, Haverford Weſt, Briſtol, Kingſwood, Bath, and "Tetherton." Their ſettlements are becoming very numerous too, but not their population, in all the different States in the American Union. TRANSLATOR.

ſawed for one farthing per foot*. This mill is near the fall of a lake which fur-

* It is remarked, that on the lands within reach of the Moravian ſettlements, the cultivation is ſuperior, and every branch of huſbandry is better carried on, firſt, from the emulation excited by theſe induſtrious people, and ſecondly, from the ſupply the countryman procures from them of every neceſſary implement of huſbandry, &c. fabricated in theſe ſettlements. Beſides thoſe the Marquis ſpeaks of, I viſited ſome others, not far from Bethlehem, at one of which, called *Nazareth*, is a famous gunſmith, from whom my friend Major Pierce Butler, bought a pair of piſtols, many of which I ſaw there of the moſt perfect workmanſhip. Nothing can be more enchanting than theſe eſtabliſhments; out of the ſequeſtered wilderneſs they have formed well-built towns, vaſt edifices all of ſtone, large orchards, beautiful and regular ſhaded walks in the European faſhion, and ſeem to combine with the moſt compleat ſeparation for the world, all the comforts and even many of the luxuries of poliſhed life. At one of their cleared-out ſettlements, in the midſt of a foreſt, between Bethlehem and Nazareth, poſſeſſing all the advantages of mills and manufactures, I was aſtoniſhed with the delicious ſounds of an Italian concerto; but my ſurprize was ſtill greater, on entering a room where the performers turned out to be common workmen of different trades, playing for their amuſement. At

niſhes it with water. A deep cut is made in a rock to form a canal for conducting the waters to the corn-mill, which is built within muſket-ſhot of the former; it is very handſome, and on the ſame plan with that of Mrs. Bowling at Peterſburgh, but not ſo large. From the mill I went to the church, which is a ſquare building, containing the houſe of the miniſter. The place where the duty is performed, and which may properly be called the church, is on the firſt floor, and reſembles the Preſbyterian meeting-houſes, with this difference, that there is an organ and ſome religious pictures *. This houſe of prayer, ſo

each of theſe places, the brethren have a common room, where violins and other inſtruments are ſuſpended, and always at the ſervice of ſuch as chuſe to relax themſelves, by playing ſingly, or taking a part in a concert. TRANSLATOR.

* The Moravians appear to me to be a ſect between the Methodiſts and the Catholics; at Nazareth, I met with an old Glouceſterſhire man, who came to America with the late Mr. Whitfield, with whom I had much converſation, and who told me that that gentleman was much reſpected, both living and dead, by the Moravians; but, indeed, beſides

ſo ſingularly placed, reminded me of a ſtory I heard at Boſton. Divine ſervice was formerly celebrated there in one of their places of worſhip, where the faithful were not aſſembled, 'tis true, on the firſt floor, but which, like this, contained the miniſter's houſe, below which were cellars. The paſtor, a very learned man in other reſpects, beſides his ſpiritual functions, carried on a trade

that, their hymns reſemble much thoſe of our Methodiſts, ſpiritualizing even the groſſeſt *carnal* tranſactions. I found that they all ſpoke of him as one of their own ſect, but utterly diſclaimed Mr. Weſley. They are very fond of pictures repreſenting the *Paſſion*, to which they pay a reſpect little ſhort, if at all, of idolatry. Their carnal alluſions are fully verified in the following hymn taken from one of their books in the Moravian chapel at Pudſey in England, in 1773, an alluſion than which nothing can be more infamous and ſhocking.

"And ſhe ſo bleſſed is,
She gives him many a kiſs:
Fix'd are her eyes on him:
Thence moves her every limb;
And ſince ſhe him ſo loves,
And only with him moves:
His matters and his blood
Appear her only good."

TRANSLATOR.

trade in wine; that is to ſay, a great deal of it went out of his cellar, but not a drop ever entered it. A ſimple negro ſervant he had, uſed to ſay, that his maſter was a great ſaint, for that he employed him every year in rolling into his cellar a number of caſks of cyder, over which, when he had preached and prayed a few Sundays, they were converted into wine.

On coming out of church I perceived Mr. Poops, who had taken the trouble to come and meet me. We mounted on horſeback together, and after paſſing through a tolerable fertile valley, in which are ſome beautiful farms, chiefly Dutch, and well cultivated fields, we arrived in the evening at his houſe. It is a charming ſettlement, conſiſting of a thouſand acres of land, the greateſt part of which is in tillage, with a fine corn-mill, a ſaw-mill, and diſtillery. The manor-houſe is ſmall, but neat and handſome. He conducted us into a parlour, where we found Mrs. Poops, his wife, Mrs. Scotland his mother-in-law, and Mr. Scotland his brother-in-law. Mrs. Poops has a pleaſing countenance, ſomewhat injured

jured by habitual bad health; her behaviour is that of an accompliſhed woman, and her converſation amiable. The evening was ſpent very agreeably, partly in converſation, and partly at play; for Mrs. Poops gave me a loſſon of backgammon, and I gave her one of *tric trac*. I had ſome converſation alſo with Mr. Scotland, a young man, who though but ſix-and-twenty, has made three campaigns, as Captain of artillery, and is now a lawyer of great practice. I have already obſerved that this is the moſt reſpectable, and moſt lucrative profeſſions in America. He told me that he uſually received, for a ſimple conſultation, four dollars, and ſometimes *half a Joe*; (thirty-ſix ſhillings ſterling) and when the action is commenced, ſo much is paid for every writ, and every deed, for in America lawyers act likewiſe in the capacity of notaries and attornies. I had much pleaſure in converſing with Mr. Poops, who is a man of a good education, well informed, and active, and concerned in a variety of buſineſs, which he conducts with great intelligence. He had been employed in the Commiſſary's department when General *Green* * was Quarter-Master General, and made extraordinary exertions to supply the army; which rendered him so obnoxious to the tories, that he was for a long time obliged to remain armed in his house, which he barricaded every night. The supper was as agreeable as the preceding part of the evening; the ladies retired at eleven, and we remained at table till midnight. Mr. Poops's brother arrived as we were at the desert; he appeared to me a sensible man, he had married in Virginia the daughter of Colonel *Fims*, who had espoused one of his sisters. He was now a widower.

The next day, the 10th of December, we breakfasted with the ladies, and set out at half past ten; Mr. Poops accompanying me

* The Gazettes have just announced the death of General Green. In him America has lost one of her best citizens, and most able soldiers. It is his greatest eulogium to say, that he stood high with General Washington, who recommended him to Congress, and that he amply justified the opinion entertained of him by that great good man.

TRANSLATOR.

me to *Eaſton*, where he had ſent to prepare dinner. I ſhould have preferred my uſual cuſtom of making my repaſt at the end of my day's journey, but it was neceſſary for a little complaiſance to return the civilities I had received. Two miles from the houſe of Mr. Poops we forded a ſmall river, and travelled through an agreeable and well cultivated country. Some miles before we came to Eaſton, we paſſed over a height from whence one diſcovers a vaſt tract of country, and amongſt others, a chain of mountains, which Mr. Poops deſired us to remark. It forms a part of that great chain which traverſes all America from South to North *. He pointed out to us two *hiatus*, or openings, reſembling two large doors or windows, through one of which flows the river Delaware; the other is a gap leading to the other ſide of the mountains, and is the road to *Wyoming*, a paſs become celebrated

* Theſe are called the Kittatinny mountains. For an account of this *hiatus*, or gap, ſee Mr. *Charles Thompſon*'s Obſervations on Mr. Jefferſon's *Notes on Virginia*, under the account of the National Bridge.

TRANSLATOR.

brated by the march of General Sullivan in 1779 * Before we got to Easton, we passed, in

* See the first Journal, where the author gives an account of his conversation with General Schuyler. In whatever manner this expedition was set on foot, which took place in 1779, after the evacuation of Philadelphia, and the diversion made by d'Estaing's squadron, the greatest difficulty to surmount was, the long march to be made through woods, deserts, and morasses, conveying all their provisions on beasts of burthen, and being continually exposed to the attacks of the savages. The instructions given by General Sullivan to his officers, the order of march he prescribed to the troops, and the discipline he had the ability to maintain, would have done honour to the most experienced amongst ancient or modern Generals. It may safely be asserted, that the Journal of this expedition would lose nothing in a comparison with the famous retreat of the *ten thousand*; which it would resemble very much, if we could compare the manœuvres, the object of which is attack, with those which have no other than the preservation of a forlorn army. General Sullivan, after a month's march, arrived, without any check, at the entrenched camp, the last refuge of the savages; here he attacked them, and was received with great courage, insomuch that the victory would have remained undecided, had not the Indians lost many of their Chiefs in battle, which never fails to intimidate them, and retreated during

in ferry boats, the eaſtern branch of the Delaware; for this town is ſituated on the fork formed by the two branches of that river. It is a handſome, though inconſiderable town, but which will probably enlarge itſelf on the peace, when the Americans, no longer under apprehenſions from the ſavages, ſhall cultivate anew the fertile lands between the *Suſquehannah* and the Delaware. Mr. Poops took us to the tavern of Mr. *Smith*, who is at once an innkeeper and lawyer. He has a handſome library, and his ſon, whom Mr. Poops preſented to me on my arrival, appeared to be a well educated and well informed young man. I invited him to dinner, as well as another youth who boarded with him, a native of Dominica, who had come to compleat his ſtudies

the night. The General deſtroyed their houſes and plantations, ſince which they have never ſhewn themſelves in a body. However ſlight and inſufficient the idea may be that I have given of this campaign, it may, nevertheleſs, aſtoniſh our European military men, to learn that General Sullivan was only a lawyer in 1775, and that in the year 1780 he quitted the army to reſume his profeſſion, and is now Civil Governor of New Hampſhire.

ſtudies amongſt the Americans, to whom he ſeemed much more attached than to the Engliſh. He had made choice of Eaſton as more healthy, and more peaceable than the other towns of America, and found all the neceſſary inſtruction in the leſſons and the books of Mr. Smith. As they knew of my coming, we did not wait long for dinner, and at half paſt three we got on horſeback, Mr. Poops being ſtill ſo good as to accompany me a mile or two, to obtain my permiſſion for which, he pretended that there was croſs road where I might loſe myſelf. At length we parted, leaving me penetrated with gratitude for his numerous civilities. Before I loſt ſight of Eaſton I ſtopped upon a hill, from whence I admired, for ſome time, the pictureſque *coup d'œil* preſented by the two branches of the Delaware *, and the confuſed and whimſical form of the mountains,

* In travelling over this hill, the Tranſlator ſtopped near an hour to view this noble and enchanting proſpect, with which it is impoſſible to ſatiate the eye. Nothing can be more delightful than the town and neighbourhood of Eaſton.

TRANSLATOR.

tains, through which they purſue their courſe. When I was ſatisfied with this ſpectacle, it was neceſſary to puſh forward to reach Bethlehem before night, and we travelled the eleven miles in two hours, but not before the day was cloſed *. We had

* The firſt time I viſited Bethlehem was from Philadelphia; and after travelling two days through a country alternately diverſified with ſavage ſcenes and cultivated ſpots, on iſſuing out of the woods at the cloſe of the evening, in the month of May, found myſelf on a beautiful extenſive plain, with the vaſt eaſtern branch of the Delaware on the right, richly interſperſed with wooded iſlands, and at the diſtance of a mile in front of the town of Bethlehem, rearing its large ſtone edifices out of a foreſt, ſituated on a majeſtic, but gradually riſing eminence, the back ground formed by the ſetting ſun. So novel and unexpected a tranſition filled the mind with a thouſand ſingular and ſublime ideas, and made an impreſſion on me, never to be effaced. The romantic and pictureſque effect of this glorious diſplay of natural beauties, gave way to the ſtill more noble and intereſting ſenſations, ariſing from a reflection on the progreſs of the arts and ſciences, and the ſublime anticipation of the "populous cities," and "buſy "hum of men," which are one day to occupy, and to civilize the vaſt wilderneſſes of the New World.

TRANSLATOR.

no difficulty of finding the tavern, for it is precisely at the entrance of the town.

This tavern was built at the expence of the Society of Moravian Brethren, to whom it served formerly as a magazine, and is very handsome and spacious*. The person who keeps

* This inn, for its external appearance, and its interior accommodations, is not inferior to the best of the large inns in England, which, indeed, it very much resembles in every respect. The first time I was at Bethlehem, in company with my friends Major *Pierce Butler*, Mr. *Thomas Elliot*, and Mr. *Charles Pinkney*, Carolina gentlemen, we remained here two or three days, and were constantly supplied with venison, moor game, the most delicious red and yellow bellied Trout, the highest flavoured wild strawberries, the most luxuriant asparagus, and the best vegetables, in short, I ever saw; and notwithstanding the difficulty of procuring good wine and spirits at that period, throughout the Continent, we were here regaled with rum and brandy of the best quality, and exquisite old Port and Madeira. It was to this house that the Marquis de la Fayette retired, to be cured of the first wound he received in fighting for America; an accident, which I am well assured gave this gallant young nobleman more pleasure than most of our European *petits maitres* would receive from the most flattering proofs of the favour of a mistress. Mr. *Charles Pinkney*, whom I have above mentioned,

keeps it is only the caſhier, and is obliged to render an account to the adminiſtrators. As we had already dined, we only drank tea, but ordered a breakfaſt for the next morning at ten o'clock. The landlord telling me there was a *Growſe*, or heath bird, in the houſe, I made him bring it, for I had long had a great deſire to ſee one. I ſoon obſerved that it was neither the *Poule de Pharaon*, nor the Heath Cock; it

is a young gentleman at preſent in Congreſs for South Carolina, and who, from the intimate knowledge I have of his excellent education and ſtrong talents, will, I venture to predict, whenever he pleaſes to exert them, ſtand forth amongſt the moſt eminent citizens of the new confederation of Republics. It is my boaſt and pride to have co-operated with him, when he was only at the age of twenty, in the defence of the true principles of liberty, and to have ſeen productions from his pen, which, in point of compoſition, and of argument, would have done honour to the head and heart of the moſt experienced and moſt virtuous politician. Should the preſent work ever fall into his hands, let him recognize in this juſt tribute to his worth, an affectionate friend, who, knowing his abilities, wiſhes to excite him to exertion, in the noble, but arduous field before him.

TRANSLATOR.

it was about the ſize of a Pheaſant, but had a ſhort tail, and the head of a Capon, which it reſembled alſo in the form of its body, and its feet were covered with down. This bird is remarkable for two large tranſverſe feathers below his head; the plumage of his belly is a mixture of black and white, the colour of his wings of a red grey, like our grey Partridges. When the Growſe is roaſted, his fleſh is black like that of a Heath Cock, but it is more delicate, and has a higher flavour *.

I could not derive much information from my landlord on the origin, the opinions, and manners of the ſociety, but he informed me that I ſhould next day ſee the miniſters and adminiſtrators, who would gratify my curioſity. The 11th, at half paſt eight, I walked out with a Moravian, given me by the landlord, but who was likewiſe ill informed, and only ſerved me as

* This bird muſt be what we call the black or grey game, and not what is known by the name of *Growſe* in England. TRANSLATOR.

as a guide *. He was a ſeaman, who imagines he has ſome talents for drawing, and amuſes himſelf with teaching the young people, having quitted the ſea ſince the war, where, however, he had no ſcruple in ſending his ſon †. He ſubſiſts on a ſmall

 eſtate

* Our company was much more fortunate, Major Butler having obtained letters from Philadelphia to Mr. Van Vleck, a man of property, living here, but formerly of New-York. TRANSLATOR.

† It is remarkable enough, that the ſon of this Moravian, whoſe name is *Garriſon*, ſhould have ſerved on board a veſſel with me, and was, without exception, the moſt worthleſs profligate fellow we had in a mixt crew of Engliſh, Scotch, Iriſh, and Americans, to all of whom his education had been infinitely ſuperior. Neither bolts nor bars could prevent, nor any chaſtiſement correct, his pilfering diſpoſition. In a long winter's voyage of *thirteen* weeks, with only proviſions and water for *five*, this fellow was the bane and peſt of officers, paſſengers, and ſeamen. Whilſt every other man in the ſhip, even the moſt licentious in proſperity, ſubmitted to regulations laid down to alleviate our dreadful ſufferings, and preſerve our lives, this hardened, unreflecting wretch, ignorant of every feeling of ſympathy and human nature, ſeemed to take a ſavage delight in diffuſing miſery around him, and adding to the diſtreſſes of his fellow ſufferers. He

eſtate he has at Reading, but lives at Bethlehem, where he and his wife board in a private family. We went firſt to viſit the houſe for *ſingle women*. This edifice is ſpacious, and built with ſtone. It is divided into ſeveral large chambers, all heated with ſtoves, in which the girls work, ſome coarſe work, ſuch as ſpinning cotton, hemp, and wool; others, work of taſte and luxury, ſuch as embrodery, either in thread, or ſilk, and they excel particularly in working ruffles, little pocket-books, pin-cuſhions, &c. like our French nuns. The ſuperintendant of the houſe came to receive us. She is a woman of family, born in Saxony; her name is Madame *de Gaſtorff*; but ſhe does not preſume upon her birth, and appeared ſurprized at my giving her my hand, as often as we went up and down ſtairs *.

She

had been well educated in the humane principles of the Moravians, but he truly verified the juſt adage of *Corruptio optimi peſſima*. TRANSLATOR.

* When the Tranſlator viſited Bethlehem, the ſuperintendant, or at leaſt her deputy, was a Mrs. Langley, a very mild pretty behaved Engliſh woman, who had been a follower of George Whitfield.

TRANSLATOR.

She conducted us to the first floor, where ſhe made us enter a large vaulted apartment, kept perfectly clean, in which all the women ſleep, each having a bed a-part, in which is plenty of feathers *. There is never any fire in this room; and though it be very high and airy, a ventilator is fixed in the roof like thoſe in our play-houſes. The kitchen is not large, but it is clean, and well arranged; in it there are immenſe earthen pots, upon furnaces, as in our hoſpitals. The inhabitants of the houſe dine in the refectory, and are ſerved every day with meat and vegetables; they have three ſhillings and ſix-pence currency per week, about four-pence per day, to the common ſtock, but they have no ſupper, and I believe the houſe furniſhes only bread for breakfaſt. This expence, and what they pay for fire and candle deducted, they enjoy the produce of their labour, which is more than ſufficient to maintain them.

 This

* The Americans in general are remarkably fond of very large ſoft feather beds, even in the hotteſt climates, and we ſuffered greatly in this particular, at the inn at Bethlehem. TRANSLATOR.

This houſe alſo has a chapel, which ſerves only for evening prayer, for they go to their church on Sundays. There is an organ in this chapel, and I ſaw ſeveral inſtruments ſuſpended upon nails. We quitted Madame de Gaſtorff well pleaſed with her reception, and went to the church, which is ſimple, and differs little from that we had ſeen at Moravian mill. Here alſo were ſeveral religious pictures. From hence we went to the houſe of the *ſingle men*. I entered the intendant's apartment, whom I found employed in copying muſic. He had in his room an indifferent *forte piano*, made in Germany. I talked with him on muſic, and diſcovered that he was not only a performer, but a compoſer. So that on his accompanying us to the chapel, and being aſked to touch the organ, he played ſome voluntaries, in which he introduced a great deal of harmony, and progreſſions of baſe. This man, whoſe name I have forgot, is a native of New-York, but reſided ſeven years in Germany, whence he had lately arrived. I found him better informed than thoſe I had yet met with, yet it was with ſome difficulty that I got from him the following details: The Moravian brethren, in whatever quarter of the world they live, are under the diſcipline of their metropolitans, who reſide in Germany*, from whence commiſſaries are ſent to regulate the different eſtabliſhments. The ſame metropolitans advance the ſums neceſſary for forming them, which are paid in proportion as theſe Colonies proſper; thus the revenue of the mills I have ſpoken of, as well as the farms and manufactures of Bethlehem, are employed in the firſt inſtance to pay the expences of the community, and afterwards to reimburſe the ſums advanced in Europe. Bethlehem, for example, poſſeſſes a territorial property, purchaſed by the Moravians in Europe, which conſiſts of fifteen hundred acres of land, forming a vaſt farm, which is managed

* The Moravians maintain a conſtant intercourſe with Germany in particular, of which country thoſe in America are chiefly natives, and think nothing of a voyage to Europe. Governor Joſeph Reed, of Philadelphia, had a ſon here, learning the German language, when I was at Bethlehem.

TRANSLATOR.

managed by a ſteward, who accounts for it to the community. If an individual wants a lot of land, he muſt purchaſe it of the public, but under this reſtriction, that in caſe of defection from the ſect, or emigration from the place, he ſhall reſtore it to the community, who will reimburſe him the original payment. As to their opinions, this ſect reſembles more the Lutherans, than the Calviniſts; differing, however, from the latter, by admitting muſic, pictures, &c. into their churches, and from the former, by having no Biſhops, and being governed by a Synod *. Their police, or diſcipline, is of the monaſtic kind, ſince they recommend celibacy, but without injoining it, and keep the women ſeparate from the men. There is a particular houſe alſo for the widows, which I did not viſit. The two ſexes being thus habitually ſeparated, none of thoſe familiar connexions exiſt between them, which lead to marriage;

* I do not ſpeak with confidence, but am inclined to think that they have Biſhops, at leaſt a perſon was pointed out to us at Bethlehem, under that denomination. TRANSLATOR.

marriage; nay, it is even contrary to the ſpirit of the ſect, to marry from inclination. If a young man finds himſelf ſufficiently at his eaſe to keep houſe for himſelf, and maintain a wife and children, he preſents himſelf to the commiſſary, and aſks for a girl, who (after conſulting with the ſuperintendant of the women) [*Tranſlator*] propoſes one to him, which he may, in fact, refuſe to accept; but it is contrary to the cuſtom, to chooſe a wife for himſelf. Accordingly, the Moravian Colonies have not multiplied, in any proportion, to the other American Colonies. That at Bethlehem is compoſed of about ſix hundred perſons, more than half of whom live in a ſtate of celibacy; nor does it appear that it has increaſed for ſeveral years. Every precaution is taken to provide for the ſubſiſtence of their brethren, and in the houſes deſtined for the unmarried of both ſexes, there are maſters who teach them different trades.

The houſe of the ſingle men which I ſaw in detail, does not differ from that of the women; I ſhall only take notice of a very convenient method they have of awakening

awakening thoſe who wiſh to be called up at any given hour; all their beds are numbered, and near the door is a ſlate, on which all the numbers are regiſtered. A man who wiſhes to be awakened early, at five o'clock in the morning for example, has only to write a figure of 5 under his number; the watchman who attends the chamber, obſerves this in going his rounds, and at the hour appointed, the next morning goes ſtraight to the number of the bed, without troubling himſelf about the name of the ſleeper.

Before I left the houſe, I mounted on the roof, where there is a Belvidere, from whence you ſee the little town of Bethlehem, and the neighbourhood; it is compoſed of ſeventy or eighty houſes, and there are ſome others belonging to the colony at the diſtance of a mile or two; they are all handſome and built with ſtone*. Every houſe has

* From this Belvidere the view is beautifully romantic, and amongſt other objects on the eaſtern ſide of the Delaware, you ſee a cultivated farm formed out of an immenſe wood and near the ſummit of a lofty mountain, which I likewiſe viſited, and every

has a garden cultivated with care. In returning home I was curious to ſee the farm, which is kept in good order, but the inſide was neither ſo clean, nor ſo well kept as in the Engliſh farm-houſes, becauſe the Moravians are ſtill more barbarous than their language. At length at half paſt ten I returned to the inn, where I was expected by my moor fowl, two woodhens, and many other good things, ſo that I was ſtill better ſatisfied with my breakfaſt than with my walk*. At twelve we ſet out to travel twenty miles farther, to *Kalf's tavern,* a German houſe very poor and filthy. We had paſſed the *Leigh*, or weſtern branch of the Delaware

ſtep of which gives you the idea of enchanted ground. Beſides the particular gardens to each private houſe, there is a large public walk belonging to the community; nay, the church-yard itſelf is a gay ſcene of beauty and regularity, the verdant turf being clad in ſummer with ſtrawberries and flowers.

TRANSLATOR.

* Notwithſtanding the good cheer at the tavern, the author, and I hope the reader, will pardon me for not crediting this declaration.

TRANSLATOR.

ware a mile from Bethlehem *; there is neither town nor village on the road, but the burghs to which the ſcattered houſes we ſaw, belonged, are called *Socconock* and *Springfield*. The 12th I breakfaſted at Montgomery, twelve miles from Kalf's tavern, and paſſing Whitemarſh and German town, we arrived towards five at Philadelphia.

Philadelphia,
24th of Dec. 1782.

* The weſtern branch of the Delaware which paſſes by Bethlehem, and forms a junction with the weſtern at Eaſton, is here called the *Lecha*. There is an excellent ferry over this rapid ſtream, of which I have ſpoken in the firſt volume. The Moravians amongſt an infinity of other ingenious inventions, have a large hydraulic machine in the middle of the town, which is at a great height from the river, for raiſing the water to ſupply the inhabitants.

TRANSLATOR.

LET-

LETTER

FROM THE

MARQUIS DE CHASTELLUX,

TO

MR. MADDISON*,

Professor of Philosophy in the University of

WILLIAMSBURGH.

I Have not forgot, Sir, the promise I made you on leaving Williamsburgh; it reminds me of the friendship with which you were pleased to honour me, and the flattering prejudices in my favour, which were the consequences of it. I am afraid that I have

* Mr. Maddison's son is a member of the Assembly, and has served in Congress for Virginia. This young man, who at the age of 30 astonishes the new Republics by his eloquence, his wisdom, and his genius, has had the humanity and the *courage*, (for such a proposition requires no small share of courage) to propose a general emancipation of the slaves, at the beginning of this year, 1786: Mr. *Jefferson*'s absence at Paris, and the situation of Mr. *Whythe*, as

have undertaken more than I am able to perform; but I ſhall at leaſt addreſs you in the language of ſincerity, in the ſort of literary bankruptcy I am now about to make.—By putting you in full poſſeſſion of my feeble reſources, however, I may perhaps obtain a ſtill further portion of that indulgence, to which you have ſo frequently accuſtomed me. The ſubject on which I rather thought of aſking information from you, than of offering you my ideas, would require long and tranquil meditation; and ſince I quitted Virginia, I have been continually travelling, ſometimes from duty with the troops, at others to gratify my curioſity in the eaſtern parts of America, as far even as New Hampſhire. But even had my time been ſubject to leſs interruption, I am

one of the judges of the State, which prevented them from lending their powerful ſupport, occaſioned it to miſcarry for the moment, but there is every reaſon to ſuppoſe that the propoſition will be ſucceſsfully renewed. As it is, the aſſembly have paſſed a law, declaring that there ſhall be no more ſlaves in the Republic, but thoſe exiſting the firſt day of the ſeſſion of 1785-6, and the deſcendants of female ſlaves.

TRANSLATOR.

I am not ſure that I ſhould have been more capable of accompliſhing your wiſhes. My mind, aided and excited by your's, experienced an energy it has ſince loſt; and if in our converſation, I have chanced to expreſs ſome ſentiments which merited your approbation, it is not to myſelf that they belonged, but to the party that ſpoke with Mr. Maddiſon. At preſent I muſt appear in all my weakneſs, and with this further diſadvantage, that I want both time and leiſure not only to rectify my thoughts, but even to throw them properly on paper. No matter; I venture on the taſk, perſuaded that you will eaſily ſupply my unavoidable omiſſions; and that the merit of this eſſay, if there will be any, will be compleated by yourſelf.

The moſt frequent object of our converſations was the progreſs that the arts and ſciences cannot fail of making in America, and the influence they muſt neceſſarily have on manners and opinions. It ſeems as if every thing relative to government and legiſlation ought to be excluded from ſuch diſcuſſions, and undoubtedly a ſtranger,

 ſhould

ſhould avoid as much as poſſible, treating matters of which he cannot be a competent judge. But in the phyſical, as in the moral world, nothing ſtands iſolated, no cauſe acts ſingle and independent. Whether we conſider the fine arts, and the enjoyments they produce, as a delicious ambroſia, the gods have thought proper to partake with us; or whether we regard them as a dangerous poiſon, that liquor, whether beneficent or fatal, muſt always be modified by the veſſel into which it is infuſed. It is neceſſary therefore to fix our attention for a moment on the political conſtitution of the people of America; and in doing this, may I be permitted to recal a principle, I have eſtabliſhed and developed elſewhere *; which is, that the character, the genius of a people, is not ſolely produced by the government they have adopted, but by the circumſtances under which they were originally formed. Locke, and after him, Rouſſeau have obſerved, that the education of man ſhould commence from the cradle, that

* *See* the author's work—*de la felicité publique.*

that is to ſay, at the moment when he is contracting his firſt habits; it is the ſame with States. Long do we diſcover in the rich and powerful Romans, the ſame plunderers collected by Romulus to live by rapine; and in our days the French docile and poliſhed, poſſibly to exceſs, ſtill preſerve the traces of the feudal ſpirit; whilſt the Engliſh amidſt their clamours againſt the royal authority, continue to manifeſt a reſpect for the crown, which recals the epoch of the conqueſt, and the Norman government. Thus *every thing that is, partakes of what has been*; and to attain a thorough knowledge of any people, it is not leſs neceſſary to ſtudy their hiſtory than their legiſlation. If then we wiſh to form an idea of the American Republic, we muſt be careful not to confound the Virginians, whom warlike as well as mercantile, an ambitious as well as ſpeculative genius brought upon the continent, with the New Englanders, who owe their origin to enthuſiaſm; we muſt not expect to find preciſely the ſame men in Penſylvania, where the firſt coloniſts thought only of keeping and cultivating the deserts, and in South Carolina where the production of some exclusive articles fixes the general attention on external commerce, and establishes unavoidable connexions with the old world. Let it be observed, too, that agriculture, which was the occupation of the first settlers, was not an adequate means of assimilating the one with the other, since there are certain species of culture which tend to maintain the equality of fortune, and others to destroy it.

These are sufficient reasons to prove, that the same principles, the same opinions, the same habits do not occur in all the thirteen United States, although they are subject nearly to the same force of government. For, notwithstanding that all their constitutions are not similar, there is through the whole a democracy, and a government of *representation*, in which the people give their suffrage by their delegates. But if we chuse to overlook those shades which distinguish this confederated people from each other; if we regard the thirteen States only as one nation, we shall even then observe, that

that ſhe muſt long retain the impreſſion of thoſe circumſtances, which have conducted her to liberty. Every philoſopher acquainted with mankind, and who has ſtudied the ſprings of human action, muſt be convinced that, in the preſent revolution, the Americans have been guided by two principles, whilſt they imagined they were following the impulſe of only one. He will diſtinguiſh, a *poſitive* and a *negative* principle, in their legiſlation, and in their opinions. I call that principle poſitive, which in ſo enlightened a moment as the preſent, Reaſon alone could dictate to a people making choice of that government which ſuited them the beſt; I call that a negative principle, which they oppoſe to the laws and uſages of a powerful enemy for whom they had contracted a well founded averſion. Struck with the example of the inconveniencies offered by the Engliſh government, they had recourſe to the oppoſite extreme, convinced that it was impoſſible to deviate from it too much. Thus a child who has met with a ſerpent in his road, is not contented with avoiding it, but flies far from the spot where he would be out of danger of his bite. In England, a septennial parliament invites the King to purchase a majority on which he may reckon for a long period; the American assemblies *therefore* must be annual; on the other side of the water, the executive power, too uncontrolled in its action, frequently escapes the vigilance of the legislative authority; on this continent, each officer, each minister of the people must be under the immediate dependence of the assemblies, so that his first care on attaining office, will be to court the popular favour for a new election. Among the English, employments confer, and procure rank and riches, and frequently elevate their possessors to too great a height: among the Americans, offices neither conferring wealth, nor consideration, will not, it is true, become objects of intrigue or purchase, but they will be held in so little estimation as to make them avoided, rather than sought after, by the most enlightened citizens; by which means every employment will fall into the hands of new and untried men, the only persons who can expect to hold them to advantage.

It

In continuing to conſider the thirteen United States under one general point of view, we ſhall obſerve ſtill other circumſtances which have influenced as well the principles of the government, as the national ſpirit. Theſe thirteen States were at firſt colonies; now the firſt neceſſity felt in all riſing colonies is population; I ſay in riſing colonies, for I doubt much whether that neceſſity exiſts at preſent, ſo much as is generally imagined. Of this however I am very ſure, that there will ſtill be a complaint of want of population, long after the neceſſity has ceaſed; America will long continue to reaſon as follows: we muſt endeavour to draw foreigners amongſt us, for which purpoſe it is indiſpenſably neceſſary to afford them every poſſible advantage; every perſon once within the State, ſhall be conſidered therefore as a member of that State, as a real citizen. Thus one year's reſidence in the ſame place ſhall ſuffice to eſtabliſh him an inhabitant, and every inhabitant ſhall have the right of voting, and ſhall conſtitute a part of the ſovereign power; from whence it will reſult, that this ſovereignty will communicate and divide itſelf without requiring any pledge, any ſecurity from the perſon who is inveſted with it. This has ariſen from not conſidering the poſſibility of other emigrants than thoſe from Europe, who are ſuppoſed to fix themſelves in the firſt ſpot where they may form a ſettlement; we ſhall one day however, ſee frequent emigrations from State to State; workmen will frequently tranſplant themſelves, many of them will be obliged even to change ſituations from the nature of their employments, in which caſe it will not be ſingular to ſee the elections for a diſtrict of Connecticut, decided by inhabitants of Rhode iſland or New-York *.

Some

* There are various opinions in America on the ſubject of encouraging emigration. Mr. *Jefferſon*, for example, a man of profound thought, and great penetration, is of opinion, that emigrants from Europe are not deſirable, leſt the emigrants bringing with them not only the vices, but the corrupt prejudices of their reſpective ancient governments, may be unable to reliſh that bold univerſal ſyſtem of freedom and toleration which is a novelty to the old world: but I venture to think,

Some political writers, eſpecially the more modern, have advanced, that property alone ſhould

and truſt, that ſuch emigrations will be attended with no bad conſequences; for who will be the emigrants to a country where there are neither gold nor ſilver mines, and where ſubſiſtence is alone to be obtained by induſtry? Men of ſmall, or no fortunes, who cannot live with comfort, nor bring up a family in Europe; labourers and artizans of every kind; men of modeſty and genius, who are cramped by inſurmountable obſtacles in countries governed by cabal and intereſt; virtuous citizens compelled to groan in ſilence under the effects of arbitrary power; philoſophers who pant after the liberty of thinking for themſelves, and of giving vent, without danger, to thoſe generous maxims which burſt from their hearts, and of contributing their mite to the general ſtock of enlightened knowledge; religious men, depreſſed by the hierarchial eſtabliſhments of every country in Europe; the friends to freedom; in ſhort, the liberal, generous, and active ſpirits of the whole world. — To America, then, I ſay with fervency, in the glowing words of Mr. *Payne*, who is himſelf an Engliſh emigrant.—" O! receive the fugitives, and prepare in time an aſylum for mankind." The hiſtory of the late revolution too, may juſtify our hopes; for it is an obſervation, for the truth of which I appeal to fact, that the Europeans ſettled in America were poſſeſſed of *at leaſt as much* energy, and ſerved that country with as much zeal and en-

ſhould conſtitute the citizen. They are of opinion that he alone whoſe fortune is neceſſarily connected with its welfare has a right to become a member of the State. In America, a ſpecious anſwer is given to this reaſoning; amongſt us, ſay they, landed property is ſo eaſily acquired, that every workman who can uſe his hands, may be looked upon as likely ſoon to become a man of property. But can America remain long in her preſent ſituation? And can the regimen of her infant ſtate agree with her, now ſhe has aſſumed the virile robe?

The following, Sir, is a delicate queſtion which I can only propoſe to a philoſopher like you. In eſtabliſhing amongſt themſelves a purely democratic government, had the Americans a real affection for a democracy? And if they have wiſhed all men to be equal, is it not ſolely, becauſe, from

thuſiaſm in the cabinet, and in the field, as the native Americans; and to ſpeak with the late Lord Chatham, who ſaid many abſurd, but more wiſe things than moſt ſtateſmen, "they infuſed a portion of new health into the conſtitution."

TRANSLATOR.

from the very nature of things, they were themſelves nearly in that ſituation? For to preſerve a popular government in all its integrity, it is not ſufficient, not to admit either rank or nobility, riches alone never fail to produce marked differences, by ſo much the greater, as there exiſt no others. Now ſuch is the preſent happineſs of America that ſhe has no poor, that every man in it enjoys a certain eaſe and independence; and that if ſome have been able to obtain a ſmaller portion of them than others, they are ſo ſurrounded by reſources, that the future is more looked to, than their preſent ſituation. Such is the general tendency to a ſtate of equality, that the ſame enjoyments which would be deemed ſuperfluous in every other part of the world, are here conſidered as neceſſaries. Thus the ſalary of the workman muſt not only be equal to his ſubſiſtence and that of his family, but ſupply him with proper and commodious furniture for his houſe, tea and coffee for his wife, and the ſilk gown ſhe wears as often as ſhe goes from home; and this is one of the principal cauſes of the ſcarcity of labour ſo generally attributed to the want

of

of hands. Now, Sir, let us suppose that the increase of population may one day reduce your artizans to the situation in which they are found in France and England. Do you in that case really believe that your principles are so truly democratical, as that the landholders and the opulent, will still continue to regard them as their equals?—I shall go still further, relying on the accuracy of your judgment to testify every thing you may find too subtle or too speculative in my idea. I shall ask you then, whether under the belief of possessing the most perfect democracy, you may not find that you have insensibly attained a point more remote from it, than every other Republic. Recollect, that when the Roman senate was compelled to renounce its principles of tyranny, the very traces of it were supposed to be effaced, by granting to the people a participation of the consular honours. That numerous and oppressed class found themselves exalted by the prospect alone which now lay open to a small number of their body, the greatest part of them remained necessitous, but they consoled themselves by saying, *we may one day become consuls*.

suls. Now obſerve, Sir, that in your preſent form of government, you have not attached either ſufficient grandeur, or dignity to any place, to render its poſſeſſor illuſtrious, ſtill leſs the whole claſs from which he may be choſen. You have thrown far from you all hereditary honours, but have you beſtowed ſufficient perſonal diſtinctions? Have you reflected that theſe diſtinctions, far from being leſs conſiderable than thoſe which took place among the Greeks and Romans, ought rather to ſurpaſs them? The reaſon of this is very obvious: the effect of honours and diſtinctions is by ſo much the more marked, as it operates on the great number of men aſſembled together. When Cneius Duillius, was conducted home on his return from ſupper to the ſound of inſtruments, the whole city of Rome was witneſs to his triumph: grant the ſame honours to Governor Trumbull *; three houſes at moſt in Lebanon will hear the ſymphony.

* Mr. Trumbull, Governor of Connecticut, inhabits the town of Lebanon, which occupies a league of country, and where there are not ſix houſes leſs diſtant than a quarter of a mile from each other.

ſymphony. Men muſt be moved by ſome fixed principle; is it not better that this ſhould be by vanity than intereſt? I have no doubt that love of country will always prove a powerful motive, but do not flatter yourſelf that this will long exiſt with the ſame ſpirit. The greateſt efforts of the mind, like thoſe of the body, are in reſiſtance; and the ſame may happen with reſpect to the State, as in matters of opinion, to which we ceaſe to be attached, when they ceaſe to be conteſted.

Behold many objects, Sir, which have paſſed in review before us. We have only glanced at them, but to diſtinguiſh them more clearly, requires more penetrating eyes than mine; you hold the teleſcope; do you apply your optics, and you will make good uſe of them. My taſk will be accompliſhed, if I can only prove to you that theſe enquiries are not foreign to my ſubject. I ſhall obſerve then that to know to what preciſe point, and on what principle you ſhould admit the arts and ſciences in your nation, it is neceſſary firſt to underſtand its natural tendency; for we may direct the courſe of rivers, but not repel them to their

ſource.

ſource. Now, to diſcover the natural tendency of a nation, not only muſt we examine its actual legiſlation, but the oppoſitions which may exiſt between the government and prejudices, between the laws and habits; the re-action, in ſhort, which theſe different moving powers may produce, one upon the other. In the preſent inſtance, for example, it is important to foreſee to what degree the democracy is likely to prevail in America, and whether the ſpirit of that democracy tends to the equality of fortunes, or is confined to the equality of ranks. It is melancholy to confeſs, that it is to a very great inequality in the diſtribution of wealth, that the fine arts are indebted for their moſt brilliant æras. In the time of Pericles, immenſe treaſures were concentred in Athens, unappropriated to any particular purpoſe; under the reign of Auguſtus, Rome owed her acquiſition of the fine arts to the ſpoils of the world, if the fine arts were ever really naturalized at Rome; and under that of the Julii and Leo the Tenth. Eccleſiaſtic pomp and riches, puſhed to the higheſt point, gave birth to the prodigies of that famous age. But these epochas, so celebrated in the history of the arts, are either those of their birth, or of their revival; and similar circumstances are not necessary to maintain them in the flourishing and prosperous state they have attained. There is one circumstance, however, which we have not yet touched upon, and which seems indispensible, as well for their preservation, as for their establishment. The arts, let us not doubt it, can never flourish, but where there is a great number of men. They must have large cities, they must have capitals. America possesses already five, which seem ready for their reception, which you will yourself name; Boston, New-York, Philadelphia, Baltimore, and Charlestown. But they are sea-ports, and commerce, it cannot be dissembled, has more magnificence than taste; it pays, rather than encourages artists.——There are two great questions to resolve, whether large towns are useful or prejudicial to America, and whether commercial towns should be the capitals. Perhaps it will be imagined, that

that the firſt queſtion is anſwered by the ſole reflection, that rural life is beſt ſuited to mankind, contributing the moſt to their happineſs, and the maintenance of virtue, without which there can be no happineſs. But it muſt be remembered, that this ſame virtue, thoſe happy diſpoſitions, thoſe peaceable amuſements, we enjoy in the country, are not unfrequently acquiſitions made in towns. If nature be nothing for him who has not learnt to obſerve her, Retirement is ſterile for the man without information. Now this information is to be acquired beſt in towns. Let us not confound the man retired into the country, with the man educated in the country. The former is the moſt perfect of his ſpecies, and the latter frequently does not merit to belong to it. In a word, one muſt have education; I will ſay further, one muſt have lived with a certain number of mankind to know how to live well in one's own family. To abridge the queſtion, ſhall I content myſelf with expreſſing to you my wiſhes? I ſhould deſire that each ſtate of America, as far as it is practicable, had a capital to be the ſeat of government, but not a commercial city. I ſhould deſire that their capital were ſituated in the center of the republic, ſo that every citizen, rich enough to look after the education of his children, and to taſte the pleaſures of ſociety, might inhabit it for ſome months of the year, without making it his only reſidence, without renouncing his invaluable country-ſeat. I ſhould deſire that at a ſmall diſtance, but more conſiderable than that which ſeparates Cambridge from Boſton, an univerſity might be eſtabliſhed, where civil and public law, and all the higher ſciences, ſhould be taught, in a courſe of ſtudy, not to be commenced before the age of fourteen, and to be of only three years duration. I ſhould deſire, in ſhort, that in this capital and its appendage, the true national ſpirit might be preſerved, like the ſacred fire; that is to ſay, that ſpirit which perfectly aſſimilates with liberty and public happineſs. For we muſt never flatter ourſelves with the hopes of modifying, after our pleaſure, commercial towns. Commerce is more friendly to individual,

dividual, than to public liberty *, it discriminates not between citizens and strangers.

* I cannot here omit an anecdote which places, in a strong point of view, the distinction between *individual* and *public* liberty, made by the mere merchant. In the early part of life I spent some years in the compting-house of one of the most considerable merchants of the city of London, a native of Switzerland, for the moderate premium of *one thousand guineas*. This happening to be the period of the violent unconstitutional proceedings against Mr. Wilkes, the foreign merchant differing from the English apprentice, entered with zeal into all the measures of the then administration, which, though a republican by birth, he maintained with all the virulence of the tools of despotism. The American war followed, and this gentleman was no less active with offers of his life and fortune, from his compting-house in the city, in support of the arbitrary views of the same set of men, accompanied on all occasions with positions destructive of every idea of *public charity*. But mark the difference, when *individual liberty* was in question.—Happening to dine with Mr. John Pringle, of Philadelphia, in 1782, the conversation fell on this merchant, who is at present one of the first in the world, and some questions were asked me respecting his politics; my answers corresponded with what I have above said of him; but, judge of my astonishment, when Mr. Pringle assured me, smiling, and gave me *ocular* demonstration of

gers. A trading town is a common receptacle, where every man tranſports his manners, his opinions, and his habits; and the beſt are not always the moſt prevalent. Engliſh, French, Italian, all mix together, all loſe a little of their diſtinctive character, and in turn communicate a portion of it; ſo that neither defects nor vices appear in their genuine light; as, in the paintings of great artiſts, the different tints of light are ſo blended, as to leave no particular colour in its primitive and natural ſtate.

Though it ſeems impoſſible to conclude this article without ſpeaking of luxury, I have, notwithſtanding, ſome reluctance to employ a term, the ſenſe of which is not well aſcertained. To avoid here all ambiguity, I ſhall conſider it only *as an expence, abuſive in its relations, whether with the fortune of individuals, or with their ſituation.* In

the fact, that America had not a better friend; producing, at the ſame time, an invoice of a cargo of *gunpowder* ſhipped by his order on *joint account*, for the *Rebels* of America, at L'Orient, by which this Mr. —, of London, cleared near £.10,000 ſterling!!

TRANSLATOR.

In the former caſe, the idea of luxury approaches that of diſſipation, and in the latter, that of oſtentation. Let us illuſtrate this thought by an example—If a Dutch merchant ſpends his property in flowers and ſhells, the ſort of luxury into which he has fallen is only relative to his means, ſince his taſte has led him further than his faculties would admit. But if, in a republic, a very wealthy citizen expends only a part of his fortune in building a noble palace, the luxury with which he is reproached, is in that caſe proportionable to his ſituation; it ſhocks the public, in the ſame manner as proud and arrogant behaviour inſpires eſtrangement and hatred.

We muſt do juſtice to commerce, it loves enjoyments more than luxury; and if we ſee the merchant ſometimes paſs the limits, it is rather from imitation than natural propenſity. In France and England, we ſee ſome oſtentatious merchants, but the example is given them by the nobles. There is another more ridiculous, but leſs culpable abuſe, from which commerce is not free; which is, faſhion. This muſt doubtleſs

 prevail

prevail wherever there are many foreigners; for what is *uſage* amongſt them becomes *faſhion*, when they eſtabliſh themſelves elſewhere. On the other hand, the numerous correſpondencies, the intereſt even of the merchants, which conſiſts in provoking, in exciting the taſte of the conſumers, tends to eſtabliſh the empire of faſhion. What obſtacle muſt be oppoſed to this? I propoſe this queſtion to myſelf with pleaſure, as it leads me back to the fine arts by an indirect road. I ſhall aſk, what has been heretofore the remedy for thoſe caprices of opinion which have begot ſo many errors, ſo many revolutions? Is it not Reaſon and Philoſophy? Well then! the remedy againſt the caprices of the faſhion is the ſtudy of the arts, the knowledge of abſtract beauty, the perfection of taſte. But, what! Do you hope to fix the ſtandard of that taſte, hitherto ſo variable? How often has it changed? How often will it not again vary? I ſhall continue to anſwer in the manner of Socrates, by interrogating myſelf, and I ſhall ſay, What ridiculous opinions have not prevailed in the world,

world, from the time of the Grecian ſophiſts to the theologians of our days? Has not Reaſon, however, begun to reſume her rights, and do you think, that when once recovered, ſhe will ever loſe them? Why are you ſo unreaſonable as to expect that objects ſo frivolous as furniture and dreſs ſhould attain perfection before religion and legiſlation. Let us never ceaſe repeating, that Ignorance is the ſource of evil, and Science that of good. —Alas! do you not ſee that the Greeks, who had ſome how acquired very early, ſuch juſt notions of the arts and taſte; do you not ſee, I ſay, that they never varied in their modes? Witneſs the ſtatues modelled at Rome by Grecian artiſts; witneſs the noble and elegant mode of dreſs ſtill retained by that people, though living amongſt the Turks. Erect altars, then, to the fine arts, if you would deſtroy thoſe of faſhion and caprice. Taſte, and learn to reliſh nectar and ambroſia, if you are afraid of becoming intoxicated with common liquors.

Perhaps, Sir, what I am about to ſay ſhould only be whiſpered in your ear. I am going to handle a delicate ſubject, I am venturing to touch the ark. But be aſſured, that during a three years reſidence in America, the progreſs of the women's dreſs has not eſcaped me. If I have enjoyed this as a feeling man, if the reſults of this progreſs have not been viewed by me with an indifferent eye, my time of life and character are a pledge to you that I have obſerved them as a philoſopher. Well, Sir, it is in this capacity I undertake their defence, but ſo long only as things are not carried to an exceſs. The virtue of the women, which is more productive of happineſs, even for the men, than all the enjoyments of vice, if there be only real pleaſures ariſing from that ſource; the virtue of the women, I ſay, has two bucklers of defence; one is retirement, and diſtance from all danger: this is the hidden treaſure mentioned by Rochefoucault, which is untouched, becauſe it is undiſcovered. The other is loftineſs, a ſentiment always noble in its relation to ourſelves. Let them learn to appreciate themſelves; let them riſe in their own eſtimation, and rely on that eſtimable pride for the preſervation of their virtue

as

as well as of their ſame. They who love only pleaſure, corrupt the ſex, whom they convert only into an inſtrument of their voluptuouſneſs; they who love women, render them better by rendering them more amiable. But, you will ſay, is it by dreſs, and by exterior charms, that they muſt eſtabliſh their empire? Yes, Sir, every woman ought to ſeek to pleaſe; this is the weapon conferred on her by Nature to compenſate the weakneſs of her ſex. Without this ſhe is a ſlave, and can a ſlave have virtues? Remember the word *decus*, of which we have formed *decency*; its original import is *ornament*. A filthy and negligent woman is not decent, ſhe cannot inſpire reſpect. I have already allowed myſelf to expreſs my opinion by my wiſhes: I deſire, then, that all the American women may be well dreſſed; but I have no objection to ſeeing that dreſs ſimple. They are not formed to repreſent the ſeverity of the legiſlation; neither ought they to contraſt with it, and convey a tacit inſult on that ſeverity. Gold, ſilver, and diamonds, then, ſhould be baniſhed from American

dreſs;

dreſs; what excuſe can there be for a luxury which is not becoming? But this indulgence, Sir, which I have expreſſed for the toilet of the women, I am far from allowing to the men. I am not afraid to ſay, that I ſhould have a very bad opinion of them, if in a country where there are neither etiquette nor titles, nor particular diſtinctions, they ſhould ever give into the luxury of dreſs; a luxury, which even the French have laid aſide, except on marriages and entertainments, and which no longer exiſts any where but in Germany and Italy, where certainly you will not go in ſearch of models.

Obſerve, Sir, that we have imperceptibly prepared the way for the fine arts, by removing the principal obſtacles which might be oppoſed to them; for, if far from rendering nations vain and frivolous, they rather tend to preſerve them from the exceſſes of luxury, and the caprices of faſhion, they can certainly be conſidered neither as dangerous nor prejudicial. Still, perhaps, you will retain ſome ſcruple on the article of luxury; but recollect, Sir, if you pleaſe, the

the definition I have given of it, and if you reflect that every fortune which exceeds the necessary demands, insensibly produces some sort of personal riches, such as valuable furniture, gold and silver trinkets, sumptuous services of plate, &c. you must perceive that this constant surplus of annual income would be infinitely better bestowed on painting, sculpture, and other productions of the arts. Luxury, we have said, is often an abusive employ of riches, relatively to the condition of him who possesses them. Now, what ostentation is there in possessing a fine painting, or a handsome statue? Surely the parade of a magnificent side-board will be more offensive to the sight of an unwealthy neighbour, than an elegant cabinet adorned with paintings. I doubt, even, whether the man who keeps a musician in his pay, be so much an object of envy as him who maintains race-horses and a pack of hounds.

But let us go farther; it is not only the production of the fine arts of which I wish to procure the possession to America; the fine arts themselves must be placed

within

within her boſom. If I am deſirous of her purchaſing pictures, it is that ſhe may have painters *; if I encourage her to ſend for muſicians, it is that ſhe may become muſical in her turn. Let her not apprehend the fate of the Romans, to whom ſhe has the apparent pride, but the real humility to compare herſelf. The Romans, ferocious, unjuſt, graſping from character, and oſtentatious

* America, in her infant ſtate, has already burſt forth into the full ſplendour of maturity in the immortal paintings of a *Copley* and a *Weſt*. Further glory ſtill attends her early progreſs, even in the preſent day, in a *Stewart*, a *Trumbull* and a *Brown*; nor is *Peale* unworthy of ranking with many modern painters of no inconſiderable fame; ages may poſſibly not elapſe before poſterity may apply to *America*, what Mr. *Tickell* has ſaid, ſo happily, heretofore of the mother country,

See on her *Titian*'s and her *Guido*'s urns,
Her fallen arts forlorn *Heſperia* mourns;
While Britain wins each garland from her brow,
Her *wit* and *freedom* firſt, her *painting* now.

For *wit*, let me refer the reader of taſte to the poem of *Mac Fingal*, written by another Trumbull of Connecticut, who is juſtly ſtiled the *American Hudibras*. *Qualis ab incepto proceſſerit, ac ſibi conſtet.*

TRANSLATOR.

oſtentatious from vanity, were able to purchaſe the maſter-pieces, but not the taſte of the arts. The Americans proceeding in general from the moſt poliſhed countries of Europe, have not to ſtrip themſelves of any barbarous prejudices. They ought rather to compare themſelves with the Greek colonies; and certainly, Syracuſe, Marſeilles, Crotona, and Agrigentum had no reaſon to envy the mother country. There is one baſe on which, all they who like you are equally attached to good taſte and to your country, may ſafely reſt their hopes. Your fellow citizens live, and will long continue to live, in the vicinity of Nature; ſhe is continually under their hands; ſhe is always great and beautiful. Let them ſtudy; let them conſult her, and they can never go aſtray. Caution them only, not to build too much on the pedantic legiſlations of Cambridge, of Oxford, and Edinburgh, which have long aſſumed a ſort of tyranny in the empire of opinion, and ſeem only to have compoſed a vaſt *claſſic* code for no other purpoſe than to keep all mankind in claſs, as if they were ſtill children.

Thus, Sir, you will have the complete enjoyment of the fine arts; ſince you will yourſelves be artiſts: but is it not to be feared, than the powerful attraction with which they operate on ſenſible minds, may divert a riſing people from ſeveral more uſeful, though leſs agreeable occupations? I am far from being of that opinion; I think, on the contrary, that the moſt diſtinctive, and moſt peculiar advantage of America is that the rapid advances ſhe is making are not laborious, that they are not due to the exceſs of labour. Every American has twice as much leiſure in the day as an European. Neceſſity alone compels our painful efforts, and you are ſtrangers to neceſſity. Beſides that, your winters are long and rigorous, and many hours may be well ſpared to domeſtic ſociety; this reflexion too is applicable only to the lower claſſes of the people. You, who live in Virginia, know what time is ſacrificed to play, to hunting, and the table; much more than is neceſſary to form a *Phidias* or a *Polycletes*.

You will inſiſt, perhaps, and you will aſk, whether a taſte for the arts and letters will not tend to render your fellow citizens effeminate?

minate? Whether it will not render them frivolous and vain? Whether the national characters and manners will not necessarily be impaired, and admitting even their utility, you will desire to have their early progress, at least, conducted with a certain measure? I think, that you will find an answer to our present enquiry in many of the preceding observations. But it is time for me to establish a general principle, the extensive consequences of which you will develop better than I can; *as long as a taste for the arts can assimilate itself with rural and domestic life, it will always be advantageous to your country, and* vice versâ.—Public spectacles, gaudy assemblies, horse-races, &c. drag both men and women from the country, and inspire them with a disgust for it. Music, drawing, painting, architecture, attach all persons to their homes. A harpsicord is a neighbour always at command, who answers all your questions, and never calumniates. Three or four persons in the neighbourhood join to pass the evening together; here is a concert ready formed. A young lady, in her irksome moments, amuses herself in drawing; when become a wife and mother, ſhe ſtill draws, that ſhe may inſtruct her children; and here is another important article, of which I had hitherto taken no notice.—Do you wiſh your children to remain long attached to you? Be yourſelves their teachers. Education augments and prolongs the relation that ſubſiſts between you; it adds to the conſideration, the reſpect they entertain for you. They muſt long be perſuaded, that we know more than them, and that he who teaches always knows more than the perſon to be taught. In America, as in England, parents ſpoil their children when they are young, and they abandon them to themſelves when they grow up; for, in theſe two nations, education is neither enough attended to, nor ſufficiently prolonged. Indulgent to children in their tender age, the people there form them into petty domeſtic tyrants; negligent of them when they attain to adoleſcency, they convert them into ſtrangers.

At preſent, Sir, it ſeems to me, that there remains no good reaſon to hinder us from attracting the fine arts to America. Unfortunately it is not the ſame with artiſts. I do not think I can better expreſs my good

opinion

opinion of the Americans, than by declaring, that they will always incur ſome riſk in receiving a foreigner amongſt them. The Europeans, it muſt be confeſſed, have vices from which you are exempt, and they are not in general, the beſt amongſt them who quit their country, eſpecially who paſs the ſeas. Let us, however, do this juſtice to painters, and ſculptors, that the aſſiduity of their labours, and above all, that the ſentiment of the beautiful, that delicacy of taſte which they have acquired, render them, generally ſpeaking, better than other men.—It is different with reſpect to muſic and dancing. Cuſtom has thought proper to place the latter among the fine arts; nor do I oppoſe it, ſince it ſeems to improve our exterior, and to give us that decorum, the ſource of which is the reſpect of others, and of ourſelves. But this apology for the art, does not conſtitute that of its profeſſors. Diſtruſt in general the maſters who come to you from Europe; be diffident even of thoſe you may yourſelves ſend for. It will always be much ſafer not to truſt to chance, but to make ſubſcriptions in each ſtate, in each town, to engage artiſts to fix themſelves amongſt you; but in this caſe apply only to correſpondents in Europe on whom you may rely. The commiſſion with which you entruſt them, ought to be ſacred in their eyes, and the ſmalleſt negligence on their parts, would be highly criminal; yet even they are liable to be deceived; and as it is much better to defer, even for a long time, the progreſs of the arts, than to make the ſlighteſt ſtep towards the corruption of your manners, it is my principal recommendation to the Americans to naturalize as much as poſſible, all foreign artiſts; to aſſimilate and identify them with the inhabitants of the country: to effect which, I ſee no better method than by ſending them huſbands and proprietors; act ſo as to induce them to marry, enable them to acquire lands, and to become citizens. It is thus that by ſecuring the empire of morals, you will ſtill further guard againſt the effect of thoſe national prejudices, of that diſdain which render foreigners ſo ridiculous and odious,

odious, and which reflect upon the art itself, the disgust inspired by the artist.

Henceforward, Sir, let us enlarge our views; the fine arts are adapted to America: they have already made some progress there, they will eventually make much greater; no obstacle, no reasonable objection can stop them in their career; these are points at least on which we are agreed. Let us now see to what purposes they may be converted by the public, the state, and the government. Here, a vast field opens to our speculation, but as it is exposed to every eye, I shall fix mine on the object with which it has most forcibly been struck. Recollect, Sir, what I have said above, relative to officers and public dignities; I have remarked that a jealousy, possibly well founded in itself, but pushed to the extreme, had made honours too rare, and rewards too moderate amongst you.——Call in the fine arts to the aid of a timid legislation; the latter confers neither rank, nor permanent distinction; let her bestow statues, monuments and medals. Astonished Europe, in admiring a *Washington*, a *Warren*, a *Greene*, and a *Montgòmery*, demands what recompence can repay their ſervices; behold that recompence, worthy of them and of you. Let all the great towns in America preſent ſtatues of Waſhington, with this inſcription: PATER, LIBERATOR, DEFENSOR PATRIÆ; let us ſee alſo thoſe of *Hancock* and of *Adams*, with only two words, PRIMI PROSCRIPTI; that of *Franklin*, with the Latin verſe inſcribed in France below his portrait—(ERIPUIT COELO FULMEN, SCEPTRUMQUE TYRANNI, *Tranſlator*) &c. &c*. what glory would not this reflect upon America! It would be found that ſhe has already more heroes, than ſhe could procure marble and artiſts—† and your public

* This verſe is of that virtuous politician and good man, Mr. *Turgot*. The Tranſlator has inſerted it, as it ſeems by the author's omitting it, to be of too high a flavour for the French *cenſure*.

TRANSLATOR.

† Although it be highly proper to inſiſt upon this ſort of recompence, it may not be amiſs that the world ſhould know that Congreſs, as far as opportunity would admit, *have not been remiſs* in beſtowing ſuch honourable rewards, which they have decreed in different forms on every ſuitable occaſion to the

public halls, your *curiæ*, why ſhould not they offer in *relief*, and paintings, the bat-

Baron de Kaalb, &c. &c. and a marble monument was voted by that body to the memory of my ineſtimable friend Montgomery, ſoon after his glorious fall, in the following words:

Extract from the Journals of Congreſs.

Thurſday, January 25, 1776.

" The Committee appointed to conſider of a pro-" per method of paying a juſt tribute of gratitude to " the memory of General Montgomery, brought in " their report, which was as follows:

" It being not only a tribute of gratitude juſtly due " to the memory of thoſe who have peculiarly diſtin-" guiſhed themſelves in the glorious cauſe of liberty, " to perpetuate their names by the moſt durable mo-" numents erected to their honour, but alſo greatly " conducive to inſpire poſterity with emulation of " their illuſtrious actions:

" *Reſolved*, That to expreſs the veneration of the " United Colonies for their late General, RICHARD " MONTGOMERY, and the deep ſenſe they enter-" tain of the many ſignal and important ſervices of " that gallant officer, who, after a ſeries of ſucceſ-" ſes, amidſt the moſt diſcouraging difficulties, fell " at length in a gallant attack upon Quebec the " capital of Canada; and to tranſmit to future ages, " as examples truly worthy of imitation, his patrio-" tiſm, conduct, boldneſs of enterprize, inſuper-" able perſeverance, and contempt of danger and

tles of *Bunker's-hill*, of *Saratoga*, of *Trenton*, of *Prince-town*, of *Monmouth*, of *Cow-*

pens,

" death a monument be procured from *Paris*, or " other part of *France*, with an inſcription ſacred " to his memory, and expreſſive of his amiable " character and heroic atchievements; and that the " continental treaſurers be directed to advance a " ſum not exceeding £.300 ſterling to Dr. Benja- " jamin Franklin, who is deſired to ſee this reſolu- " tion properly executed, for defraying the expence " thereof."

This reſolve was carried into execution at Paris by that ingenious artiſt, Mr. *Caffiers*, ſculptor to the King of France, under the direction of Dr. Franklin. The monument is of white marble, of the moſt beautiful ſimplicity, and inexpreſſible elegance, with emblematical devices, and the following truly claſſical inſcription, worthy of the modeſt, but great mind of a Franklin.

To the GLORY of
Richard Montgomery, Major General
of the Armies of the United States of America,
Slain at the Siege of Quebec
the 31ſt of December, 1775, aged 38 years.

The academy of inſcriptions and Belles Lettres, have compoſed medals for the Generals Waſhington, Greene, Gates, Morgan, &c. The State of Virginia alſo ſent for Monſieur *Houdon* the ſtatuary from Paris to America ſince the war, expreſsly to take a model, in order to form the ſtatue of General

pens, of *Eutaw Springs?* Thus would you perpetuate the memory of theſe glorious

Waſhington — an example however which Congreſs do not think proper to follow, *during the life-time* of the General, for reaſons which may poſſibly not be diſapproved of, by the Marquis de Chaſtellux, even in ſo unexceptionable an inſtance.

Over this monument, the Tranſlator who was the intimate friend of this excellent young man, ſhed an affectionate tributary tear, when at Paris in the year 1777. He had long known and looked up to him with admiration, for he was deep in the ſecrets of his head and heart. His attachment to liberty was innate, and matured by a fine education, and a glorious underſtanding. The Tranſlator whilſt he indulged his private ſorrow at the ſight of this ſad, though noble teſtimonial of his friend's tranſcendent virtues, felt his mind awed and overwhelmed with the magnitude of the event which led to this cataſtrophe, and with reflections on the wonderful revolutions, and extraordinary diſpenſations of human affairs.——But a few months, and he had ſeen the deceaſed hero, an officer in the ſervice of England, an officer too of the moſt diſtinguiſhed merit, who had fought her battles ſucceſsfully with the immortal Wolfe at Quebec, the very ſpot on which fighting under the ſtandard of freedom, he was doomed to fall in arms againſt her; but a few months, and he ſees his dead friend the ſubject of a monument, conſecrated to his memory

deeds; thus would you maintain, even through a long peace, that national pride, so

by the united voice of a free people, and his monument, and his fame, as a victim to tyranny, and a champion of freedom, consigned to be celebrated by an enslaved people, against whom he had often fought in defence of the same cause, in which he sacrificed his life. There is a remarkable circumstance connected with his fall, which merits to be recorded. One of General Montgomery's Aides de Camp, was Mr. *Macpherson*, a most promising young man, whose father resided at Philadelphia, and was greatly distinguished in privateering in the war of 1756. This gentleman had a brother in the 16th regiment in the British service, at the time of Montgomery's expedition into Canada, and who was as violent in favour of the English government, as this General's Aide de Camp was enthusiastic in the cause of America; the latter had accompanied his General a day or two previous to the attack in which they both lost their lives, to view and meditate on the spot where Wolfe had fallen; on his return, he found a letter from his brother the English officer full of the bitterest reproaches against him for having entered into the American service, and containing a pretty direct wish, that if he would not abandon it, he might meet with the deserved fate of a rebel. The Aide de Camp immediately returned him an answer full of strong reasoning in defence of his conduct, but by no means attempting

ſo neceſſary to the preſervation of liberty; and you might, without alarming even that liberty, laviſh rewards equal to the ſacrifices ſhe has received *.

It would be injurious Sir, to you and to your country, to inſiſt longer on theſe reflections: my attention is excited by a freſh

to ſhake the oppoſite principles of his brother; and not only free from acrimony, but full of expreſſions of tenderneſs and affection; this letter he dated, "from the ſpot where Wolfe loſt his life, in fighting the cauſe of England, *in friendſhip with America.*" This letter had ſcarcely reached the officer at New York, before it was followed by the news of his brother's death. The effect was inſtantaneous; nature, and perhaps reaſon prevailed; a thouſand, not unworthy ſentiments ruſhed upon his diſtreſſed mind; he quitted the Engliſh ſervice, entered into that of America, and ſought every occaſion of diſtinguſhing himſelf in her ſervice!

TRANSLATOR.

* Mr. *Trumbull*, ſon to Governor Trumbull of Connecticut, who was impriſoned in England as a traitor, whilſt he was ſtudying painting under Mr. Weſt, is now at Paris reſiding with Mr. Jefferſon, and has finiſhed two capital pictures of the death of *Warren* and *Montgomery*. They are eſteemed *chef d'œuvres* by all the connoiſſeurs in this ſublime art.

TRANSLATOR.

fresh object, but I should regard it also as an offence, to entertain an idea that it is necessary to call the attention of America to this object, you are desirous that the progress of the sciences also should enter into your deliberations. It is impossible not to foresee their progress in a country already so celebrated for its academies and universities, which rival those of the old world for its learned men; I will go further, for its men of distinguished genius, whose names alone will mark famous epochas in the history of the human mind *. Doubt not,

* Mr. Jefferson in answer to a prejudiced remark of the Abbé Raynal, who says, " on doit être etoné " que l' Amerique noit pas encore produit un bon " poëte, un habile mathematicien, un homme de " genie dans un seul art, ou une seule science." Mr. Jefferson, amidst abundance of good reasoning, says in answer, " In war we have a *Washington*, " whose memory will be adored while liberty shall " have votaries, whose name will triumph over time, " and will in future ages assume its just station " among the most celebrated worthies of the world, " when that wretched philosophy shall be forgotten " which would have arranged him among the *de-* " *generacies* of mankind, (see *Buffon*'s system re- " specting animals in America.) In physics we have

not, Sir, that America will render herſelf illuſtrious by the ſciences, as well as by her arms and government; and if the attention of the philoſopher be ſtill neceſſary to watch over them, it is leſs to accelerate than to remove the obſtacles which might poſſibly retard their progreſs. Let the univerſities, always too dogmatical, always too excluſive,

"produced a *Franklin*, than whom no one of the "preſent age has made more important diſcoveries, "nor has enriched philoſophy with more, or more "ingenious ſolutions of the phænomena of Nature. "We have ſuppoſed Mr. *Rittenhouſe* ſecond to no "aſtromomer living: that in *genius* he muſt be the "firſt, becauſe he is ſelf-taught. As an artiſt he has "exhibited as great a proof of mechanical genius as "the world has ever produced. He has not, indeed, "made a world; but he has by imitation approached "nearer its Maker than any man who has lived from "the creation to this day, &c. &c." There are various ways, Mr. Jefferſon adds, of keeping truth out of ſight. Mr. Rittenhouſe's model of the planetary ſyſtem has the plagiary appellation of an *orrery*; and *the quadrant*, invented by *Godfrey*, an *American* alſo, and with the aid of which the European nations traverſe the globe, is called *Hadley*'s quadrant.—Thus too, the Tranſlator adds, is the great *Columbus* robbed of the honour of giving his name to *America!*

TRANSLATOR.

exclusive, be charged only to form good scholars, and leave to an unrestrained philosophy the care of forming good men. In England, the universities have laboured to destroy scepticism, and from that period philosophy has been visibly on the decline; it seems as if the English, in every thing, wish only for a *half liberty*. Leave owls and bats to flutter in the doubtful perspicuity of a feeble twilight; the American eagle should fix her eyes upon the sun. Nothing proves to me that it is not good to know the truth, and what has error hitherto produced?—the misery of the world.

As for academies, they will always be useful, whilst they are very numerous. An academician is a senator of the republic of letters; he takes an oath to advance nothing he cannot prove; he consecrates his life to truth, with a promise to sacrifice to it, even his self-love. Such men cannot be numerous; such men ought not to be thrown into discredit, by associates unworthy of them. But if academical principles tend to make science austere and scrupulous, the encouragements proposed

to

to the public ought to excite every mind, and furniſh a free channel for opinion. Of this nature are prizes propoſed by the academies; it is by their means that the activity of men's minds is directed towards the moſt uſeful objects; it is to them that firſt efforts are indebted for celebrity; it is by them alſo the young man thirſting for glory is diſpenſed with ſighing long after her firſt favours. The more the ſciences approach perfection, the more rare do diſcoveries become; but America has the ſame advantage in the learned world, as in that which conſtitutes our reſidence. The extent of her empire ſubmits to her obſervation a large portion of heaven and earth. What obſervations may not be made between Penobſcot and Savannah? between the lakes and the ocean? Natural hiſtory and aſtronomy are her peculiar appendages, and the firſt of theſe ſciences at leaſt, is ſuſceptible of great improvement.

Morals are a branch of philoſophy lately in great repute. As for myſelf, it appears that wherever the legiſlation is good, morals are already formed; and where the legiſlation

giſlation is defective, I know not the uſe of morals. It is in this caſe in general, as with health, little attention is paid to it until it be loſt. Moraliſts too are like phyſicians and apothecaries, whom a good regimen would render uſeleſs, and who not unfrequently ſerve but to amuſe our anxiety, and to treat our imagination. Preſerve a good government, render the people mild and ſenſible, and they will make morals for themſelves.

With reſpect to religion, its object and end, conceal it from our obſervations: as it conſiders not the relations of men with each other, but their connection with God alone, its influence ought to be internal and perſonal; and whenever it extends further, it is invariably at the expence of public order. I cannot, therefore, but congratulate America on being the only country poſſeſſing true toleration; which has not only triumphed over ſuperſtition, but which makes even the enemies of ſuperſtition bluſh at the ignominious compromiſes they have made with her. But that none of thoſe objects which intereſt you, Sir, may paſs before

fore our eyes without inducing ſome reflections, I ſhall allow myſelf to make one, which, I truſt, will meet with indulgence from a philoſopher.

All the religions eſtabliſhed in America, agree in one very important point; they proſcribe all ſuperſtition, all dependence on any external power; but they agree alſo in a practice which ſeems to me to have no neceſſary connection with the Proteſtant tenets. I mean the extreme ſeverity with which they obſerve the Sunday. This day is conſecrated to divine worſhip: be it ſo; but it is alſo conſecrated to reſt, and what is this repoſe without gaiety, without relaxation? I venture to ſay, that in America, you neither know the pain of labour, nor the pleaſure of repoſe. What a gloomy ſilence reigns in all your towns on Sunday! a ſtranger would imagine that ſome epidemic or plague had obliged every one to confine himſelf at home *.—Tranſport yourſelf to Europe,

* Whilſt I was at Boſton, in 1782, there were violent debates in the aſſembly, and the ſenate, reſpecting the duration of the Sabbath—one party were

Europe, and especially to a Catholic country; behold, on the same day, when divine service is over, the people deluging the squares,

for having it consist of *six and thirty* hours, commencing at six o'clock on the Saturday evening, whilst the others insisted on abridging it to *eighteen*, reckoning from the midnight of Saturday, and finishing at six on the Sunday evening; the former proposition passed the assembly where the country interest prevailed, but was thrown out in the senate by the predominant interest of the merchants, aided by good sense, and the palpable absurdity of such a regulation in a commercial country abounding with strangers. Mr. *Cobbet*, a very sensible man, and a rich merchant of Beverley, distinguished himself on this occasion by a speech full of eloquence and wit. As far as my memory serves me, the sabbath is at length wisely limited to eighteen hours; I say wisely, for not even travelling is permitted on a Sunday in the New England States, insomuch that you are at every instant liable to be stopped by force, and carried by the *deacons* before a magistrate, who inflicts a fine, and puts an end to your journey for the day. This ridiculous and unmeaning austerity, will probably be some day put an end to, by the fatal exit of one of these bigotted officers of the church tribunal, who may possibly be mistaken by some sturdy traveller or stranger, by seizing his horse by the bridle, for a *knight of the pad*; for, pleasantry apart, this is by no means an improbable prediction. TRANSLATOR.

ſquares, and public walks, and hurrying in crowds towards the ſuburbs, towards the neighbouring villages, where a thouſand taverns are open to receive them; every where your ear is ſaluted with ſongs, and inſtrumental muſic; every where your eyes are entertained with gay and animated dances. It is a truly affecting ſpectacle to ſee the artizan preſſing towards the *Guinguettes*, or houſes of entertainment; under one arm he holds his wife, dreſt in her beſt array, the other ſerves him to carry the youngeſt of his children, whilſt the remaining one, who is able to walk, faſtens on his mother's hand, and ſtrives to follow her; this whole family are going to rejoice together. If the wine gives riſe to ſome quarrels, they are appeaſed by the women, who prevent that exceſs of drinking to which men are but too ſubject; the family drink and dance amongſt themſelves, and this happy day frequently encroaches on the night, and always terminates too ſoon. In America, it is the reverſe; as there is nothing but idleneſs without the reſource of either ſport or dance, the ſexes ſeparate, the women at a loſs what to do with their fine dreſs, which has ſhone only at the church or meeting, fall into a ſtate of wretched liſtleſſneſs, which is only to be diverted by frivolous diſcourſe and ſcandal ; whilſt the men, wearied with reading the bible to their children, aſſemble round a bowl, not prepared by joy, and at the bottom of which they find nothing but ſtupid intoxication.

I know not, Sir, whether the following principle be that of a philoſopher, or only of a Frenchman ; but I am of opinion that every amuſement which ſeparates the women from the men, is contrary to the welfare of ſociety, is calculated to render one of the ſexes clowniſh, and the other ſlovenly, and to deſtroy, in ſhort, that ſenſibility, the ſource of which Nature has placed in the intercourſe between the ſexes.

Weigh theſe reflections, Sir, which are not ſo frivolous, perhaps, as they appear. Happineſs is only compoſed of enjoyments ; now, Sundays make the ſeventh part of our lives, and if you deduct from the people their days of extraordinary labour, you will

ſee

ſee that they conſtitute the half of our beſt time. Make happy days, then, of Sundays, give them to America, and you will have conferred on them an ineſtimable preſent.

Theſe obſervations on the ſabbath, on the day of repoſe which ſucceeds to labour, ſeem to apprize me that mine is at an end. May it not appear longer to you, than it has to myſelf; and may you, after beſtowing on me ſome moments of attention, not feel too ſenſibly the want of that diſſipation I have juſt been extolling. Recognize at leaſt, Sir, in this feeble eſſay, my devotion to your will, and the ſincere attachment with which I have the honour to be, &c. &c.

On board the frigate L'Emeraude, in the Bay of Cheſapeak, the 12th of January, 1783.

Description of the Natural Bridge, called in Virginia, Rocky Bridge.

On my return from my journey in Upper Virginia, I regretted not having been able to take the dimensions of the Natural Bridge. I was anxious that some person, who was at once a designer and geometrician, should undertake an expedition to the Apalachians for that sole object, and that he should be provided with the instruments necessary for accomplishing it with accuracy. No man was more capable of this than the Baron de Turpin, Captain in the royal corps of *Génie*; for in him were united all those branches of knowledge, which are carried to so great a height in the corps to which he belongs, with the talent of designing with as much facility as precision; besides which, he was well enough acquainted with the English language to dispense with an interpreter. I proposed, therefore, to the Comte de Rochambeau, to charge him with this commission, which I was confident he would acquit with pleasure.

ſure. The General thought that it would be rendering a freſh ſervice to the Americans, to make them acquainted with one of the wonders which render their country celebrated, and that it would be pleaſant enough for Frenchmen to be the firſt to give them a preciſe idea and a correct plan of it *. The Baron de Turpin ſet out, therefore, in

 the

* So intereſting an object could not eſcape the curioſity and obſervations of Mr. *Jefferſon* †. He had meaſured the height and breadth of the natural bridge, of which he ſpeaks, in an excellent memoir compoſed in 1781, a few copies of which he printed laſt year under the modeſt title of *Notes upon Virginia*, or rather without any title, for this work has never been made public. We hope, however, the precious documents on natural philoſophy, as well as politics, contained in that work, will not be loſt to the

† The following is Mr. JEFFERSON's account of the Natural Bridge alluded to in this note, which I am happy in being able to lay before the reader.

" The *Natural Bridge*, the moſt ſublime of Nature's works, is " on the aſcent of a hill, which ſeems to have been cloven thro' " its length by ſome great convulſion. The fiſſure, juſt at the " bridge, is by ſome admeaſurements 270 feet deep, by others only " 250. It is about 45 feet wide at the bottom, and 90 feet at the " top; this of courſe determines the length of the bridge, and its " height from the water. Its breadth in the middle is about 60 " feet, but more at the ends, and the thickneſs of the maſs at the " ſummit of the arch, about 40 feet. A part of this thickneſs is " conſtituted by a coat of earth, which gives growth to many large

the beginning of May, and in three weeks brought me back five plans, three of which are

public. A well-known man of letters ‡ has made use of them, and we recommend the perusal of a work, which will speedily make its appearance under the title of *Observations on Virginia.*

" trees. The residue, with the hill on both sides, is one solid rock " of limestone. The arch approaches the semi-elliptical form; " but the larger axis of the ellipses, which would be the chord of " the arch, is many times longer than the transverse. Though the " sides of the bridge are provided in some parts with a parapet of " fixed rocks, yet few men have resolution to walk to them, and " look over into the abyss. You involuntarily fall on your hands " and feet, creep to the parapet, and look over it. Looking down " from this height about a minute, gave me a violent head-ach. " If the view from the top be painful and intolerable, that from " below is delightful in the extreme. It is impossible for the " emotions arising from the sublime to be felt beyond what they " are here: on the sight of so beautiful an arch, so elevated, so " light, and springing as it were up to heaven, the rapture of the " spectator is really indescribable! The fissure continuing narrow, " deep, and streight for a considerable distance above and be- " low the bridge, opens a short but very pleasing view of the " North Mountain on one side, and Blue Ridge on the other, at " the distance each of them of about five miles. This bridge is in " the county of *Rockbridge*, to which it has given name, and affords " a public and commodious passage over a valley, which cannot " be crossed elsewhere for a considerable distance. The stream " passing under it is called Cedar Creek. It is a water of James " river, and sufficient, in the driest seasons, to turn a grist mill, " though its fountain is not more than two miles above."

TRANSLATOR.

‡ Monsieur *De Meunier*, in his new article of *Etats Unis* in the last *Livraison* of *La Nouvelle Encyclopedie*, and the Abbe de *Morlaix*, who is translating them into French.

TRANSLATOR.

are engraved and annexed to this work. Two of them preſent perſpectives, taken from the two ſides of the Natural Bridge, and from the bottom of the valley from whence it ſprings. The third is a bird's-eye view, and repreſents a part of the country in which it is. The two others being only ſuppoſed ſections of this bridge where it holds by the bank, and which may be conſidered as its abutment, I have not thought proper to have engraved, to avoid multiplying the plates neceſſary to be given with this work. As to the dimenſions, they are as follows, as given me by M. de Turpin:

"The Natural Bridge forms an arch of fifteen toiſes (ſix feet Engliſh) in length, of that ſpecies we denominate *the Cow's Horn*: the chord of this arch is ſeventeen toiſes at the head of *Amont*, and nine at that of *Aval*, and the right arch is the ſegment of an ellipſe, ſo flat that the ſmall axis is only a twelfth of the large one. The maſs of rock and ſtone which loads this arch is forty-nine feet ſolid on the key of the great centre, and thirty-ſeven on that of the ſmall one; and as we find about the ſame difference in taking the level of the hill, it may be ſuppoſed that the roof is on a level, the whole length of the key. It is proper to obſerve, that the live rock continues alſo the whole thickneſs of the arch, and that on the oppoſite ſide it is only 25 feet wide, in its greateſt breadth, and becomes gradually narrower.

"The whole arch ſeems to be formed of one and the ſame ſtone, for the joints which one remarks at the head of *Amont*, are the effect of lightning, which ſtruck this part in 1779; the other head has not the ſmalleſt vein, and the *intrados* is ſo ſmooth, that the martins, which fly round it in great numbers, cannot faſten on it *. The abutments, which have a gentle ſlope, are entire; and, without being abſolute planes, have all the poliſh which a current of water would give to unhewn ſtone in a certain time. The four rocks adjacent to the abutments ſeem to be perfectly homogeneous, and to have a very trifling ſlope. The two rocks on the right bank of the rivulet

* See at the end of this article a note, which was too long to be inſerted under the text.

vulet are 200 feet high above the ſurface of the water, the *intrados* of the arch 150, and the two rocks on the left bank 180.

" If we conſider this bridge ſimply as a pictureſque object, we are ſtruck with the majeſty with which it towers in the valley. The white oaks, which grow upon it, ſeem to rear their lofty ſummits to the clouds; whilſt the ſame trees, which border on the rivulet, appear like ſhrubs. As for the naturaliſt, he muſt content himſelf with ſuch obſervations as may guide a more hardy philoſopher to form ſome probable conjecture on the origin of this extraordinary maſs.

" From every part of the arch, and of its ſupporters, cubic pieces of three or four lines dimenſion were taken, and placed ſucceſſively in the ſame aqua fortis; the former were diſſolved in leſs than half an hour; the others required more time, but this muſt be attributed to the diminution of ſtrength of the aqua fortis, which loſt its activity in proportion as it became ſaturated.

" We ſee that theſe rocks being of a calcareous

careous nature, excludes every idea of a volcano, which besides cannot be reconciled with the form of the bridge and its adjacent parts. If it be supposed that this astonishing arch is the effect of a current of water, we must suppose likewise that this current has had the force to break down, and carry to a great distance, a mass of 5000 cubic fathoms, for there remains not the slightest trace of such an operation. The blocks found under the arch, and a little below it, have their interior positions marked on the collateral pendents on the side of *Aval*, and are occasioned by no other demolition than that of the bridge itself, which is said to have been one third wider.

"The excavation of eight or ten inches, formed in the *pied droit*, or supporter, on the left bank of the stream, under the spring of the arch, lengthens it into the form of a crow's beak. This decay, and some other parts which are blown up, give reason to presume, that this surprizing edifice will one day become a victim of that time which has destroyed so many others."

Such

Such are the obſervations the Baron de Turpin brought back with him, and with which he was pleaſed to favour me. As their accuracy may be relied on, perhaps it would be ſufficient to tranſcribe them here, and leave the reader to exerciſe his thoughts on the cauſes which could produce this ſort of prodigy. This was in fact the reſolution I had taken, when, abandoned to my own powers, of which I was juſtly diffident, I was writing at Williamſburgh, and for myſelf alone, the Journal of my late expedition. A Spaniſh work, however, which fell into my hands, confirmed me in the opinion I at firſt had entertained, that it was to the labour only of the Creator that we owe the magnificent conſtruction of the Natural Bridge. The opinion of the Count de Buffon, whom I have ſince conſulted, has left me no doubt upon the ſubject. His ſublime conceptions of the different epochs of nature ſhould have been ſufficient to put me in the way; but the diſciple, who knows how to do juſtice to himſelf, is timid, even in the application of his maſter's principles. But, whoever has travelled in America,

America, becomes a witneſs entitled to depoſe in favour of that genius whoſe oracles frequently meet with too many opposers. If it be neceſſary to juſtify what the Monteſquieus, the Humes, the Voltaires have ſaid on the fatal effects heretofore produced by ſuperſtition, by ignorance, and prejudice, we might ſtill, in ſurveying Europe, find whole nations which would preſent to us the picture of what we were 300 years ago. Nations, which are, ſo to ſpeak, the contemporaries of paſt ages, and the truth of hiſtorical facts would be demonſtrated by thoſe to which we ourſelves are witneſſes. It is the ſame in America with reſpect to the epoch of Nature, and all the documents of natural hiſtory. In viſiting this part of the world, you think yourſelf removed back a whole epoch; the lower grounds, the plains are watered by ſuch large rivers, and interſected by ſo many creeks; the coaſts are ſo frequently divided by gulphs, and arms of the ſea, which ſeem to conduct the waves to the very heart of the country, and to the very foot of the mountains, that it is impoſſible not to be perſuaded

persuaded that all this part of the Continent is not of new creation, and produced entirely by successive ebbings of the water. On the other hand, if we observe that all the high mountains form long chains parallel with each other, and almost in a direction North and South; that the greatest part of the rivers, which fall into the ocean, take their origin in the narrow vallies which separate these mountains, and that after following their direction for a considerable space, they turn suddenly towards the East, pierce the mountains, and at length reach the sea, acquiring magnitude as they proceed; we shall be apt to think ourselves, if not contemporaries, at least not far removed from that epoch of Nature, when the waters collected to an extraordinary height in hollow vallies, were striving to break down their dykes, still uncertain of the means to be adopted for making their escape; we shall be led to think that the motion of the earth on its axis, or the westerly winds, which in North America correspond with the trade winds of the Tropics, and of which they are possibly the effect, have at length

length determined the motion of the waters towards the East. In which case, one of these two circumstances might happen; either that the waters having exceeded the heights of the least lofty summits which opposed their passage, formed a sort of gutters, by which the superfluity escaped; or that unable to attain the height of these mountains, they met with some softer parts of the greater mass itself, which they first sapped, and then entirely penetrated. In the first case, if the declivity was very steep, and the rock which served by way of apron was very hard, they would form a cataract; but where the declivity was less rapid, and the soil less compact, the waters not only will have formed the gutter which served them as a passage, but have overthrown and hurried along with them the lands, forming them into long *glacis*, which would lose themselves finally in the plains. Thus Hudson's River, the Delaware, the Potowmack, James River, and many others, have opened ways for themselves to the sea, by piercing the mountains at angles, more or less approaching to right angles, and forming,

ing, more or leſs, ſpacious vallies. In the ſecond caſe, the waters unable to paſs the mountains, unleſs below their ſummits, muſt have left above them a ſort of *calotte*, or arch, ſimilar to that of the Natural Bridge. But how many chances are there, both that theſe arches muſt fall down after a certain time, eſpecially when the beds of the rivers becoming deeper and deeper, the burthen becomes too weighty, and they have loſt their baſes*!

* Mr. *Jefferſon*, in his excellent *Notes on Virginia*, ſeems to lean to the ſyſtem of *Buffon*, in the following ſublime and animated deſcription:

" The courſes of the (following) great rivers of " Virginia, ſays he, are at right angles with the " long chain of mountains, known in the *European* " *maps* by the name of the Apalachian Mountains. " James and Potama penetrate through all the " ridges of mountains eaſtward of the Alleghaney. " That is, broken by no water-courſe, it is in fact " the ſpine of the country between the Atlantic on " on ſide, and the Miſſiſippi and St. Laurence " on the other. The paſſages of the Patowmac " through the Blue Ridge is perhaps one of the " moſt ſtupendous ſcenes in nature; you ſtand on " very high point of land. On your right comes " up the *Shenandoah*, having ranged along the foot " of the mountains an hundred miles to ſeek a

Do we ſtill doubt of the probability of this hypotheſis? Do we wiſh for more ſtriking

" vent. On your left approaches the *Patowmac*, " in queſt of a paſſage alſo. In the moment of " their junction they ruſh together againſt the " mountain, rend it aſunder, and paſs off to the " ſea. The firſt glance of this ſcene hurries our " ſenſes into the opinion that this earth hath been " created in time, that the mountains were formed " firſt, that the rivers began to flow afterwards, that " in this place particularly they have been dammed " up by the Blue Ridge of mountains, and have " formed an ocean which filled the whole valley; " that continuing to riſe, they have at length broken " over at this ſpot, and have torn the mountain " down from its ſummit to its baſe. The piles of " rock on each hand, but particularly on the She-" nandoah, the evident marks of their diſrupture, or " evulſion from their beds, by the moſt powerful " agents of Nature, corroborate the impreſſion. " But the diſtant finiſhing which Nature has given " to the picture, is of a very different character. It " is a true contraſt to the fore-ground. It is as placid " and delightful as that is wild and tremendous. " For the mountain being cloven aſunder, ſhe pre-" ſents to your eye, through the cleft, a ſmall catch " of ſmooth blue horizon, at an infinite diſtance in " the plain country, inviting you, as it were, from " the riot and tumult roaring around, to paſs through " the breach, and partake of the calm below. Here

ſtriking tokens, more evident traces of the operation of the waters, let us continue to

" the eye ultimately compoſes itſelf; and that way " too the road happens actually to lead. You croſs " the Patowmac above the junction, paſs along its " ſide through the baſe of the mountain for three " miles, its terrible precipices hanging in fragments " over you, and within about twenty miles reach of " Frederic Town, and the fine country round it. " This ſcene is worth a voyage acroſs the Atlantic. " Yet here, as in the neighbourhood of the Natural " Bridge, are people who have paſſed their lives " within half a dozen miles, and have never been to " ſurvey theſe monuments of a war between rivers " and mountains, which muſt have ſhaken the earth " itſelf to its centre."

Mr. *Charles Thompſon*, Secretary to Congreſs, in an Appendix to Mr. Jefferſon's work, adds the following remarks on the ſame ſubject. The reader will pardon, I am confident, the length of theſe extracts from a work ſo highly intereſting, and which is not yet given to the public.

" The reflections," ſays Mr. Thompſon, " I was " led into on viewing this paſſage of the Patowmac " through the Blue Ridge were, that this country " muſt have ſuffered ſome violent convulſion, and " that the face of it muſt have been changed from " what it was probably ſome centuries ago: that the " broken and ragged faces of the mountain on each " ſide the river, the tremendous rocks which are left " with one end fixed in the precipice, and the others

travel in America; let us go into the vicinity of the Ohio, on the banks of the river

" jutting out, and seemingly ready to fall for want " of support; the bed of the river for several miles " below obstructed and filled with the loose stones " carried from this mound; in short, every thing on " which you cast your eye, evidently demonstrates a " disrupture and breach in the mountain; and that, " before this happened, what is now a fruitful vale " was formerly a great lake or collection of water, " which possibly might have here formed a mighty " cascade, or had its vent to the ocean by the Sus- " quehanna, where the Blue Ridge seems to termi- " nate. Besides this, there are other parts of this " country which bear evident traces of a like convul- " sion. From the best accounts I have been able to " obtain, the place where the Delaware now flows " through the Kittatinny mountain, which is a con- " tinuation of what is called the North Ridge or " Mountain, was not its original course, but that it " passed through what is now called, " The Wind " Gap," a place several miles to the Westward, and " above an hundred feet higher than the present bed " of the river. This Wind Gap is about a mile " broad, and the stones in it such as seem to have " been washed for ages by water running over them. " Should this have been the case, there must have " been a large lake behind that mountain, and by " some uncommon swell of the waters, or by some " convulsion of Nature, the river must have opened

ver Kentucké; we may there obſerve what follows, or rather what the recent hiſtorian

" its way through a different part of the mountain,
" and meeting there with leſs obſtruction, carried
" away with it the oppoſing mounds of earth, and
" deluged the country below with the immenſe col-
" lection of waters to which this paſſage gave vent.
" There are ſtill remaining, and daily diſcovered,
" innumerable inſtances of ſuch a deluge on both
" ſides of the river, after it paſſed the hills above the
" falls of Trenton, and reached the Champaign.
" On the New Jerſey ſide, which is flatter than the
" Penſylvania ſide, all the country below Creſſwick-
" hills ſeems to have been overflowed to the diſtance
" of from ten to fifteen miles back from the river,
" and to have acquired a new ſoil by the earth and
" clay brought down and mixed with the native ſand.
" The ſpot on which Philadelphia ſtands evident-
" ly appears to be made ground. The different
" ſtrata through which they paſs in digging to wa-
" ter, the acorns, leaves, and ſometimes branches
" which are found above twenty feet below the ſur-
" face, all ſeem to demonſtrate this *. I am in-

* From an accurate topographical obſervation of the mountainous parts of England, and other countries, on theſe principles, might we not be able to ſolve various phænomena which preſent themſelves in the plains bordering upon rivers, that is to ſay, within reach of ſuch a ſuppoſed overflow of waters; the quantity of large ſolid oak-timber, for example, found in *Walker Colliery* near Newcaſtle, on the banks of the river Tyne, at the prodigious depth of 120 fathoms. TRANSLATOR.

of that country * has written. " Amongſt
" the natural curioſities of this territory,
" the

" formed that at York-Town in Virgina, in the " bank of York river, there are different ſtrata of " ſhells and earth, one above another, which ſeem " to point out that the country there has under- " gone ſeveral changes, that the ſea has for a ſuc- " ceſſion of ages occupied the place where dry land " now appears, and that the ground has been ſud- " denly raiſed at various periods. What a change " would it make in the country below, ſhould the " mountains at Niagara, by any accident, be cleft " aſunder, and a paſſage ſuddenly opened to drain " off the waters of lake Erie and the upper lakes! " While ruminating on theſe ſubjects, I have often " been hurried away by Fancy, and led to imagine " that what is now the bay of Mexico was once a " champaign country, and that from the point or " cape of Florida, there was a continued range of " mountains through Cuba, Hiſpaniola, Porto Rico, " Martinique, Guadaloupe, Barbadoes and Tri- " nidad, till it reached the coaſt of America, and " formed the ſhores which bounded the ocean and " guarded the country behind: that by ſome con- " vulſion or ſhock of Nature the ſea had broken " through theſe mounds, and deluged that vaſt plain " till it reached the foot of the Andes; that being " there heaped up by the trade winds, always blow-
" ing

* Mr. Filſon, whoſe work is lately tranſlated into French. TRANSLATOR.

" the winding banks, or rather the preci-
" pice of Kentucké, and of the river Diek,
" merit the firſt rank. The aſtoniſhed
" eye beholds, almoſt on every ſide, 3 or
" 400 feet of a calcareous rock, perpendi-
" cularly cut; in ſome places a beautiful
" white marble, curiouſly ſhaped in arches
" or in columns, or piled upon a fine
" ſtone for building. Theſe precipices,
" as I have already obſerved, reſemble the
" ſides of a deep trench, or a canal, the
" earth around being level, except in the
" courſe of the rivulets, and covered with
" groves of red cedar; you can only croſs
" this river at certain places, one of which
" is worthy of admiration: It is a high-
" way formed by the buffaloes, and wide

 " enough

" ing from one quarter, it had found its way back, as
" it continues to do, through the gulph between Flo-
" rida and Cuba, carrying with it the loom and ſand
" it may have ſcooped from the country it had occu-
" pied, part of which it may have depoſited on the
" ſhores of North America, and with part formed the
" banks of the Newfoundland.——But theſe are only
" the viſions of Fancy." The Tranſlator adds, but
they are the ſublime viſions of a great and enlightened
mind. TRANSLATOR.

" enough for waggons, in a gentle ſlope, " from the ſummit of the foot of a very " ſteep eminence, cloſe to the river above " Lees-Town."

But let us conſult Don *Joſeph d'Ulloa*, already ſo celebrated by his Voyages; he is the author of the above-mentioned Spaniſh book, entitled, *Noticias Americanas*, in which he gives very curious and minute deſcriptions of all Spaniſh America. In the article I am going to tranſlate, he begins by remarking a very ſenſible difference between the mountains in America, ſituated under the torrid zone, and thoſe we obſerve in other parts of the globe; for although the height of the latter be often very conſiderable, as the ground riſes gradually, and their combined ſummits form immenſe countries, they who inhabit them may be ignorant of their elevation above the level of the ſea; whereas thoſe of America being ſeparated, and ſo to ſpeak, cloven their whole height, give inceſſantly the idea, and even the meaſure of their prodigious altitude. " In this part of the world, " adds he, the earth is interſected by pro-

" found

" found trenches (*quebradas*) of a very " conſiderable width, ſince they form the " ſeparation of the mountains from each " other, and form frequently an opening, " of more than two leagues, at the upper " part of them. This ſpace becomes con- " tracted in proportion as they are more " or leſs profound; and it is in the bottom " of this kind of vallies that the rivers " flow, which almoſt regularly occupy the " middle, leaving an equal extent of level " ground on each ſide of them. But what " is moſt remarkable, is, that the angles " or ſinuoſities formed by theſe rivers, cor- " reſpond perfectly with thoſe we obſerve " to the right and left in the ſegments of " theſe mountains; ſo that if we could at " once bring together the two ſides of theſe " vallies, we ſhould have a ſolid maſs, " without any interruption. The rivers " purſue their courſe in theſe embank- " ments, until they reach the plain, and " from thence the ocean. In this latter " part of their career, their bed is not deep, " and their bottom is nearly on a level " with the ſea. Thus it may in general

" be remarked, that the more lofty the " mountains of the Cordelliers, the more " profound is the bed of the rivers which " flow through their vallies."

" In the province of *Angaras*, amongſt " the *luſus Naturæ*, with which theſe coun- " tries abound, there is one which me- " rits particular attention. This province, " which is a dependency of *Guancavelica*, " is divided into ſeveral departments; in " one of theſe departments, called *Coniaca*, " is the ſmall village of *Vinas*, ſituated at " nine leagues diſtant from *Conaica*. " About midway between them, is a moun- " tain known by the name of *Coroſunta*: " On arriving at the foot of this moun- " tain, you enter into a cleft, or if you " will, an opening, through which flows " the rivulet of *Chapllancas*; this rivulet " enters an embarkment, the breadth of " which is from twenty to five and twenty " feet, and its height upwards of forty, " without being perceptibly wider at the " ſuperior than the inferior part. This " gap, which is occupied in its whole " width by the ſtream, forms the only

" commu-

" communication that exiſts between *Vinas* " and *Coniaca*. You can only croſs the ri- " ver in thoſe places where, as I have already " ſaid, the opening is twenty feet broad; " and you are obliged to croſs it nine times, " taking advantage of thoſe places where " it departs a little from the rock, which " only happens where it has formed ſome " ſinuoſities; for when its courſe is direct, " it exactly fills the opening through which " it paſſes. This trench is formed out of " the live rock, and with ſo much regu- " larity, that all the prominent parts of " one ſide correſpond perfectly with the " recipient parts or indentures of the other " in its whole height; inſomuch that it " might be taken for a canal cut expreſs- " ly for the paſſage of the water, and " which had been executed with ſo com- " plete a ſymmetry, as that the two ſides " might exactly fit each other, without " leaving the ſmalleſt interſtice between " them. There is no danger in travelling " this road, for the rock is too ſolid to " give any apprehenſion of its crumbling, " and the ſmall river is not rapid enough

" to

" to endanger boats; yet it is difficult to " ſuppreſs a ſentiment of terror, on find- " ing yourſelf engaged in this narrow gap, " the two ſides of which, from their per- " fect correſpondence, preſent the idea of " a box half opened for a moment, and " always ready to cloſe upon you."

" The cavity I have been deſcribing " is ſo much the more worthy our obſer- " vation, as it may be looked upon as a " model, or example of what the vallies of " the Cordilleras have been, when in their " origin they did not exceed the depth of " this; for their ſides, which now form a " gentle ſlope, were then doubtleſs per- " pendicularly cut, and it was not until " the waters undermined them to a great " depth, that the upper parts being over- " loaded, have ſucceſſively crumbled down. " This analogy is even confirmed by the " decay to be obſerved in the embank- " ment formed by the *Chapllancas*; a waſte " occaſioned by the ſlow and ſucceſſive " effect of the rains and froſt, and the " crevices produced by the ſun, but which " are leſs ſenſible there than elſewhere, be- " cauſe

" cauſe the rock is harder, more ſolid, " and more continuous, not being inter- " rupted by any bed of earth, or other " matter eaſily to be diſſolved or crumbled. " Every thing therefore leads to a con- " cluſion, that the waters alone have form- " ed this canal in the form we now ſee it, " and that they will continue to augment " its depth, ſince we know that time alone " is ſufficient to reduce the hardeſt ſtone " to a fine and almoſt imperceptible ſand, " and that this progreſs is already diſcover- " able from the little fragments of ſtone " viſible at the bottom of the river, as well " as from thoſe it carries to the plain; " when, finding a more extenſive range, it " begins to enlarge its ſurface."

" Whether we attribute the origin of " this canal to the friction of the waters " which have gradually deepened it, or " whether we ſuppoſe the mountain to have " been rent aſunder by an earthquake, ſo " as to open a new paſſage for this river " which flowed antecedently in another di- " rection; it is ſtill certain that ſuch an " aperture cannot have exiſted at the epo-

" cha

" cha immediately ſubſequent to the de-
" luge. It is the ſame with reſpect to the
" larger embankments of this kind, known
" by the name of *Quebradas*, and which are
" frequently to be met with in the upper
" part of South America. It is evident that
" they have been formed equally by the la-
" bour of the waters; for on the one hand,
" we know that the rapidity of their cur-
" rent is capable of wrenching off ſtones
" of an extraordinary ſize; and on the
" other, we have manifeſt proofs of the
" continual effort made by them to deepen
" their bed, an effort the traces of which
" are diſcovered in the huge blocks they
" have formed into the ſhape of dice, or
" cubes, as often as the rocks oppoſe too
" much exiſtence to them to admit of their
" dividing and clearing away the whole ex-
" tent of the bottom on which they exerciſe
" their activity. In the river of *Iſuchaca*,
" near the village of that name, is a large
" maſs of ſtone, of a regular ſquare form,
" and each ſide of which may be above five
" and thirty or forty feet. When the wa-
" ters are low, it riſes five-and-twenty
" feet

" feet above their level. But to account " for the form of theſe large cubic maſſes, " as well as of other ſmaller ones, which " are often to be found in the bed of ri- " vers, and which are all regularly ſhaped, " we muſt ſuppoſe that the waters have ſuc- " ceſſively torn and wrenched off the rocks " by which they were ſurrounded, thus " leaving them ſingle, and iſolated, in their " preſent form; but this only until the " beds of the rivers becoming deeper and " deeper, the waters meet at their baſes " with ſome veins of earth or other mat- " ter eaſy of diſſolution; for in that caſe " they will undermine and unſet them, " (ſo to ſpeak) ſo as one day to diſplace " them entirely and hurry them along. " Theſe maſſes, once in motion, will ſhock " either thoſe on the banks, thoſe they " meet with in the bed even of the ri- " ver, which breaking and being reduced " to various maſſes of leſs dimenſion, will " be the more eaſily drifted. Such is with- " out doubt the origin of all thoſe ſtones " we ſee under the water, or on the banks, " ſome of which are very ſmall, and others

" ſo

" ſo enormous, that no human effort is " able to remove them. As to the extra- " ordinary profundity of thoſe vallies or " *Quebradas*, one example will be ſuffi- " cient to give an idea of it. The town " of *Guanvelica* is built in a valley form- " ed by different chains of mountains; " the barometer there ſtands at eighteen " inches, one line and an half (this mean " term is taken between eighteen inches " and a quarter, and eighteen inches one " third, which form the greateſt variation " of the barometer at that place;) accord- " ing to this height of the mercury, the " elevation above the level of the ſea " ſhould be 1949 toiſes. On the ſum- " mit of the mountain in which is the " mine of *Aſoguès*, a ſpot ſtill habitable, " and which is itſelf as much lower than " other adjacent heights, as it is higher " than the town of *Guanvelica*, the mer- " cury only ſtands at ſixteen inches juſt, " which gives 2337 toiſes above the level " of the ſea, and about 500 toiſes for the " depth of the *Quebrada*, or valley of *Guan-* " *velica*, which ſeems to be no other than

" the

" the deepened bed of the river we now " ſee flowing through the middle of it."

After ſo many obſervations on the extraordinary effects of the waters, have we not ſome foundation for ſuppoſing that the Natural Bridge is alſo their production, and ought we not to regard it as a ſort of *Quebrada?* When the vallies of the Apalachians were only vaſt lakes, in which the waters were retained priſoners, this little valley, whoſe depth they traverſe, may have ſerved as a partial reſervoir, wherein they have remained even after thoſe of the large vallies made their eſcape. The maſs of the rock out of which the Natural Bridge is excavated, may have ſerved them as a barrier; but whether it be that they have not riſen to the ſummit of the rock, or whether they ſucceeded more eaſily in ſapping the lower part of it, they will in either caſe have left ſubſiſting that immenſe gap which form the arch ſuch as we now ſee it. It would be uſeleſs, and perhaps raſh, to endeavour minutely to explain the manner in which the bending of this vault has been ſo regularly traced out; but the cauſe once underſtood,

underſtood, all the effects, however varied, and however aſtoniſhing they may appear muſt have the ſame origin. We may obſerve beſides, that the greateſt bend of this vault correſponds with the angle formed by the valley in this place, inſomuch that the rock ſeems to have been the more worked upon, as the effort of the waters have been more conſiderable. However this may be, I leave every one at liberty to form ſuch conjectures as he pleaſes *, and as I have ſaid

* Mr. *Jefferſon*, after ſpeaking of the above paſſage of the Spaniſh author, differs from him and from the Marquis de Chaſtellux, in their reaſoning on the probable cauſes of its production, as follows: "Don Ulloa inclines to the opinion, that this "channel has been effected by the wearing of the "water which runs through it, rather than that the "mountain ſhould have been broken open by any "convulſion of Nature. But if it had been worn "by the running of the water, would not the rocks, "which form the ſides, have been worn plain? or "if, meeting in ſome parts with veins of harder "ſtone, the water had left prominences on one "ſide, would not the ſame cauſe have ſometimes, "or perhaps generally, occaſioned prominences on "the other ſide alſo? Yet Don Ulloa tells us, "that on the other ſide there are always correſpond-

ſaid above, my deſign has been leſs to explain this prodigy of Nature, than to deſcribe it with ſuch accuracy as to enable the learned to form a judgment on the ſubject *.

" ing cavities, and that theſe tally with the promi-
" nences ſo perfectly, that were the two ſides to
" come together, they would fit in all their inden-
" tures, without leaving any void. I think that
" this does not reſemble the effect of running wa-
" ter, but looks rather as if the two ſides had part-
" ed aſunder. The ſides of the break, over which
" is the Natural Bridge of Virginia, conſiſt of a veiny
" rock which yields to time, the correſpondence
" between the ſatient and re-entering inequalities,
" if it exiſted at all, has now diſappeared. This
" break has the advantage of the one deſcribed by
" Don Ulloa in its fineſt circumſtance, no portion
" in that inſtance having held together, during the
" ſeparation of the other parts, ſo as to form a bridge
" over the abyſs." TRANSLATOR.

* They who wiſh to form an exact idea of the Natural Bridge, muſt not judge of the ground plan of it, from the aſpect preſented by its ſegments in the two landſcapes which are engraved. The ground over which travellers paſs is almoſt level, but the parapets formed by the rocks are not ſo; beſides that their declivity is exaggerated by an optical effect, the views having been taken from the banks of the rivulet, and very near the bridge.

NOTE.

Though the ſpring was far advanced when I viſited the Natural Bridge, and it was then the 20th of April, I do not recollect having ſeen a ſwallow of any kind. Mr. Le Baron de Turpin did not go thither till the 15th of May, by which time the martins, which appear later than the ſwallows, had had time to arrive; but I have reaſon to think that the bird he here deſcribes, is no other than the *ſwallow with the white rump*, and which is improperly called a martin in ſome provinces of France.

I ſhall take this opportunity to obſerve, that the bird, called in America a *martin* (martinet) is a peculiar ſpecies, not known in Europe, and which is no where deſcribed, not even in *Cateſby*, at leaſt, if he means this bird, in ſpeaking of a Carolina martin, which he calls the *purple martin* *, unfortunately I am not ſo able as I could wiſh to ſupply this deficiency. Many reaſons have prevented me from profiting by my reſidence in America, by abandoning myſelf to ſuch obſervations as the trifling knowledge I have gained of natural hiſtory would have allowed me to make. In fact, the little room aſſigned even to general officers for tranſporting

* *Peter Kalm*, a Swediſh traveller, who has certainly not been ſparing of details, ſpeaks very ſuccinctly of this bird: he not even obſerves that the female is not of the ſame colour with the male, and ſeems to confound it with the European, which he calls the *Engliſh martin*. See volume III. p. 113. German Edition.

porting their effects, on our departure from Europe, did not allow me to carry any more books than were necessary for the political and military knowledge of the continent, where I was going to make war, and it was beyond my powers to work from memory, and after my own ideas; besides that, I had conceived an erroneous notion, that every thing was already known and written on a country so well understood and so much frequented as North America. I found, too late however, that I was deceived; the little success attending my efforts to derive some advantage, either from my own curiosity, or from the information of some persons I employed, have convinced me, that it would even now be of great use to send a little caravan, composed of naturalists, geographers and designers, to America. But whilst this project, which has already been proposed, is carrying into execution, I shall here submit a few observations I have made on the *martin* of America.

This bird differs from our European martin in its form, its colour, and its manners; in its form, as its body is pretty large, and similar to that of many other birds of different species, such as the blackbird and the starling: in its colour, because if the male be quite black like other martins, the female is of a cindery grey, a little clearer than that of our female blackbird, whilst its breast is of a dirty and mixed white; in its manners, for that instead of being wild like our martin, it is still more familiar, and more domestic, if possible, than our chimney swallow. The Americans have an almost ſuperſtitious reſpect for theſe birds; not only do they prepare for them, at the commencement of the ſpring, earthen pots like thoſe we affix to our walls to attract the ſparrows, but they ſuſpend, beneath the projection of the roof, little cages for them to build in. The more credulous of the Americans ſay that theſe birds bring good luck to the houſes that they viſit; the moſt ſenſible imagine they are uſeful, not only in deſtroying the flies, which are very troubleſome in ſummer, but becauſe by their boldneſs and their cries they drive away the birds of prey, when they come to attack the poultry. Theſe animals are ſo familiar, that with a little adroitneſs, one may take them with the hand; their ſong is far removed from the diſagreeable cry of our martin; it reſembles rather that of the chimney ſwallow, but is much more melodious. I never ſaw them but at liberty, for I confeſs that having a hundred times reſolved to kill at leaſt one or two of them, that I might inſpect them more narrowly, I never had the courage; ſo much did I reſpect the kind hoſpitality afforded them, and which they accept with the ſame confidence.

I do not know why Cateſby calls this bird the *purple martin*, for I have never obſerved the ſlighteſt ſhade of that colour in their wings; thoſe of the male are of the moſt beautiful black, and as I have already ſaid, thoſe of the female are of a cindery grey upon the back, and the belly is white, mixed with grey. If this bird was not a bird of paſſage, and a bird, which like all thoſe of the ſame ſpecies, muſt travel very rapidly, it would appear probable, that

that in approaching the tropics it aſſumes a purple colour. For we remark a ſenſible difference in the manner in which different birds, of the ſame ſpecies, are coloured as they approach nearer the tropics, or the equinoctial line. The humming-birds we ſee in Virginia, and which proceed even into Penſylvania and the Jerſeys, are of a grey colour, and their neck alone diſplays the colours of the ruby, whilſt thoſe of *Guiana*, and Brazil diſplay, in their whole plumage, that brilliancy which Nature has beſtowed only partially on the others. No ſpecies would furniſh more examples of this progreſſion in brilliancy and integrity of colours than that of the ſtarling, were not theſe birds emigrants, and could we but know with accuracy from what country thoſe ſwarms arrive which we ſee in the ſpring. The moſt beautiful variety of theſe ſpecies is the black ſtarling, called the *blackbird* in America: when perched he appears quite black, but in the folds of his wings he has ſeveral feathers of a very lively red, but ſhaded withal, ſo as to be compared only to the carbuncle; and, in his flight, his brilliant colours produce an effect ſo much the more agreeable as it is unexpected. Another variety immediately follows, in the grey ſtarling, which has alſo ſeveral red feathers, but fewer in number, and of a leſs lively red; a third is of a brown colour inclining to red, ſomething like the hen pheaſant: it has alſo in the fold of the wings three feathers abſolutely red, but of a gloomy red, and without éclât; a fourth ſpecies, in ſhort, would be abſolutely ſimilar to our European ſtarling, had it not, at the fold of the wing, three or four reddiſh feathers, which ſeem to atteſt its American origin, and may be regarded as the facings of an incomplete uniform, but which is ſufficient to indicate to what army this legion belongs. There is every reaſon to believe, that if we could aſcertain from whence theſe birds come, which appear only at the commencement of the ſpring, throughout North America, and even in Virginia and Carolina, we ſhould be able to determine that the greater or leſs brilliancy of their feathers is owing to the greater or leſs height of latitude they inhabit during the winter. We read in natural hiſtory, that the ſtarling is not a bird of paſſage; this may be true, of European ſtarlings, but I can affirm, that from Boſton to the bay of Cheſapeak, I have never ſeen one arrive but at the end of winter.

I have not ſpoken of a ſort of ſtarling not mentioned in the natural hiſtory of Buffon, but which is to be ſeen in the King of France's cabinet, and is deſcribed by Cateſby; it is with this however I ſhould have begun, as being the bird which has led me to this long digreſſion. It is called in America the *ſtarling crow*. This bird is a great deal larger than other ſtarlings, and on conſidering its beak, one is tempted to rank it with the jackdaw; but there is no doubt of its being a real ſtarling, of which it has the cry and the manners; it dwells in marſhes, and mixes with all the ſpecies of ſtarlings I have mentioned. Its colour is of a mixed and changeable red, which affords, according to the manner in which it is enlightened, bluiſh and purple ſhades: now it is probable enough that theſe birds, whoſe colour

is

is originally black, may acquire, from the vicinity of the ſun, theſe purple or blue ſhades which we remark in the ſtarling crow; and in this caſe it is poſſible that the purple martin of Cateſby may exiſt in South Carolina, though I have never ſeen it in Virginia: but it would ſtill be difficult to explain why this martin, whoſe origin muſt be more ſoutherly, ſhould not extend his emigration as far as Virginia and Penſylvania; for though we have obſerved that ſtarlings are birds of paſſage in America, their emigrations muſt be diſtinguiſhed from thoſe of the ſwallows and the martins. There is a great appearance that the ſtarlings content themſelves with retiring in winter to the neighbourhood of the lakes and rivers which abound between the Pacific ocean and tlantic, from 35 to 33 degrees of latitude. It is enough for them, in fact, to avoid the froſt which would hinder them from finding ſubſiſtence in the marſhes; whereas the ſwallows muſt return to countries where volatile inſects do not ceaſe to flutter in the air during the winter. The following obſervation however was made by Mr. Fleming, Chief Juſtice of Virginia, a man worthy of credit, and reſpectable in every point of view; he aſſured Mr. Jefferſon, that on a winter's day, as he was occupied in ſuperintending the felling of ſome trees on a ſpot he was about to ſow, he was ſurprized to ſee fall, with a large cleft oak, a great number of martins, which had taken refuge and were benumbed in the crevices of the tree, as bats are found in holes of rocks and caverns. Does this fact, which it is difficult to conteſt, prove that martins do not emigrate like quails and ſtorks; or only that a lazy troop of theſe birds, having delayed their departure too long, were ſurprized by the froſt, and compelled to ſeek an aſylum for the winter?

Since I have ſuffered myſelf to be led into the diſcuſſion of ſubjects relative to natural hiſtory, I ſhall not terminate this long note without adding another article, on which however I can throw no new light, as it has been treated by the Count de Buffon; but where I ſhall have the ſatisfaction at leaſt of confirming, by irrefragable proofs, what was revealed to him by mere dint of genius alone; happy to find at once the opportunity of rendering a particular homage to the moſt illuſtrious man of the age, and of boaſting of that friendſhip which has ſo long connected us; a friendſhip already of ancient date, ſince it is coeval with my admiration of his immortal works. We know that one of the moſt intereſting articles of the hiſtory of quadrupeds, is that of the *opoſſum*. Obſervation diſcovered, that the female of this animal has under its belly a ſort of pouch in which it carries its young ones; that they are never ſeen out of this pouch, before they are able to run about and ſeek their food, and that they remain, until that period, always attached to their mother's teat: but ignorance and credulity had adopted all ſorts of ridiculous tales reſpecting the manner in which generation is performed between theſe animals. I found the opinion eſtabliſhed in Virginia, even amongſt phyſicians, that the young of the opoſſum came out of their mother's belly

belly by the teats. Their extreme ſmallneſs, at the moment of their birth, alone could give ſanction to this opinion, which anatomy would ſo eaſily have belied, on the ſlighteſt attention. My firſt occupation in the winter of 1781 to 1782, was to procure ſome of theſe animals, and have them diſſected. Mr. Robillard, firſt ſurgeon to our army, and one of the moſt expert in France, was pleaſed to undertake it. Having diſſected a male and female, he found the organs of generation ſimilar to thoſe of other quadrupeds, with this only difference, that he obſerved a bifurcation in the glans penis of the male and the clitoris of the female, and that he diſcovered in the matrice of the latter a ſort of partition or mediaſtine, which divided it into two departments, but without being continuous enough for the two cavities not to be ſeparate from each other. This was ſufficient to confirm and to explain the moſt eſſential articles of a deſcription, which Mr. D'Aubenton had an opportunity of taking only from one which was preſerved in ſpirits of wine. But Mr. de Buffon, who with admirable ſagacity concluded, that Nature, in forming this animal, had proceeded in a peculiar manner, and given it the faculty of reproducing itſelf, intermediately, ſo to ſpeak, between that of quadrupeds and that of birds, in order that the brevity of geſtation might correſpond with their long incubation in the pouch they are preſerved in; Mr. de Buffon added: "Nobody has obſerved the length of the geſtation of "theſe animals, which we preſume to be much "ſhorter than in others; and as this premature

"excluſion

" exclusion is an example singular in Nature, we " exhort such as have the opportunity of seeing " opossums alive in their native country, to endea- " vour to discover how long the females bear them, " and how long also, after their birth, the young " remain attached to the teat before they quit it. " This observation, curious in itself, may become " useful, by pointing out to us possibly some means " of preserving the lives of children born before " their time." Here the *interpreter of Nature*, as it often happens to Asiatic drogomans, was under the necessity of diving into his master's thoughts before he attempted to express them in intelligible language; but when the interpreter is both minister and confidant, it matters little whether he translates or pronounces of himself; accordingly, the only apprehension I had was of not being able to procure the means necessary to prove to the Americans a truth of which I was myself thoroughly persuaded. For to attain this object, it was necessary that tame opossums should be brought to copulate in this domestic state, or rather state of slavery; it was necessary that this union should be productive, and that we should have an opportunity of observing the result. Now, nobody in this country had ever thought of rearing one, and we could only obtain those caught by the soldiers in the woods. I had possessed one, which was become very familiar, but I had sent it to the Comte de Buffon, in the frigate *L'Hermione*; the Comte de la Touche, who commanded it, having been so kind as to charge himself with several animals and other objects of natural history I wish-

ed

ed to ſend to Europe. But chance fortunately ſupplied me better than I could have been by all my endeavours: The Chevalier d'Aboville, *Brigadier des Armees du Roi*, and commander of our artillery, availing himſelf of our preſent ſtate of repoſe, employed, in augmenting his knowledge in phyſics and natural hiſtory, the ſame talents, and the ſame activity which had been of ſuch eminent ſervice during the campaign. He reared at his houſe ſeveral animals, and amongſt others a female opoſſum, which he had the good fortune to ſee conceive, become a mother, and bring up her young in his own houſe, nay even in his own chamber. I cannot do better than tranſcribe the obſervations he made, and with which he has been pleaſed to favour me.

" The opoſſum, ſays he, is more timid than untractable, and very readily becomes tame. I had a ſhe one ſome time before I could get a male. At firſt ſhe appeared to be afraid of him; and, to avoid a quarrel, I tied up the new comer in a box near my chimney. The female enjoyed the full liberty of the chamber, where ſhe had likewiſe a box from whence ſhe came out only at night to eat and drink, and void herſelf. The evening of the ſecond day, after the arrival of the male, whilſt I was writing before my fire, I ſaw the female advance ſlowly towards the box in which was the male, run under my bed, come towards the box, and return, advancing each time a little nearer, and at length became hardy enough to enter the box of the male, who, inſtantly, threw himſelf

upon

upon her with ſuch precipitation, that having hitherto obſerved him very indifferent, I concluded it aroſe from anger. I drew her out, and beat him. A few minutes after ſhe returned to the charge, and the male hearing her approach, came out of his box, and the length of the cord allowing him to join her on the middle of the hearth, he fell upon her with the ſame impetuoſity, and I ſoon perceived, that as the female was not afraid, I ought not to meddle with their affairs. She was ſquatted, and the male upon her, with all his feet reſting upon the ground, and both of them in a ſtate of perfect immobility. I regarded them in this poſition near half an hour; I paſſed my finger between them, and could perceive that there was no intromiſſion. My preſence did not ſeem to embarraſs them in the leaſt; but that nothing might interrupt them, I went to bed. The fire before which I left them, gave light enough for me to obſerve them, which I continued to do for above half an hour in bed, and ſaw them ſtill remain immoveable. I cloſed my eyes for a few moments, and the female had mounted on my bed; I careſſed her, and paſſing my hand towards her poſteriors, found them wet, from whence I concluded, that notwithſtanding appearances, the act of copulation had been fully compleated, and the next day I found ſome ſpots upon the floor, which were a ſecond proof of it. But I was ſoon confirmed in my opinion, by the change I perceived in the pouch of the female. They coupled on the 7th of February, and ten days after I remarked that the edge of the orifice of the pouch

was

was rather thicker; this appeared more ſenſibly the following days, and I obſerved that the pouch alſo became larger, and its aperture more widened than before. The night of the 20th, that is to ſay, thirteen days after the copulation, ſhe did not leave the box till the night was far advanced, and then only to eat, and drink, and void herſelf, after which ſhe returned immediately to her box, ſo that I had not time that day to continue to obſerve the progreſs of the alteration in her pouch. The fourteenth day towards the evening, ſeeing that ſhe did not come out of her box, I put my hand into it, which ſhe greatly careſſed, licking it, and gnawing it very gently; ſhe embraced my fingers with her little hands, and endeavouring to retain mine when I attempted to withdraw it; I gave her ſome pieces of meat, which ſhe ate, continuing to careſs my hand, and ſeeing that ſhe could not retain it, ſhe determined to follow it, and came out of her box ſtill keeping hold of my finger. I was anxious to examine the pouch, and the change I perceived in it convinced me, that I had loſt much in having miſſed obſerving it one day, and that I had ſuffered the moſt intereſting moment to eſcape. This pouch, which had been gradually widening the preceding days, was then almoſt cloſed, preſenting only a ſmall round aperture, in the middle of a cavity ſimilar to a navel. The orifice of it was rather moiſt, and the hair round the orifice was wetted with a glairy humour common to the anus and the vagina. It ſeemed to me as if I could ſtill have been able to introduce one of my fingers into the pouch; but I thought that

that this could not be effected without forcing the paſſage, and hurting it, perhaps too, without deſtroying the delicate embryos it contained. The fifteenth day, whether it was that my impatience got the better of my fears, or whether the orifice of the pouch was really more open than the day before, I introduced my finger, and found, at the bottom of the pouch, a little round body, which appeared to be of about the ſize of a pea. The mother, who had before allowed me without much difficulty to put my fingers in her pouch, now became very unquiet, and endeavoured to eſcape, which prevented me from examining with ſufficient accuracy to aſcertain whether the body was ſpherical, whether it was adherent, and if there were ſeveral of them; but it appeared to me adherent, and ſituated on one ſide of the pouch, from whence I concluded that there was a ſecond upon the other ſide. The ſixteenth night ſhe only came out to eat, and returned immediately. The ſeventeenth day in the evening ſhe came out, and on examining her pouch, I found two bodies ſituated at the bottom, the one beſide the other, and adherent to the body of the mother; their volume did not exceed that of a pea, and as far as I could judge of their form, by the touch, it appeared to me to reſemble that of a fig, with the ſmall end implanted in a baſe of the form of a ſegment of a ſphere, and exhibited to the finger, inequalities upon its ſurface. Although I had felt only two bodies, I had no doubt of this pouch containing a great number. The twenty-fifth day after the copulation, conſequently the

the twelfth of the residence of the young in the pouch, I began to feel them move under the finger, and a month after the second epocha, I could plainly discover them on half opening the pouch. Fifteen days later it remained naturally open enough to see them freely: and at the end of two months, the female lying down, and the opening of the pouch being in a more lax situation than when she walked, the young ones were partly out of the pouch, and might easily be reckoned: they were to the number of six, all holding to the mother by a canal which enters the maw of the young one, and which cannot be withdrawn, but by such violence as might destroy it, if this should happen at an early period; for the young one is then unable to take hold again of the teat. But when six weeks old, it can resume it by strong suction, the aperture at the end of the muzzle being barely large enough to receive the pap, which is about two lines in length, and the size of the second or third cord of a violin. The opossum notwithstanding has a very wide maw, but as it remains attached to the mother, Nature has joined the two jaws by a membrane, which dries up and disappears as soon as the young one is three months old, at which term it begins to eat and to walk.

" The number of the young varies greatly; I have seen females with ten or eleven, others which had only five or six. There are never more paps than young ones, and when they are weaned, these paps dry up, and detach themselves, as in other animals; the umbilical string detaches itself from the young,

 with

with this difference, that the latter preserve the mark of the spot where the string was, whereas the female opossum retains no trace of the points where the teats have been, and which are not, as in other animals, placed in two parallel lines, but irregularly, and as if by accident. It appears as if they formed themselves in those places where the embryos happen to touch the mother's belly when she has conveyed them into her pouch, successively, as she *lays* them; for that is the most proper expression, undeveloped embryos being comparable only to eggs."

THE END